TRANSPORTING ATLANTA

SUNY series in Urban Public Policy

C. Theodore Koebel and Diane L. Zahm, editors

TRANSPORTING ATLANTA

The Mode of Mobility under Construction

MIRIAM KONRAD

STATE UNIVERSITY OF NEW YORK PRESS

Published by
State University of New York Press, Albany

For information, contact
State University of New York Press, Albany, NY
www.sunypress.edu

Production, Laurie Searl
Marketing, Anne M. Valentine

Library of Congress Cataloging-in-Publication Data

Konrad, Miriam Fiedler.
Transporting Atlanta : the mode of mobility under construction / Miriam Konrad.
p. cm. — (SUNY series in urban public policy)
Includes bibliographical references and index.
ISBN 978-1-4384-2677-8 (hardcover : alk. paper)
ISBN 978-1-4384-2678-5 (pbk. : alk. paper)
1. Local transit—Georgia—Atlanta. 2. Metropolitan Atlanta Rapid Transit Authority. 3. Georgia Regional Transportation Authority. 4. Regional planning—Georgia—Atlanta Metropolitan Area. I. Title.

HE310.A7K66 2009
388.409758'231—dc22 2008043247

10 9 8 7 6 5 4 3 2 1

For my dear ones,

Leslie, Eric, Ruth, Marilyn, Margaret, and Andrea—

who all took the ultimate journey during the writing of this book.

CONTENTS

ACKNOWLEDGMENTS

I wish to express my thanks to Dr. Charles Jaret, without whom this book would not have been written. He, along with Dr. Wendy Simonds and Dr. Charles Gallagher, inspired and instructed me throughout this demanding and rewarding journey. Thanks also to Georgia State University for providing a small grant which in part supported my research. I also want to thank the many transportation experts and advocates who kindly gave their time to speak with me and educate me regarding their areas of expertise. Their input was invaluable to the process of writing this book. I owe a debt of gratitude as well to my enormous support network (what did I do to deserve it?)—friends, family, colleagues, the entire Georgia State Sociology Department—and foremost always, my precious Bob.

LIST OF ACRONYMS AND ABBREVIATIONS

Association County Commissioners of Georgia—ACCG
Atlanta Regional Commission—ARC
Bus Rapid Transit—BRT
Central Business District—CBD
Citizens for Progressive Transit—CPT
Clayton County Transit—C-Tran
Cobb Community Transit—CCT
Congestion Mitigation and Air Quality—CMAQ
Compressed Natural Gas—CNG
Development of Regional Impact—DRI
Environmental Impact Statement—EIS
Environmental Protection Division—EPD
Federation for American Immigration Reform—FAIR
Freeing Alternatives for Speedy Transportation lanes—FAST lanes
Gwinnett County Transit—GCT
Georgia Emergency Management Agency—GEMA
Georgia Department of Transportation—GDOT
Georgia Regional Transportation Authority—GRTA
Georgians for Better Transportation—GBT
Geographic Information System—GIS
High Occupancy Toll lanes—HOT lanes
High Occupancy Vehicle lanes—HOV
Intermodal Surface Transportation Efficiency Act—ISTEA
Metropolitan Atlanta Rapid Transit Authority—MARTA
Metropolitan Planning Organization—MPO
National Ambient Air Quality Standards—NAAQS
Pedestrians Educating Drivers on Safety—PEDS
Regional Transit Action Plan—RTAP
Regional Transportation Plan—RTP
State Implementation Plan—SIP
State Road and Tollway Authority—SRTA
Tax Allocation District—TAD
Transit Oriented Development—TOD
Transportation Equity Act for the Twenty-first Century—TEA-21
Transportation Improvement Program—TIP

ONE

INTRODUCTION

Begin at the Beginning

WHY TRANSPORTATION?

It is astonishing how many of the world's great struggles may be framed in terms of mobility issues, from forty years in the desert, to the middle passage, the Trail of Tears, diasporas, dislocation, expatriation, repatriation, immigration, emigration, access to work, school, play, home, and so much more. Transportation options serve as both a barrier and a bridge, literally and figuratively, and may truncate or elongate both time and space for all denizens of the planet. The wherewithal to move about is increasingly packaged as an item that may be bought and sold whose exchange value buys more than simple arrival at destinations. The cultural cachet of being able to traverse a great deal of space and consume time at a rapid rate affords one a favored position in society, smoothing the road for a successful life. This commodification of movement and the consequent privileging and punishing, mobilizing and miring, conferring and crippling, produced and reproduced by the systematized transportation complex, evident globally, fine-tuned in the United States, and well illustrated in the Atlanta case, is what I refer to as the mode of mobility.

Both preference for and access to transportation options are created through overt and subtle processes that include: creating spaces that only lend themselves to certain forms of mobility (namely, the automobile) and preclude in many instances any alternatives; fetishizing high-speed, privatized forms of mobility; and privileging those forms that have been accommodated and fetishized, and also those persons who advocate them. The built environment both proscribes and describes where and how we are going, and the discourse that both reflects and creates that environment too often goes unexamined. This reflexivity is manifest in all aspects of our movement as well as in our immobility. We learn what we "need" in part from reading the landscape that we are given (which was created by people's choices or lack thereof at some point), which in turn gives those very needs life. Ever more roads call for ever more cars and we become increasingly less able to distinguish what we created from what is a "natural" and "obvious" trajectory of progress.

The human hand becomes invisible as creator and director of transportation options, in such a way as to allow us to believe, often, that we are merely following the road as it stretches before us, rather than shaping its twists and turns as we go. In this vein, then, the mode of mobility not only determines where we go and how we get there, (as if that were not enough) but further confers value added to (or subtracted from) the means that we choose or are forced to employ, and simultaneously obscures from us our power in the production of those means. Deciphering the hieroglyph of the mode of mobility and its ability to conflate physical movement and social position is the aim of this book.

Mine is fundamentally a neo-Marxian perspective: "Marxian" in that I take relations of power as central to all social processes, and "neo" in that I conceive these relations as situated not only in the economic sphere. Production is not purely an economic notion, but also applies to the production of knowledge, culture, and space. I see the concepts of ideology (the legitimization of the status quo via a predominant system of signs, symbols, and discourse); hegemony (the cultural domination of ideology by the elite); multiple oppressions, operating sometimes simultaneously and sometimes at odds with each other; and spatiality (how space is created, negotiated, manipulated, and dominated) as salient issues in reading the mobility landscape.

My central concept of the mode of mobility is fashioned after and extended out from Karl Marx's conception of the mode of production in which the mode indicates the method of producing the necessities of life. This method is a complex and recursive exchange between external conditions and internal conceptions determining what we as a society need, want, and do. Marx ([1859] 1978) asserts, "It is not the consciousness of men that determines their being, but, on the contrary, their social being that determines their consciousness" (4). I extend on and transform this assertion by removing the "not" and transforming the "but" to an "and." In so doing, this supposition discloses its deeply reflexive character, revealing the dialectical nature of the process, becoming: "It is the consciousness of men [humans] that determines their being, and their social being that determines their consciousness." Thus, I seek to investigate the interplay between discourse and the built environment, mindful that each recursively affects the other, culminating in transportation policies and practices that both mirror and manufacture the mode of mobility.

More specifically, I ask how the mode of mobility is produced and reproduced in Atlanta, Georgia. This overarching question leads to a set of sub-questions:

> What motivates groups of individuals to fight for, or against, a particular transportation policy?
> How does this motivation and the action(s) in response to it, vary temporally, geographically, by race, class, gender, age, and so forth?
> How are transportation decisions arrived at?
> Who are the key players in setting the agendas and making the decisions?

Car-centered Growth advocates; Green (environmental) proponents; and Equity (social justice) actors emerge as the triumvirate in the region determining transportation and land-use practices. Attention to these forces leads to questions such as:

> Under what circumstances do each of these goals intersect with the others?
> When are they mutually exclusive?
> What makes them at times mutually supportive?
> When they are at odds, what forces result in the privileging of one over the others?

WHY ATLANTA?

When one person's mobility is mired in gridlock, lack of access, pollution, impossibly circuitous routes, or danger, it is a private trouble. When one million people are consistently so mired . . . it is Atlanta! The transportation crisis in Atlanta has reached such epic proportions that it is the topic of not only much scholarship but also of street-corner and tabloid discussions. Illustrative is a Web site simply entitled Atlanta Jokes. If one visits this virtual location, sixteen of the twenty jokes listed have to do with Atlanta's transportation issues. Two examples give not only the flavor of the site but also well reflect sentiments often heard expressed around town:

> Atlanta is comprised entirely of one way streets. The only way to get out of downtown Atlanta is to turn around and start over when you reach Greenville, South Carolina.
>
> The 8 a.m. rush hour is from 6:30 to 9:30 a.m. The 5:00 p.m. rush hour is from 3:30 to 6:30 p.m. Friday's rush hour starts Thursday morning and lasts through 2:00 a.m. Saturday (AHAJokes.com).

Joking aside, the inconveniences, annoyances, and hardships created in Atlanta by too many automobiles and overcrowded roads, and not enough alternatives for movement, have reached untenable levels:

> In metro Atlanta, the number of miles driven each day on the area's roads was expected to rise by about forty-two million miles by 2005——about half the distance from the earth to the sun. The vice chairman for transportation of the Metro Atlanta Chamber of Commerce predicts that by 2010, Atlantans will spend more time in traffic than at home. Traffic congestion in Atlanta has become so bad that the Chamber of Commerce called it the greatest threat to the city's prosperity ("Traffic Congestion," FAIR 2003:1–2).

Efforts to rectify the myriad problems associated with this impasse have for too long focused on individual pieces of the puzzle and behavior modification with little attention to the ideological framework that undergirds the entire system. For example, growth-oriented policies (and the political actors associated with them) look to ever more roads to alleviate the traffic congestion. Those with a "greener" orientation seek greater walkability, bikability, and more public transit options to address the needs of both those who must move about and the space in which they move. Citizens concerned primarily with issues of equity organize their efforts around policies that will increase the mobility of marginalized members of society, reminding us that, "solutions guided by a tendency which ignores that fact of inequality will inevitably place the greatest burdens of adjustment on those least able to carry them" (Irrante 1980:516). While all of these actors are in pursuit of relief for pains arising from the same source, their proposed solutions can at best be palliative and never curative because they attend to symptoms rather than the disease.

To further complicate matters, groups of people with the above-mentioned primary interests often find themselves at loggerheads with one another, either in overt conflict (as with the growth and equity groups); in an uneasy and volatile game of concessions and compromises (as with the green and growth groups); or in a strange and often confoundingly strained relationship in which ostensibly compatible goals clash despite the best intentions of the parties involved (as with the equity and green groups). The tensions arising from the open enmity in some instances, the veiled friction between interests in others, and the unsettled alliances created in still others could perhaps be eased if all parties had a more profound understanding of the foundations on which their assumptions about mobility are predicated.

Getting at what lies beneath the asphalt, as it were, will shed light on its seemingly unstoppable space, energy, and money consumption and perhaps allow for future decision making that includes a more nuanced reading of the landscape. This exploration will therefore include, but not be limited to, a cataloguing of the components of policy formulation as commonly understood—i.e., the agenda-setting process, the actors invited to the table, and the outcomes. It will further be an examination of what precedes all of this; the taken for granted assumptions about the meanings and possibilities of mobility. For example, all researchers are aware that the questions we bring to a study in part determine the answers. This is no less true with how transportation policy is created. In terms of equity issues, for instance:

> How transportation is defined and measured can often determine how equity is evaluated. The use of vehicle mileage, as a measure of travel and traffic congestion, tends to favor more spending on infrastructure improvements and less on other transportation alternatives. Also, transportation planners use other variables in their transportation modeling such as vehicle miles traveled, which favors people who drive their automobile more miles than average, or passenger miles traveled, which favors people who travel more than average (Bullard et al. 2000:68).

If mobility is defined and hierarchically structured in such a way as to marginalize some modes, and even preclude others, we would do well to identify how that construction came into being. As with any social problem, seeking a way out must begin with understanding how we arrived there in the first place.

This investigation engages a wide literature on race, space, and place; attendance at transportation and land-use meetings and symposia; archival data; and in-depth interviews with twenty area transportation experts and interested parties, including planners and designers, authority staff and board members, conservationists and environmentalists, transit and pedestrian advocates, environmental justice actors, lobbyists, and Chamber of Commerce staff and members. As race and regionalism are so central to understanding power and procedure in metro Atlanta, particular attention will be given to racial and spatial practices. (See appendix A for a full detailing of methodology.)

The macro analysis, meaning how these local transportation and land-use policies and practices reflect and inform the mode of mobility on a global scale, will be largely addressed in chapter 2 and in the concluding chapter. What I discover through scrutinizing the particular cases in chapters 3 on MARTA, 4 on GRTA, and 5 on the Beltline will also be—though not generalizable—situated in the larger context to understand how Atlanta's mobility practices are both products and producers of global ones.

As this is an examination of transportation-related policies and practices and the suppositions upon which they are based at the local and regional levels, the microanalysis of how individuals personally negotiate space shall be mostly left to other works or other scholars. My investigation will focus largely on meso-level processes through the examination of the creation, trajectories, and current positioning of three major Atlanta transportation projects: the Metropolitan Atlanta Rapid Transit Authority (MARTA), the Georgia Regional Transportation Authority (GRTA), and the Beltline, an enormously popular current proposal to build a twenty-two-mile loop of greenspace, transit, and other amenities around an inner loop of the city built on existing rail beds.

These three projects exemplify the region's struggles with transportation and land-use policy development over the last thirty years and hold the key to understanding how transportation is "done" in metropolitan Atlanta. The examination of MARTA's life course especially reveals the intersection of race and place in transportation planning. GRTA's history gives us a clear window into spatial disputes—particularly the urban/suburban split and how regionalism becomes so central to policy decisions. The examination of the evolving Beltline project is an excellent site from which to view issue framing around a currently popular enterprise in which developers, politicians, environmentalists, and public transit actors all have a clear and articulated stake. All three cases provide insight into the interplay between Growth, Green, and Equity issues in the region.

Transportation policies and procedures are not developed in a vacuum. It is increasingly recognized that land-use patterns are both informed by and informative of transportation practices. Consequently, much of this investigation focuses on the intersections between the development and implementation of land-use policies and transportation decisions. How land is configured shapes how we move about on it, and how we move about determines how we delineate space. Growth and development, environmental concerns, and issues of equity—both geographic and social—all play major roles in these determinations. Thus, land use and transportation negotiations are highly politicized and hinge largely on ideological positions for their existence. Consequently, they rely heavily on paradigm shifts if they are to transform. In this work, I trace the conceptual and tangible trails, especially in the metropolitan Atlanta region, of the mode of mobility over the last several years. Through the interrogation of MARTA, GRTA, and the Beltline, and the ideologies that have driven them, I disentangle the "spaghetti junction" that comprises Atlanta's mode of mobility.

CHAPTER OVERVIEWS

In chapter 2, I invoke the pertinent literature. This inquiry engages a number of discourses and perspectives. For convenience and clarity I have loosely subdivided the literature relevant to the mode of transportation into three groups: Race; Place; and Space. These categories are merely an artifice with much overlap and other shortcomings. Nonetheless, it is my hope that this necessarily oversimplified classification system will allow me as the author and you as the reader to make sense of the salient works as they pertain to this one. Toward that end, I will define the terms as I am using them here.

The Race literature refers to those works that primarily focus on race or ethnicity as either most or highly salient in the trajectory of urban development, especially as it relates to transportation issues. I interrogate global, national, regional, and local discourses on race and its application to mobility, with an emphasis on Atlanta's issues. As Atlanta's theme song could be dubbed, "We Built This City on Race and Roads," there is no better site for such an inquiry.

The Place research touches on urban inquiries that situate location, both physical and social, at the heart of their arguments. In addition to invoking race, class, gender, age, disability, and other markers of difference from the dominant in the examination of urban mobility, the place research invites an interrogation of the role of transportation in the negotiations between the ideological bastions of pro-growth and slow-growth groups (facile yet useful distinctions). In this review, I examine place conceptions such as sprawl, Urban Regimes and issue framing, Smart Growth, New Urbanism, Market-based growth, and automobility.

The Space narratives involve those discourses that problematize the very notion of place, inviting us to dig beneath the surface and discover how space is created, manipulated, defined, and undergoes metamorphosis through the processes of human perception, commentary, and action. If we conceive of place research as examining location—both physical and social and the interconnections between the two—we may think of the space narratives as deconstructing, or de-locating if you will, location itself. This can be understood through discourses that uncover both the globalization of the local and the localization of the global. By the former, I mean the stripping away of the cultural identity of places—marked by the indistinguishability of various aspects of cities, such that in strip malls and chain restaurants around the world you might be anywhere at all—deprived of local flavor and steeped in Starbucks coffee. The relentless paving of space, reconfiguring vast quantities of it into freeways leading to intersecting and bisecting further freeways, is also emblematic of this phenomenon. Rutheiser (1996) speaks of this phenomenon in the Atlanta context, noting that both the local and the global have been subsumed under the mantle of progress and image-making, resulting in a place that is "the inverse of both globality and locality, the ultimate nonplace that belongs to everywhere, yet is located nowhere in particular and which has little to offer but Planet Hollywood, the Hard Rock Café, and other sites of serialized uniqueness" (73).

By localization of the global, I refer to those aspects of city life aimed at the reappropriation of regional identity. In Atlanta, the current excitement and advocacy around the Beltline project speaks vividly to this concept. It is an effort to combine greenspace, land use, and transit options as a means to localize the global need for community and identity, by creating a connected series of parks and amenities that, allegedly, no other city in the United States, or perhaps the world, has. Similarly, the push for sustainable communities (discussed at length farther on in this book) is another means by which people attempt to incorporate global concerns, such as environmental consciousness, into local, daily practices.

These two often competing but occasionally complementary aspects of spatiality—one gobbling up place through homogenization and the other struggling to rescue it from obliteration via local identity claims—comprise the essence of the space narratives as I utilize them here. This lopsided equation with (as we shall see in the ensuing discussion) the attempts at retrieval often resulting in the unintended consequence of reproducing that which they aim to escape—reveals an important component of the mode of mobility. That is to say, the space narratives help us to understand how the mode of mobility is deeply implicated in the orchestration of space. Mobility's infrastructure is informed by pushes and pulls toward the vacuous and the meaningful, the artificial and the authentic.

Space narratives use the place research as their jumping-off point, further problematizing notions of location by placing them in a broader context. For example, in examining the new "planned communities," both the place research and the space narratives can help us to identify whose interests are served by "new" spatial configurations. The space narratives can also take us farther into the recognition that places are symbols for something else (affluence, poverty, individuality, private property) and that at the same time that "something else" gets finally devoured by the symbols themselves. LeFebvre ([1974] 1991) explains: "The 'world of signs' is not merely the space occupied by space and images . . . It is also that space where the Ego no longer relates to its own nature, to the material world, or even to the 'thingness' of things (commodities), but only to things bound to their signs and indeed ousted and supplanted by them" (311).

Through this lens, then, we begin to apprehend the ways in which, for instance, the supremacy of the automobile has resulted in "city life [that] is subtly but profoundly changed, sacrificed to that abstract space where cars circulate like so many atomic particles" (312). The examination of these three intimately related literatures will set the stage for the analysis of the three transportation cases I explore: MARTA, GRTA, and the Beltline.

Chapter 3 takes an in-depth look at MARTA. I begin by situating MARTA's current station in historical context. I look at its evolution from the perspectives of Atlanta's black and white communities and other interested parties, including the transit dependent, the business community, political actors, and environmental and equity groups. I examine the interactions, negotiations, and outcomes among these several actors. This exploration places MARTA squarely in the center of Atlanta's racial and spatial disputes, and highlights the ways in which politics continue to be deeply implicated in its trajectory.

MARTA, often read as both symbol and carrier of Atlanta's poor and left behind, has, at times, been alternately framed as Atlanta's beautiful centerpiece. Its current hideous reputation, to elucidate this point, caused one of my respondents to proclaim, "It's hard to believe now, but it's only been nine years since MARTA was the darling of this town! I mean, the Olympics would never have come to Atlanta without MARTA!" In tracing MARTA's path to its current brink of transformation, it becomes clear that the contest over what it becomes is more dependent on what it means than what it is.

The investigation of the Georgia Regional Transportation Authority (GRTA) in chapter 4 reveals the deeply conflicted relationships between land-use planning and transportation modality. From its inception to its present state of being, GRTA has conjured up both the best intentions and the worst fears of area actors regarding a vision for Atlanta's mobility future. Implemented at the behest of Governor Roy Barnes in response to issues of nonattainment of air quality standards, GRTA's powers (though, as we shall see, sparingly used) have become emblematic of the tightrope between liberty and license, or, seen from another perspective, between urban planning and social engineering.

Shot through with language allowing for unprecedented regulation on area transportation plans, the GRTA statute moves our inquiry to a deep place, poignantly pitting notions of free-market ideology against those of limited, sustainable growth. Those who favor unfettered mobility are passionate in their defense, not only of its benefits, but also of its position in our lives as an inalienable right. Those who see setting some limits as necessary in leaving our children a livable planet are equally ardent in their beliefs and efforts. The contestation over GRTA's role is an excellent site in which to view this intense divide, which profoundly influences local, regional, national, and global discourses and performances.

Chapter 5 explores the current proposal to build on a belt line of existing railroad tracks in Atlanta. The proposal was based on a Georgia Institute of Technology graduate student's master's thesis, and then strongly advocated by developers, city government, various transportation agencies, and pedestrian and bicycle-oriented groups. The proposition is essentially a twenty-two-mile loop of greenspace, transit, and transit-oriented development within the city of Atlanta. This is a particularly significant case, because its proponents frame it as advantageous to all parties—promoting it as tantalizing to growth, green, and equity groups alike.

Despite seemingly ubiquitous support, the Beltline is no more unidimensional than the other cases studied. Notwithstanding the rhetoric, it is as unlikely to be a panacea for all the city's ills as it is to bridge the ideological chasm already referenced between area actors. Thus, its physical manifestation and symbolic meanings will be negotiated on the same playing field as the other instances examined. The Beltline project is gathering steam every day and appears to be remarkably popular with a broad cast of players. (Critics have also begun to appear on the scene, as we shall see in Chapter 5.) Yet there are really multiple versions of what it may become floating around the city. Its neonatal status makes it distinct from MARTA, which we are perhaps capturing in its swan song phase, and from GRTA, which we are analyzing six years into its existence. The Beltline affords us an opportunity to speculate, based on evidence from the other cases and from application of the sociological imagination, on which version will ultimately emerge.

The concluding chapter will examine the ways in which taken together these three cases provide an optimum window through which to view the Atlanta Metropolitan Area's transportation policies and practices over the last several years. Ideally, it will also give us the theoretical tools to assist in the formulation of a vision that will move us forward, as the transportation lingo goes, in a "seamless, linked, and coordinated" fashion. This chapter will also go beyond the lessons of the preceding ones, and be a safe haven in which to richly imagine a different mode of mobility. In it, while not entirely suspending reality, I invite us to envision with fewer cynical constraints a world of movement within spaces created by and for the people. After acknowledging some of the mighty forces that we find ourselves up against, I will draw on examples from inspirational, experimental, and visionary persons and communities that seek to create, in the words of Lefebvre ([1974] 1991), "an architecture of pleasure and joy, of community in the use of the gifts of the earth" (379). I will examine some alternatives to the auto-cratic landscape that has been so painstakingly crafted. Examining contemporary mobility patterns—central and marginal, actualized and fantasized, with and against the current—I will take a glimpse into the potential futures of transportation. Shifting our gaze from the horrific probable to the promising possible, we round off our tour through the labyrinth of the mode of mobility, ultimately returning to what is likely to actually be the transportation future of the region.

TWO

THE TRANSPORTATION TRIO

Race, Place, and Space

RACE LITERATURE

Any attempt to comprehend transportation options and policy decisions anywhere in the United States, and in Atlanta in particular, must take race into consideration. "Racism has kept the Atlanta region geographically divided. Indeed, race is at the heart of Atlanta's regional transportation dilemma" (Bullard et al. 2000:69). African Americans, who comprise about two-thirds of the city of Atlanta's population (and a little under one-third of the greater MSA), remain the heirs of transportation disadvantages on a number of levels. Increasingly, as the Hispanic and other minority populations grow in the area, some members of these groups are being treated to the same hindrances. Bullard et al. (2000) distinguish three varieties of inequity regarding transportation projects:

> Procedural inequity results when transportation decisions are not carried out in a uniform, fair and consistent manner with the involvement of diverse public stake holders.
>
> Geographic inequity results from the geographic and spatial impacts—both positive and negative—of transportation decisions. These impacts affect urban, rural, and central-city neighborhoods differently. Some communities are physically located on the wrong side of the tracks and often receive substandard services. Environmental justice concerns arise when transportation systems disproportionately favor one geographic area or spatial location over another.

> Social inequity results when transportation benefits and burdens are not randomly distributed across population groups. Generally, transportation benefits accrue to the wealthier and better educated segments of society, while transportation burdens fall disproportionately on people of color and individuals at the lower end of the socioeconomic spectrum. (67–68)

Examples of such inequities include:

A greater likelihood of pedestrian fatalities: "People of color account for less than a third of the Atlanta region's population and nearly two-thirds of all the pedestrian fatalities in the region" (72). This is also true nationally, and is partially due to the fact that people of color are more likely to walk than whites.

National studies show that blacks walk 82 percent more than whites, and Hispanics walk 58 percent more than non-Hispanic whites (U.S. Department of Transportation 1997). The Surface Transportation Policy Project (STPP) reports that walking is thirty-six times more dangerous than driving (with Atlanta being one of the most dangerous cities for pedestrians) . . . on average, states spend just fifty-five cents per person of their federal transportation funds on pedestrian projects, less than 1 percent of their total federal transportation dollars. Average spending on highways came to $72 per person (Bullard et al. 2000:13).

A decreased likelihood of car ownership: although automobile possession is extremely high among the U.S. population (91.7 percent of households as of 2001), there are differences in terms of primary reliance on the automobile by race. 87.6 percent of whites, 83.1 percent of Asians and Hispanics, and 78.9 percent of blacks principally depend on private vehicles for their mobility (EJRC 2003:2). More specifically, in the area served by the Metropolitan Atlanta Rapid Transportation Authority (MARTA), a whopping 26.5 percent of blacks versus only 6.3 percent of whites are without a car (Bullard et al. 2004:61).

The inconveniences that are part and parcel of greater public transportation dependence: ("People of color are twice as likely as their white counterparts to use non-auto modes of travel—public transit, walking, bicycles—to get to work" [Bullard et al. 2000:68]). For instance, "[G]enerally, people who commute using public transit spend twice as much time traveling as those who travel by car" (68). The exodus of jobs from central cities, where public transportation is far more likely to be accessible, is another burden of greater public transit dependence. Higher rates of the physical ailments associated with transportation fall out: a national study conducted by the Center for Disease Control and Prevention between 1980 and 1993 determined that "African Americans are two to six times more likely than whites to die from asthma" (71).

Also, poor people of color suffer greater economic burdens both in terms of their own mobility and in terms of subsidizing others' mobility:

As regards the former, "Americans spend more on transportation than any other household expense except housing. On average, Americans spend 19 cents out of every dollar earned on transportation expenses . . . The nation's poorest families spend more than 40 percent of their take home pay on transportation . . . Nationally, African Americans earn only $649 per $1,000 earned by white households" (EJRC 2003:2). As regards subsidizing others' mobility, the MARTA case is illustrative. It is only residents of DeKalb and Fulton counties that pay the one cent MARTA sales tax, yet "A recent license tag survey, 'Who Parks- and -Rides,' covering the period 1988–1997, revealed that 44 percent of the cars parked at MARTA lots were from outside the Fulton/DeKalb County service area" (Bullard et al. 2004:55).

Underpinning all of these disadvantages is the reality that Atlanta is a deeply segregated city, with a startling north (white)/south (black) split. "For years, I-20 served as the racial demarcation line in Atlanta, with blacks located largely to the south and whites to the north" (Bullard et al. 2000:69). This racialized component of Atlanta's spatial configuration is by no means a new phenomenon. While recent rhetoric proudly proclaims Atlanta to be a city "too busy to hate," history says otherwise. In her eloquent book on Atlanta's post-Emancipation African American laundry women's efforts to gain control of their political and social lives, Tera Hunter (1997) speaks to the push-me pull-you mentality of race relations in Atlanta that has remained so characteristic and continues to reflect in transportation politics:

> As long as blacks were living in close contact as servants or subordinates, physical proximity was not only acceptable but desirable. It was usually when blacks moved into white neighborhoods on equal footing that physical proximity became an aberration. (105)

This "geography of privilege" (Logan and Molotch 1988:197) has stubbornly persisted into the current Atlanta landscape. It is reflected, for instance, in the notion of "work-force housing," which is the latest appellation for low-income housing. The implication being that it is socially useful for the non-poor to keep laborers close at hand or easily transportable. The "work force" in question tends to consist of nonwhites.

While Atlanta is known for its unusually high numbers of middle- and upper-class African Americans, this does not mean that blacks and whites are unusually integrated in the region. On the contrary, with the aid of modern transportation options, omnibuses, trolleys, and so forth, segregation became more stark and entrenched in the form of the urban/suburban split as the twentieth century got underway. But it was finally the meteoric rise of the private automobile (all over the nation) that concretized this polarization. In 1899, there were a total of about four thousand cars manufactured in the United States. By 1919, nearly two million were produced (Chinoy 1955:12). The explosive increase was partly due to Henry Ford's insight that sales would increase if workers could afford the products they manufactured and had partly to do with powerful oil and rubber interests, which I will treat more fully later in this book. Relevant here is that cars to some extent democratized mobility and yet simultaneously (and paradoxically) aided in the further segregation of people by race and class and other social markers.

The American Dream, epitomized by automotive freedom, was (and remains) widely shared by people of all hues. Sikivu Hutchinson (2003) notes, "For blacks who had protested Jim Crow on street railways and railroads, automobiles were a means of liberation from the dehumanization of public transit in particular and public space in general" (92).

Tracing two family histories in *Where Peachtree Meets Sweet Auburn*, Pomerantz (1996) demonstrates the geographical and social disconnects and interdependence of blacks and whites in Atlanta. In the following passage, some of the meanings of driving an automobile for John Wesley Dobbs (a prominent Atlanta figure and grandfather of former Atlanta mayor Maynard Jackson), affectionately known as "the Grand," are described:

> During the early 1940s, the Grand streaked across the single-lane highways of Georgia in his green Lincoln Zephyr. He was bound for his Masonic meetings where he intended to spread the gospel of voter registration. He drove his automobile hard and fast, just as he drove his masons. His daughters feared riding in the car when the Grand was behind the wheel. He adored speed in an automobile. It was, after all, one of the few ways in which a southern black could make progress quickly. (144)

For Dobbs, and perhaps for many others like him, race, gender, and power meet behind the wheel. A device used largely for racial separation, the automobile, having carried millions of whites away from blacks physically and metaphorically, is used in this instance as a tool to escape the very feelings of oppression that its use at times creates. Concomitantly, the force and speed transferred from the engine to the man allow him to feel powerful in an otherwise powerless milieu.

As identity issues become intertwined with mobility issues, it is not a simple matter of power and economics controlling how people traverse space in cities. As Mann et al. (2001) note: "The power of the auto/highway lobby is legendary, but the problem goes deeper because the working class itself is hooked on the auto for both transportation and cultural reasons" (9). If and what we drive becomes a matter of "taste" in our minds because the built environment and the dominant discourse leave us few choices beyond color and shape. Taste, as Bourdieu (1984) informs us, "continuously transforms necessities into strategies, constraints into preferences . . . through taste, an agent has what he likes because he likes what he has" (505–506).

How those "choices," born of "taste" and implemented (or not) due to economic and cultural resources, are read by ourselves and others informs our social status. First whether, and then what, you drive becomes saturated with symbolic cues about who you are. This is hardly lost on the advertising industry whose creative geniuses spend untold hours developing and perfecting just the right "hooks" to target every conceivable niche in the driving market. In all car advertising, whether in print or on screen, there is an underlying assumption that everyone must have a car. The only objective then is to let us know why it must be this one. The barrage of automobile advertisements linking driving with freedom helps to reinforce the already profoundly entrenched linkage in most people's minds between driving and the American Dream. The privileging and valorizing of car ownership and the consequent devalorization of other forms of movement make it doubly difficult for those who cannot afford to drive. As Henderson (1999) asserts, "[T]he Montgomery Bus Boycotts and the Rosa Parks episode resulted in more cynical white racist reactions that implicitly created an anti-transit ideology. Transit became associated with the poor, and more significantly, with blacks, and because of this it was considered inferior by many whites" (5), and I would add, by people of all colors as well.

In a class assignment asking each student to engage in a discussion of how race, class, and gender had personally affected him or her (nothing about transportation was suggested in the assignment) one of my African American female students wrote:

> When High School hits, economics takes over. Then you have—what a guy can drive and if he drives, what kind of car did his parents buy him? You tend to look at the kids who ride the city bus as a lower class. I remember I would not be caught dead on a bus—I'd rather walk.

Yet, perhaps it is not public transportation itself that is degrading, but rather the notion that one "must" use it. A respondent in a study done by Jensen (1997) noted, "It is not low status to take the bus, but it is low status not to have the choice. It is not low status to choose to take the bus if you have a car in your garage . . . If you chose public transportation yourself there is nothing embarrassing about it" (in Ger et al. 1999:17). Thus, the meanings of mobility are not only read in the ways in which we move about but also in the reasons for employing the modes that we do. The price of conformity is higher for those who must struggle to maintain the symbols of achievement, in this case the car, than for those who do not. In our country this burden falls more heavily on people of color. As Veblen ([1973] 2001) noted, "No class of society, not even the most abjectly poor, forgoes all customary conspicuous consumption. The last items of this category of consumption are not given up except under stress of the direst necessity" (497). And this attitude has been applicable regarding the car for a long time, as early as the late 1920s, when the Lynds engaged in their famous study, some of their respondents had this to say about their priorities: "[A] mother of nine told them, 'We'd rather do without clothes than give up the car.' Another said, 'I'd go without food before I'll see us give up the car.' A woman explained why her family had purchased a car before indoor plumbing: 'Why, you can't go to town in a bathtub' " (in Baxandall and Ewen 2000:15).

The notion that everyone can (and implicitly should) have an automobile has increasingly become pervasive and persuasive. But this democratization of the American Dream, embodied in the sweet freedom ubiquitously linked to the automobile by no means suggests either that access becomes likewise democratized nor that ownership and usage carry the same social meanings—or physical locations—for different races. Or as Irrante (1980) puts it, "A range of social and economic considerations for example, the proportion of family income which could be spent on a car, shaped people's identities as consumers and their uses of cars. In other words, inequality continued to affect the ability to consume even though the opportunity to consume became more widespread" (509).

While nearly everyone may want a car, not everyone can have one, for a variety of social and economic reasons. Yet race seems to be stubbornly salient in this determination. Raphael and Stoll (2000) break down car ownership by age, educational attainment, and race (three categories) in a study conducted in the early 1990s, demonstrating that disparities in ownership by race persist across categories of age and educational attainment (while by no means a perfect proxy for income, at least informative). I have reproduced their chart below in a modified form (from Table 1, 12):

Table 2.1. Car-Ownership Percentages by Race/Ethnicity, Educational Attainment, and Age 1993/1994

	White	*Black*	*Latino*
All	75.7	46.8	52.2
Educational Attainment			
Less than 12 years	50.7	28.4	43.5
12 years	76.7	45.5	52.0
13 to 15 years	77.3	52.6	61.1
16 years	82.3	70.0	71.4
More than 16 years	87.3	74.0	74.6
Age			
16–19	14.3	3.6	8.8
20–24	52.2	20.6	33.0
25–34	80.3	48.9	58.9
35–44	87.0	61.2	69.3
45–54	89.1	67.9	68.5
55–65	87.4	70.5	63.8

The sample combines the fourth wave of the 1992 and 1994 Survey of Income and Program Participation.

These data show us that racial differences in car ownership persist across all age and educational attainment levels, with the greatest differences being for people with lower levels of education and for those between the ages of twenty and thirty-four (with more than thirty percentage point differences for those categories). While ownership begins to level out with higher education and at the youngest and oldest ages, it never fully equalizes. With greater than sixteen years of education, for example, about 87 percent of whites, 75 percent of Latinos, and 74 percent of blacks own cars, and for people between the ages of sixteen and nineteen about 14 percent of whites, about 3.5 percent of blacks, and nearly 9 percent of Latinos own cars.

In addition to disparate meanings and access to mobility modes, transportation planning itself has been used as a weapon against people of color. Using transportation infrastructure for social control and specifically as a tool of racial segregation and containment has long been a feature of urban planning. A Chicago planner, Daniel Hudson Burnham, asserted in the 1890s that "broad thorough fares" should be cut "through the unwholesome district" in order to forcibly relocate residents "so degraded by long life in the slums that they have lost all power of caring for themselves" (Bayer 1978:272). This linking of a culture of poverty argument to transportation policies is by no means unique. Massey and Denton (1993:56) note that "urban renewal" and the road and highway construction frequently associated with it have often been tantamount to "negro removal" in many U.S. urban centers. In Atlanta, transportation policies have long been used in a project of systematic exclusion. The back-alley dwelling law of 1955,[1] in conjunction with the elimination of many alleys themselves, ostensibly to improve the housing quality in certain in-town neighborhoods had the added bonus/burden (depending on which side of the alley you were standing on) of driving large numbers of African Americans out of these areas (Keating 2001:48). Along with practices and policies that dispersed or isolated both poverty-stricken and middle-class African Americans, there was the concurrent automobile-driven exodus of Atlanta's white elite from the urban core. As Roth and Ambrose (1996) inform us, at the turn of the twentieth century Atlanta's white and wealthy mostly lived in the central city. They began to move to the north over the next couple of decades, such that by 1930 nearly 50 percent of those in the Social Register lived north of Ansley Park. Consequently, "Racial distance and separation in Atlanta was now not only political and social, it was increasingly spatial as well" (152).

As elsewhere in the United States, shifts in neighborhood racial composition in Atlanta have generally meant more segregation rather than more integration. For example, "Between 1960 and 1970, (these) neighborhoods changed from being almost 100% white to almost 100% black. In Kirkwood, for example, 91% of residents were white in 1960; by 1970, 97% of the population was black" (Reid and Adelman 2003:8). Roads were specifically and strategically used to ensure this continued divide. The 1946 Lochner plan, commissioned by the City of Atlanta and Fulton County, was a study of traffic and highway patterns and locations in the Atlanta area aimed at developing subsequent road systems to enhance the flow of traffic and increase business and neighborhood development. "However, wherever the highway/road system could possibly serve a racial function, it was developed with that in mind also" (Bayor 1996: 61). Sometimes the use of roads as racial barriers has been made quite explicit, as in a 1960 Bureau of Planning report, which stated, "[A]pproximately two to three years ago there was an 'understanding' that the proposed route of the West Expressway [I-20 West] would be the boundary between the White and Negro communities" (in Bayor 1996:61). The closing off of roads was yet another measure employed to ensure segregation, even at the expense of leaving perfectly usable land as dead space. Bayor (1988) tells us:

> In the late 1950s the city and county agreed to cut Willis Mill Road five blocks south of Martin Luther King Jr. Drive (formerly Gordon Road) so that it would be impossible to drive from that street to Cascade Road. Willis Mill begins again north of Cascade . . . To prevent the southward migration of blacks into the white section, part of the road was abandoned and over 100 acres of land were left undeveloped between the dead-ended parts of the road. (14)

The placement and layout of roads (or in some instances the non-placement of them) and the availability of transit options not only served as racial barriers to ensure continued segregation but also often resulted in spatial mismatch, the physical distance between jobs and those who need them. When Georgia Power owned the transit lines in the 1940s and 50s, their refusal to provide service in black neighborhoods placed a heavy burden on black commuters who needed to get downtown. Similarly, in the 1970s suburban counties outside Atlanta (such as Cobb and Gwinnett) would not allow MARTA entrée. These decisions were likely racially driven, since, as Bayor (2000) points out, "It makes little sense economically to hamper easy travel throughout the metro area. But a fixation on race explains much, racial concerns in this situation took precedence over economic considerations" (53).

This situation persists, as the Brookings Institution 2000 report tells us: "MARTA has over 1,600 miles of rail and bus lines and serves over half a million people each weekday, yet it does not reach three out of the five counties (Cobb, Gwinnett, and Clayton) in which the region's employment in concentrated" ("Moving Beyond Sprawl":22). These uniquely MARTA-related causes and effects of race and place-making will be more fully drawn in chapter 3.

In addition to shaping mobility options and access to employment opportunities, the racially motivated placement of transit options can also be hazardous to one's health or even life threatening. As mentioned earlier, both asthma rates and pedestrian fatalities are higher for people of color. Take the case of Cynthia Wiggins, an African American seventeen-year-old from Buffalo, New York. She was killed by a dump truck while crossing a seven-lane highway to get to a suburban mall because the bus that came closest, serving predominantly black riders, was forbidden to stop at the mall. Cynthia had a job in a fast food restaurant at the mall, and the stop was about three hundred arduous yards away (Bullard et al. 2000: 68).

In Atlanta too, much can be learned about the racial practices as opposed to the racial promises by looking at transportation policies, and specifically those around public transit. A *Creative Loafing* article (Feaster 2003) describes an artist named Epstein, who depicts his vision of MARTA. Epstein is quoted as saying:

> Almost all of the east-west riders were black. There were a few more white riders on north-south trains, mostly headed to the airport. Soon I put this together with information about the racial politics of the system, how the suburban counties declined to be part of it, how when the system was first built, some whites joked that the acronym stood for "Moving Africans Rapidly Through Atlanta." (47)

Feaster offers this insight: "Within Epstein's nicely melancholy work is a bitter truth that all of the city's progress suddenly backslides on MARTA and in Atlanta's car-dependent culture, which keeps the races segregated" (47). Just as throughout the nation our mythology about integration and equality is brutally exposed when we look at residential patterns, in Atlanta, the superficiality of our "city too busy to hate" rhetoric is also laid bare on the bus.

PLACE RESEARCH

Since its inception, urban sociology has linked the role of transportation to the fate of places. In many instances, the very survival of a community has hinged upon its accessibility, technological transit achievements or failures, and its ability or inability to adapt to broader changes in that technology. For example, Cottrell (1951) demonstrated that the switch from steam powered trains to diesel powered ones spelled doom for many small Southwestern towns whose "reason for existence was to service the steam locomotive" (360). New transportation technologies, or shifts in dependence on one mode over another, while not always resulting in death of place, certainly always alter it and reflect its alteration. In the current landscape, this is most evident when observing how use of the automobile has monumentally transformed not only the ways in which we traverse space, but also the social structures that underpin its traversal. Many of the resulting phenomena arising from these changes are referred to under the rubric of sprawl.

There is widespread agreement that sprawl must be addressed if people are going to continue to move about in urban spaces, and this is nowhere a more salient issue than in Atlanta, which has been variously dubbed the "megasprawl" center, "the sprawl poster child" and "Sprawlanta" (Bullard et al. 2000:2). Where widespread agreement ends is with both the definition of sprawl and decisions regarding how it ought to be addressed. In a recent study aimed at water resource management, the Towson University Center for Geographic Information Sciences (CGIS) notes that definitions of sprawl vary by interest group with some drawing on "disease analogies," the Sierra Club focusing on issues of irresponsibility and inadequate planning; less invidious descriptions invoke notions of "low density urbanization and discontinuous development." According to the Towson Center's interpretation, "Sprawl occurs when the rate of land conversion and consumption for urban uses exceeds the rate of population growth for a given area over a specified period of time" (CGIS Report 2004:1).

Regardless of definition used or emphasis in description of sprawl, it is clear that Atlanta fits the bill. Low density combined with high energy consumption, which are the hallmarks of Atlanta's growth patterns, are the very definition of sprawl. While this has resulted in fantastic benefits for some people and some areas, it has done so at the expense of others. Specifically, the inner city has suffered as the suburbs have prospered:

> Most of metro Atlanta's sprawl has occurred in the counties on the north side of the city in the so-called "favored quarter," roughly located in the wedge between I-75 and I-85. In 1980, the northern suburbs accounted for 44 percent of the Atlanta Regional Commission's planning population. This share increased to 52 percent by 1990. In contrast, the southern suburbs' share of total population declined from 33 to 32 percent over the same ten-year period. (Brown 1998:1)

This of course adversely impacts the entire region in terms of environmental quality, not to mention transportation patterns. Despite the obvious traffic hours, Atlanta continued to choose roads over transit. Between 1982 and 1987 there were more than nine hundred miles of freeway added to the metropolitan region, which rapidly filled up. By the late nineties the average metropolitan Atlanta driver was covering thirty-five miles per day. "Atlanta's 'Thelma and Louise transportation policy,' as it was dubbed was headed for a cliff" ("Stuck in traffic," startribune.com 2000). One important Atlanta response to these issues of sprawl will be addressed in detail in chapter 4; the implementation of the Georgia Regional Transportation Authority.

The ills of sprawl are of course not restricted to the city, with suburbia taking a huge hit often in the form of isolation, the most miles logged by residents to get to destinations, and other problems such as excessive speeding. Duany et al. (2000) note, for instance, "Generally, the only time that people don't speed in modern suburbia is when they are lost, which is, fortunately, quite often" (119–20). This ironic quip summarizes two suburban pitfalls. And it would appear that at least through the 1990s not much had transpired to change suburban myths or realities. Baxandall and Ewen (2000) resolved to take a fresh look at suburbia in their book Picture Windows, suspending reductionist images of cloned cottages and isolated white housewives. What they found, for the most part, were cloned cottages and isolated white housewives, rewrit for the nineties as doppelganger condos and sequestered (mostly white) individuals.

But this book is meant neither as a descriptor of sprawl nor as a litany of its myriad attendant miseries. Both of these projects have been well carried out by others. Yet sprawl and its tentacles are inseparable from this work in that it is simultaneously the result of and the inspiration for transportation policies and practices, with the car as the centerpiece from which these agendas radiate. The love affair with the automobile (and how this relationship shapes all aspects of the mode of mobility) is unquestionably central to both issues of sprawl and to my guiding concerns.

America's love affair with the automobile can be seen through various lenses. First, there is the view that it is the ideal adult, healthy relationship—the culmination of years of work and technology resulting in the logical and most efficient means of getting about—in other words, progress. For the purposes of this discussion we shall call this position Pro-Car Growth. Secondly, there are those who hold that the love affair is in need of marriage counseling, essentially beneficial to society and to individuals, but in need of reform. This will be here referred to as Sustainable Growth. Finally, there are those who believe that this tryst has grown altogether codependent and dysfunctional, bolstering greed and unchecked accumulation for some, deeply discrediting and disadvantaging others, and first and foremost an orchestrated affair, or, if you will, an arranged marriage, created by late capitalism with the express result (if not intent) of reproducing itself. I call this view of the car-person pairing Equitable Growth. Let us examine each of these viewpoints in turn.

Pro-Car Growth

The pro-car growth, or conservative view, is not shared by most scholars and is generally denigrated in academia as politically incorrect, shortsighted, and backward thinking. Nevertheless, paradoxically, it remains the predominant perspective from which policy decisions are rendered and the platform on which many politicians stand. From this dais venomous diatribes are hurled at those holding other viewpoints, serving both to simplify and marginalize dissent and transgression. Progress and growth are linked as not only obvious but inevitable bedfellows, and to be against unfettered growth is akin to being against progress and downright anti-American. What's good for General Motors is good for America is hardly a bygone philosophy.

Atlanta has a long and renowned history of "pro-growth politics," with strong ties between the business elite and elected officials. William Hartsfield (Atlanta mayor through the 1940s and 1950s) once noted, "The secret of our success [is that] we roll a red carpet out for every damn Yankee who comes in here with two strong hands and some money. We break our necks to sell him" ("Moving Beyond Sprawl" 2000:32). This spirit persists, not only in Atlanta, but in the American ethos in general. It is often linked specifically to the car and sometimes centered around a defensive stance and an indignant reproach against those who may seem to differ. In this view, automobile dependency is not only understandable but also desirable, and it is efforts to separate people from vehicles that are seen as irrational and counterproductive. Automobiles make life easier, more exciting, and allow us to do more and go farther. From such a lens, proponents of reduced spending on roads and greater expenditures on public transport are misguided and backward thinking. Samuel (1999) remarks:

> We must come to terms with the automobile. The failed effort to pry drivers from their cars has produced a vast waste. More important, it has prevented us from adopting measures to fit the motor vehicle into the environment, to make it serve human purposes with fewer unwanted side effects. The problems on the roads must be tackled on the roads. (55)

Samuel is far from alone in feeling that automobiles must be protected against heretics and that we can and must build our way out of sprawl. In a 2001 article in the *Atlanta Journal-Constitution (AJC)* by the editorial board, they, "called for an end to 'petty vendettas against suburbanites' and 'lifestyle choices pejoratively called 'sprawl,'' urging the design of a transportation system mindful that "the internal combustion engine" has transformed the nation by freeing us "to live where we choose" and "is here to stay." Among their suggestions for improved conditions in the area was "double-deck critical freeways," a vertical alternative to more horizontal lanes (from Georgia Smart Growth News Articles 2004:39). Relatedly, in another 2001 *AJC* article, a Rutgers University political science professor, James Dunn Jr. is cited as saying that he sees "real dangers and costs hidden in the anti-sprawl agenda." Two recounted in the article are "the demonization of the automobile," and the "costly overselling of public transit's capability." "The professor concludes that . . . blaming cars 'for suburban angst and spending large amounts of public money to re-create the passenger rail system of the pre-auto era are bad ideas' " (from Georgia Smart Growth News Articles 2004:47–48).

Similarly, Wendell Cox, a noted researcher on urban policy, transportation, and demographics, who heads up a consultancy firm on these and related topics, asserts on his Web site that smart growth is a delusion, not a vision. He advocates a "pro-choice" stance when it comes to urban development, meaning that if the will of the people is for more cars then what we need to build is more space for them (2001 www.demographia.com).

For the final examples of this kind of reasoning, I draw on James Wilson's article in Commentary entitled "Cars and Their Enemies," in which he dichotomously frames the automobile argument as a public versus private debate in which privatization will "naturally" and "inevitably" be the winner. Wilson (1997) suggests that the disagreement between those he labels "car haters" and those he terms "car defenders" is really "a debate between private benefits and public goods" (Wilson 1997:20). He goes on to aver that when we weigh the costs to society (pollution, energy consumption, noise levels, and safety issues) against the personal gains of flexibility, comfort, privacy and time saving, the automobile wins in this cost-benefit analysis (20). As expressive of the profound "rightness" of the bond, Wilson exquisitely reifies the human relationship to the car, "If people can afford it, they will want to purchase convenience, flexibility, and privacy. These facts are as close to a Law of Nature as one can get in the transportation business. When the industrial world became prosperous, people bought cars. It is unstoppable" (Wilson 1997:19). More of how this viewpoint plays out in the Atlanta context will be explicated in chapter 4 in the discussion of GRTA.

Sustainable Growth

The second position runs along a continuum from those who hold that our transportation policies need tweaking and minimal reform to those who feel the system is desperately ailing and in need of serious and fundamental revamping. This category includes the slow-growth, smart growth, livable communities, sustainable development, and New Urbanism promoters. In addition to widely varying degrees of reform perceived as necessary for viability, there is also a wide range of guiding principles among promoters of these various strategies. Some are most concerned with environmental issues. Some see safety as most salient. Some place health concerns front and center, still others focus on aesthetics and authentic connections to nature. Some emphasize social costs and benefits. And some see economic viability as the heart of the matter. Most planners, scholars, and other interested parties who subscribe to some version of smart-growth ideology have a combination of these concerns in mind and may accentuate one aspect or another in a variety of ways.

In a 1987 report put forth by the World Commission on Environment and Development, sustainability was defined as follows: "development that meets the needs of the present without compromising the ability of future generations to meet their own needs" (in Whitelegg 1997:99). In this broad sense, sustainability can be taken to include most if not all of the concerns referred to in the preceding paragraph. The notion of "needs" is, of course, not unproblematic. How and by whom they are defined is often central to policy decisions as well as to everyday understandings of mobility, as shall be amply demonstrated in chapters 3, 4, and 5. Let us here briefly examine some aspects of sustainability.

The environmental concerns associated with the burning of fossil fuels are myriad and well documented (for a full discussion of these hazards see, for example, Whitelegg 1997). I will only note at this point that, "[c]arbon dioxide is responsible for about 50 per cent of global warming. The main source of CO_2 is from fossil fuel combustion" (Whitelegg 1997:115). And more specific to Atlanta, "Every week some 500 acres of green space, forest, and farmland in the Atlanta region are plowed under to make way for new housing subdivisions, strip malls, shopping centers, and highways" (Bullard et al. 1999:19). While most of us are not aware of this land, air, and water destruction in an ordinary daily context, the health and safety aspects of automobility are more tangible.

Air pollution is associated with "asthma, nasal congestions, throat irritation, respiratory tract inflammation, reduced resistance to infection, changes in cell function, loss of lung elasticity, chest pains, lung scarring, formation of lesions within the lungs, and premature aging of lung tissues . . . Air pollution claims 70,000 lives a year, nearly twice the number killed in traffic accidents" (EJRC 2003:4). Increasingly, obesity, a serious national health concern, is linked to sprawl and automobile use. "The study of nearly 11,000 people in the Atlanta area found that people living in highly residential areas tend to weigh significantly more than those in places where homes and businesses are close together . . . for residents, this meant that the relative risk of being obese increased by about 35 percent between the most mixed and least mixed areas" (Stein 2004:1–2). As for safety, a 2003 study revealed that "In the United States, 70.8% of all deaths among persons aged 10–24 years result from only four causes: motor-vehicle crashes, other unintentional injuries, homicide, and suicide" (Grunbaum et al. 2003:1). In Georgia, citizens are more likely to be killed by a car than by a stranger with a gun (Hinkelman 1997:1). In 1997, there were a total of 1,607 motor vehicle deaths in the state, with the highest rates being among the elderly. In that same year, there were 184 traffic-related pedestrian deaths (Georgia Injury Mortality Statistics 1997). As of 1999, the CDC reported that Atlanta was the second most dangerous large metropolitan area for pedestrians (behind Miami) ("Georgians fear traffic crashes," Traffic Safety Digest 1999).

From a sociological perspective, my interest is in how our everyday understandings and practices allow for such a state of affairs. I ask, What impact do these practices have on producing and reproducing societies and individuals? Are pollution, land destruction, and the other negatives enumerated necessary evils in the inevitable march toward technological rationalization of time and space, ultimately bringing the most rewards to the greatest number of people? Or, are there viable alternatives that take into account "needs" that cannot be met through more spatial consumption, more speed, greater mobility for mobility's sake? As Joni Mitchell intoned, "They paved paradise, and put up a parking lot."

Long before Mitchell was decrying the asphalting of our nation's treasures, others were already anticipating the disastrous effects:

> What if we fail to stop the erosion of cities by automobiles? . . . In that case Americans will hardly need to ponder a mystery that has troubled men for millennia: What is the purpose of life? For us, the answer will be clear, established and for all practical purposes indisputable: The purpose of life is to produce and consume automobiles. (Jacobs [1961] 1992:370)

In 1958, Lewis Mumford articulated similar sentiments. He went so far as to speak of the American obsession with the automobile as a religion, thus "stand[ing] outside the realm of rational criticism" (in Marshall 2000:106). He notes that we retain our reverent fervor even when presented with evidence that the very things we rely on the automobile to provide, such as escape from urban dreariness, are, ironically, exacerbated by it. Thus, when the motorist "reaches his destination in a distant suburb, he finds the countryside he sought has disappeared: beyond him, thanks to the motorway, lies only another suburb, just as dull as his own" (107).

As early as 1941, Herbert Marcuse offers an eloquent disquisition on the transformation of both space and consciousness wrought by automobile travel, and most especially by the advent of the highway. He notes that in this reshaped landscape, those items that were once the pastoral destinations (lakes, mountains, and so on) now become obstacles to get by, through, or around. Additionally, the built environment informs us what is worth seeing, and how to feel about what we observe and do. We can now know that a view is "breathtaking" because there is a sign or an overlook telling us so. Similarly, we are not only told that we are tired, hungry, or thirsty at convenient intervals, but also what to do about it: "[G]iant advertisements tell [us] when to stop and find the pause that refreshes." Spontaneity is replaced by rationality, safety, and convenience. And finally, the highway becomes for Marcuse Weber's iron cage:

> There is no personal escape from the apparatus which has mechanized and standardized the world. It is a rational apparatus, combining utmost expediency with utmost convenience, saving time and energy, removing waste, adapting all means to the end, anticipating consequences, sustaining calculability and security. (Marcuse [1941] 1982:143)

Marcuse's disquisition demonstrates that the noose of rationality that the automobile society epitomizes was already drawn so tightly by this historical period that it nearly strangled any possibility of retreat. And yet, astonishingly, there was room enough for it to get still tighter. In the 1940s, this preplanned and packaged auto-driven society was as yet a choice among several. More work lay ahead to pave the way for absolute rule by automobile interests. In a more recent work aimed at explaining the notion of hegemony, Mark Surman (1994) uses the automobile as an example. He notes that changes in various institutions had to take place in order for North Americans to "joyously shout in unison 'the car is the only way to get around and we love it!' " (p. 1 in appendix). These changes included enormous injections of highway money from the government, the consequent car-oriented configuration of shopping centers, the almost total disappearance of public transit, and the mythological link to freedom and the American ethos that the automobile has been imbued with for a century (p. 1 in appendix).

Most of the scholars, past and present, warning us about the dangers embedded in unquestioned reliance on the automobile are not anti-progress fanatics pushing a Luddite agenda. In fact, many of them also caution against vilifying, scapegoating, or reifying the automobile as in itself capable of creating havoc and degradation. Jane Jacobs, for instance, after advising us to be wary of allowing cars to become the meaning of life, also counsels, "Automobiles are often conveniently tagged as the villains responsible for the ills of cities and the disappointments and futilities of city planning. But the destructive effects of automobiles are much less a cause than a symptom of our incompetence at city building" (7). Attempts (such as GRTA) to address this incompetence are often met with resistance, as shall be addressed in full in later chapters.

Overreliance on the automobile as the preferred mode of mobility is both emblematic and causative in levying a hefty social tax on the American consumer. Situated as it is in the context of a hierarchical, capitalistic, patriarchal society, this dependency plays its part in furthering various social gaps. The salience of race in this configuration, already addressed, is undeniable and will be revisited throughout this work. Mobility issues also need to be understood in terms of gender, age, class, and physical ability. For instance, Feagin (1998) writes, "Heterogeneous central cities provide more opportunities for women to resist patriarchy and develop independently from men, while homogeneous suburbs enshrine a more incapacitating and entrenched form of patriarchy" (16). Large urban centers also provide more opportunity for disappearing in the crowd. This is an aspect of city life that for some immigrant women in particular imbues them with a different kind of power. Hirsch (2000), in her study of Mexican immigrants in Atlanta notes in this regard: "[In Mexico] very few women own cars. For migrant women, mobility is power. The Mexican women I know in Atlanta who do drive never tire of the thrill of the freedom to go wherever they want without having to ask, of their new mastery of the street" (379).

Hirsch goes on to explain that it is the obscurity that lends to this sense of empowerment. For some, the privacy associated with automobile transport transforms their sense of the possible. "[In Mexico] a woman seen riding in a car with an unknown man would have some serious explaining to do, but in all likelihood her transgression would pass completely unnoticed amid Atlanta's urban anonymity" (379). Thus, both access and opportunity equate to mobility, and can mean the difference between dependence and autonomy.

Yet with gendered power relations remaining relatively entrenched, more independence from men for many women means more dependence on the automobile. This is because women are more likely to need variable path transportation options in order to run errands. The 1997 Personal Mobility Transportation Statistics Annual Report notes that the Nationwide Personal Transportation Survey (NPTS) defines person-trips as one-way travel from one destination to another. The annual report notes that while this is adequate for the simplest of journeys, it misses the complexity of many journeys. In real life, much travel is comprised of "chain trips," that is trips that involve multiple stops, for instance, dropping the kids off at school and then going grocery shopping, stopping at the cleaners, and then going to or from work. Trip chaining is a very common form of travel (about 46 percent of trips in 1990), with women more likely than men to practice it (42 percent versus 31 percent). The report further avers that it is difficult to determine causal direction in terms of car use and trip chaining; "It is unclear whether automobile use encourages trip chaining or if the desire to trip chain encourages automobile use" (154). Either way, however, the ubiquity of trip chaining clearly privileges automobile travel over other modes. Trip-chaining behavior appears to put other modes of transportation, such as transit, at a disadvantage.

In addition to these extra burdens, women's choices about how, where, and when to move about are also constrained by fear of danger in public spaces. This is true as well for the elderly and disabled. An aging driving population with greater night-blindness and slower reaction times also increases road hazards (Wolf 1996:188). Paltry (at best) accommodations for the disabled on public transportation render many people virtually immobile. Additionally, the everyday lives of children have been dramatically transformed by automobile domination. Wolf (1996) speaks of the enormous changes that have taken place for children in regard to use of space. At the beginning of the last century it was common for children in Western societies to play and roam up to four kilometers from their homes. Today they are largely driven to their increasingly scheduled activities (sports, ballet, art classes) and have less and less direct contact with nature. The child's view of the world is now filtered "through a car window while strapped into the backseat" (190). Wolf laments that this new relationship with the world results in a defensive rather than an exploratory mentality for children: "Previously, the child itself had to conquer the world; today, the most important thing the child has to learn in order to survive is not to cross the road" (190).

I would be remiss if I did not say a few words about class issues when speaking of the social costs of transportation options. Class will be more fully addressed in the following section on equitable growth, but there are a couple of points that should be articulated here. Class has everything to do with where we go and how we get there, from the cradle to the grave. As noted earlier in this paper, the democratization of space that transportation options may afford is an aspect that is both feared and hoped for, depending on the actor's position in the social strata. Fear from the upper class of lower-class encroachment being aided and abetted by new mobility technologies is long-standing, causing the Duke of Wellington to remark in the early 1800s regarding affordable public transit that it would "only encourage the common people to move about needlessly" (Jackson 1985:42). Such sentiments seem to have remarkable staying power. The proliferation of gated communities, panopticonic surveillance techniques, and transportation policies that favor race and class segregation regardless of the rhetoric are clear material manifestations of the same conception. The mode of mobility is essential in increasing the social distance between the haves and the have-nots and has dramatic effects on how daily living patterns differ for those with and those without. Vasconcellos (1997) writes about the effects in São Paulo, but could easily be speaking of anywhere in the world, including Atlanta, Georgia. Like Wolf, Vasconcellos speaks to the privatization of consumption patterns and the corresponding privatization of the means to arrive at them. Middle-class children must be chauffeured to school and to play. This is no surprise as, "These new forms of consumption derive from the 'commodification' of social relations proper to capitalist modernization" (251).

Working-class households have very different life styles. Children still play in the streets. Shopping is done largely locally. Health care is local as well. And schools are generally within walking distance. It was once the minority for whom the private car afforded the most benefits. Yet social and fiscal policy have followed the needs of the affluent. So much so in fact that, "the resulting travel behavior—in particular mode of travel, is practically preordained" (255), and because the built environment follows these needs, car ownership consequently becomes a necessity for nearly everyone. Yet here in the United States, class still deeply informs mode of transport. "Nationally, in more affluent neighborhoods, close to nine in ten people use motor vehicles to get to work, compared with approximately two-thirds in poor neighborhoods" (Jargowsky 1997:105). Nevertheless, on a psychological level, to be middle class becomes equated with car ownership and to give it up would be tantamount to giving up that status, an unacceptable proposition for most who consider themselves that class, or aspire to it (all but everybody).

I have looked at environmental concerns; safety and health issues; aesthetics and genuineness of connection with nature; and social costs put forth by critics calling for reform of the mode of mobility. The last piece of sustainability that I promised to touch on is its financial viability, or, that is to say, its practical application: the "what do we do about it" portion of all the criticisms of the current state of affairs. One vision of where we might go from here is frequently described under the designation of New Urbanism. Katz (1994) asserts (in normative language) that New Urbanism mandates two related practices: "First, urbanism—defined by its diversity, pedestrian scale, public space and structure of bounded neighborhoods—should be applied throughout a metropolitan region regardless of location: in suburbs and new growth areas as well as within the city" (xi). He says the second precept is that an entire region must be "structured by public space" (xi), in which the pedestrian is well positioned and the area must have an end point—that is, recognizable boundaries.

The Beltline project elaborated in chapter 5 is envisioned to incorporate these precepts. New Urbanism is meant to redress the ill effects of sprawl, which have configured cities, suburbs, and rural environments in such a way as to disadvantage residents of each. Duany and Plater-Zybeck (1994) have been instrumental in detailing the principles as well as the practical applications of New Urbanism. The Web site Newurbanism.org succinctly lays these out, providing us with the full flavor of New Urbanism. Here I will merely note the headings: Walkability; Connectivity; Mixed-use and Diversity; Mixed Housing; Quality Architecture and Urban Design; Traditional Neighborhood Structure; Increased Density; Smart Transportation; Sustainability; and Quality of Life. Under the last of these the authors assert: "Taken together these add up to a high quality of life well worth living and create places that enrich, uplift, and inspire the Human spirit" (NewUrbanism.org).

These recommendations have the distinct flavor of Jane Jacobs's earlier visions of livable communities. They are, in part, an attempt to recapture those elements of past neighborhoods (real or imagined) that were warmer and less alienating than those we have recently created and at the same time move forward incorporating technology and global understandings that are part and parcel of our current landscape. Jacobs's (1961) notion of "exuberant diversity" was closely akin to New Urbanist precepts. She posited that four conditions were necessary for this diversity to be transformative:

> 1. The district, and indeed as many of its internal parts as possible, must serve more than one primary function; preferably more than two. These must ensure the presence of people who go outdoors on different schedules and are in the place for different purposes, but who are able to use many facilities in common.
>
> 2. Most blocks must be short, that is, streets and opportunities to turn corners must be frequent.
>
> 3. The district must mingle buildings that vary in age and condition; including a good proportion of old ones so that they vary in the economic yield they must produce. This mingling must be fairly close-grained.
>
> 4. There must be sufficiently dense concentration of people, for whatever purposes they may be there. This includes dense concentrations . . . of people who are there because of residence. (151)

For these visions (and their contemporary cousins) to be viable, they must be marketable. Planned communities, such as Florida's Seaside and Celebration, have been successful, as have other efforts at smart growth, because they have been able to attract investors and customers with the wherewithal to maintain them. While such projects seem to have achieved some of their aims—greater walkability, more cohesive communities, less traffic congestion, and so on—this has often been at the expense of some of the other goals of sustainability. For example, criticisms of such planned communities are that they are sterile and cookie-cutter despite efforts to avoid these qualities; they reproduce inequality because only those with a particular social status can afford to live in them; and they ironically commodify the very things that they were seeking to salvage from commodification—turning walkability into a consumable and sense of community and pride in locality into glitzy products. This concept of the commodification of place, (and the high profile of mobility within it), brings us to the next section of the place research dealing with notions of equitable growth, turning to those scholars for whom reform is not enough.

Equitable Growth

The indispensability of ever-greater mobility is, arguably, not an intrinsic attribute of human beings. Rather, as Sawers ([1978] 1984) points out, "capitalist accumulation" both creates and reflects "high demand for mobility" (223). There are those who would argue that economic interests are solidly in the driver's seat when it comes to the built environment. In the debate over whether automobiles are ubiquitous because of efficiency and convenience or because of favoritism and privilege, those reading the landscape through the Equitable Growth lens would clearly favor the latter explanation. The notion of Equitable Growth challenges the dominant laissez-faire growth paradigm. This conception invites us to rethink mobility's distribution, and to notice hidden subsidies and privileges. Nathan Strauss, once head of the United States Housing Authority (USHA),[2] reminds us that "the automobile industry in the United States became great largely by reason of government subsidy." Rather than giving families aid so that they could more reasonably pay tolls to get to work, local and federal governments chose instead to subsidize the automobile industry:

> This was the largest subsidy ever granted by the government in the history of our country and produced the most notable results. The average amount expended for this purpose by federal and state governments annually in the period from 1935–1940, was nearly a billion dollars. (in Baxandall and Ewen 2000:114)

In his famous treatise, "American Ground Transport: A Proposal for Restructuring the Automobile, Truck, Bus and Rail Industries," Bradford Snell "describes how General Motors, Ford and Chrysler reshaped American ground transportation to serve corporate wants instead of social needs" (Snell 1974:1). Snell and others believed that General Motors and associates, Standard Oil, Phillips Petroleum, and Firestone successfully conspired to drive out the electric railway systems in the United States in order to amass unprecedented fortunes. Wolf (1996) notes, "By 1949, General Motors had been involved in the replacement of more than 100 electric transit systems with General Motors buses in 45 cities, including New York, Philadelphia, Baltimore, St. Louis, Oakland, Salt Lake City, and Los Angeles" (84). These accusations were substantiated by a lawsuit brought by the government against General Motors at the urging of the founder of the Electric Railroader's Association, which was upheld, albeit with miniscule recompense. Nonetheless, they were so controversial that they reverberate still. In 1998, for example, an anonymous piece was posted on the Internet entitled, "Who shudda shot the author of 'American Ground Transport' "–which is a scathing diatribe accusing Snell of being a mendacious, anti-American heretic. For instance, the author writes, "Not content with resorting to crude 'post hoc ergo propter hoc' fallacies, simpleminded economic calculations, distortions of fact, invented quotations, and other sophomoric tactics, Snell even finds it necessary to link General Motors with Nazism" (1).

There are others who less venomously disagree with Snell's proposition, not perhaps with the spirit so much as with his oversimplification of how the built environment came to be dominated by automotive interests. Sawers

([1978] 1984) offers an alternate view of the trolley decline. He suggests that rather than trolleys being conspiratorially driven out by automobile interests, "competition from the automobile initiated a process of cumulative decline which became self-reinforcing once begun" (230). In this view, trolleys were gradually forced out due to loss of revenue with cutbacks in service and quality leading to further declines in ridership. Then, as people increasingly purchased cars, this added to road congestion making it even more difficult for trolleys to operate. Ultimately, they were phased out of existence (230).

In his nuanced analysis, Sawers demonstrates how transportation policies in general are driven by multiple factors and various interests. He remarks that the role of the highway lobby in creating overreliance on motor vehicles has been well established and "widely decried by liberal critics" (233). He asserts that the role of the business community, since the 1920s, has been equally influential in shaping use of space and transportation policies but far more invisible from the public eye. Specifically, Sawers notes that the business elite hoped to drive downtown business district property values up, in part by changing land-use patterns to favor functions other than manufacturing (233).

Specific to Atlanta, the interplay between politics and business in shaping transportation policies is well documented. Keating (2001) tells us that in spite of all the shifts in politics and in the economy in Atlanta over time, what has remained fairly constant over the last several decades is the domination of city government by business interests (196). As a case in point, Keating notes that it was pressure from real estate interests that crushed the push for "land-use regulations that would have concentrated high-density commercial development around MARTA rail lines and stations," despite the fact that such regulations would have conceivable gone far in staving off the transportation and air quality nightmares the city currently faces, which was ostensibly its raison d'être in the first place, at least so voters were told (197).

These issues, not addressed by MARTA as some had envisioned, were later not addressed by GRTA in a similar vein despite an even more explicit agenda, as shall be further explained in chapter 4. Thus, many scholars posit that the shaping of the built environment to almost exclusively serve the needs of the automotive industry is not conspiratorial in nature but rather a matter of what Reiman (2001) refers to as "historical inertia." "By 1922, 135,000 suburban homes in 60 cities were already wholly dependent upon cars for transportation . . . By 1940, 13 million people lived in communities beyond the reach of public transportation" (Irrante 1980:3). In the countryside, "The reorganization of rural space which widespread car ownership facilitated changed farmers' needs for transportation. Within the specific context of those changes, the automobile was transformed from a rural convenience to a rural necessity" (4). Public transportation is often the last thing on the agenda in terms of the use of public monies. In response to fiscal crises in the late 1960s, everything but public transportation was considered worthy of funding. "By 1968, 28 states had approved diverting highway users' taxes for everything from welfare payments to mosquito control. In fact, of $8.2 billion of state highway construction, only $0.8 billion went to non-highway transportation uses" (Yago 1978:353).

Public transportation, which had in its turn fed the machine, turned out to be only an appetizer in the mobility feast, "By the end of the 1920s, the first era in U.S. urban mass transit drew to a close. The demand for mobility was not sated by the trolleys and subways; they only whetted capitalism's appetite. But it was the internal combustion engine that dominates the next era in urban transportation history" (Sawers [1978]1984: 229). Even in the "internal combustion" form, buses and trains have had, as is glaringly obvious, a hard time competing with the automobile. Yet municipalities' relationships with transit are not uncomplicated. It has proved necessary for cities to retain some form of transit in order to both serve the needs of their citizens and to bolster their reputations as world-class cities. In this regard, urban trains have been privileged over buses, which many argue is to the distinct disadvantage of those who rely most heavily on transit.

While there is much debate over the efficacy of rapid rail (fixed route) versus buses (variable route) transportation, many scholars and social activists argue that the former primarily benefits the non-poor while the latter assists those with fewer financial resources. This bus versus rail debate will be well documented in the coming chapters. Here, I will note that some aver that the expansion of rapid rail hinders the poor by detracting from bus service, cutting through cities in ways that decrease mobility, and even increasing automobile traffic in response to such sectionalizing. Sawers ([1978] 1984) notes in this regard that the anticipated beneficiaries of the system would be those commuting from the suburbs and the central city businesses. Downtown residents would actually be hindered in many cases, because access to frequently traversed parts of the city (by foot or bus) may be cut off. Rail stations are positioned on busy streets, and new growth centers around them. As cars remain the heavily favored mode of transportation, this can result in increased as opposed to decreased auto congestion. Even if more people get out of their cars as a result of the transit, uneven growth results in uneven congestion. This is the case even where rail lines are built specifically in order to reduce traffic congestion, and inner-city residents bear the brunt of these uneven congestion patterns (247).

This is a possible unintended consequence that farsighted planners of the Beltline project are realizing they must contend with. Concentration inevitably leads to congestion if all else remains equal. This dilemma will be further elucidated in chapter 5.

It is not only "new" rapid rail that has been perceived in this negative light. As early as 1938, Lewis Mumford saw inner-city public transportation systems as little more than cesspools created to bolster image and torture riders; Marcuse depicts the sometimes hour-long commute as sheer torture and refers to the subways as "man-sewers." He notes that it deprives workers of much needed exercise, and warns that the subway is the ultimate:

> Metropolitan waste . . . a vast expenditure, of time, energy, money, human vitality upon an activity that has flatly no value in itself; an activity whose main use is to uphold the crowd-prestige of the metropolis and increase the pecuniary values garnered by the ground landlords and the financiers. (242–43)

Sawers ([1978] 1984) suggests that rail is privileged explicitly because it is not only less likely to infringe on automotive interests, but actually likely to enhance them. He maintains that new rapid rail systems bolster the "preeminence of the automobile" and thus are the preferable mode of public transit (over bus or trolley) for highway lobbyists (250).

Yet, the dominance of the automobile is not unequivocally good for business either, particularly not for small businesses. "One Atlanta drugstore owner, forced out of business in 1926 lamented, 'The place where trade is, is where automobiles go . . . A central location is no longer a good one for my sort of business' " (Irrante 1980:504). And in a 2003 speech, Atlanta Mayor Shirley Franklin quoted Tom Pitts, an Atlanta Five Points Pharmacist (perhaps the same one Irrante was citing) as noting in 1925, "Hundreds dropped in, now thousands drive by."

The mode of mobility as it currently operates clearly has myriad drawbacks that counteract its superficial apparent "convenience." Yet it persists tenaciously, in part because of the dominance of big business whose interests it primarily serves, but also through profound persuasion and seduction. For the most part, "The coordinated masses do not crave a new order, but a larger share in the prevailing one" (Marcuse 1964:151). We justify as inevitable side effects of convenience, efficiency, and unprecedented freedom, the danger, disadvantage, and defilement that private ownership of automobiles brings to us all in different ways. Pockets of resistance and visions of more communitarian modes of existence are hard to realize in a national milieu of wanting to have one's cake and eat it too. Most of us long for a greater sense of community, more connection with our neighbors, justice for all, and so on, but are either unable to see the sacrifices necessary for their achievement, or unwilling to make them, or both. Marshall (2000) exposes this dilemma, noting that our nostalgia and our willingness to sacrifice do not always align. For instance, people want shops in their neighborhood, but fail to recognize that this would mean destruction of existing infrastructure, higher prices on gas and consumables, and possibly downsizing of homes. The easiest means to this end would be higher gas taxes, which "would push people out of their cars and densify communities" (193), yet most people are not eager for increases in their gasoline tax. We want the "saner, more livable lifestyle" (193), but do not want to pay the requisite costs.

It comes down to a matter of what is most important to us as a society and what we are willing to give up in order to make those wants a reality. It also might mean needing to recognize that lifestyle choices imply political choices, and this is a connection that many are reluctant to draw. Marshall clearly draws this connection, speaking of the poverty of American community as directly linked to the individualism of our political spirit (or lack thereof). He notes that time and time again, as a collective, Americans opt for the self-centered choice over the communal one, saying no to universal health care, mass transit, family leave policies, equitable school funding, and so forth (193). The resultant isolation from our neighbors, increased crime, delinquency and substance dependency are both unwelcome to the general public and unconnected in the collective mind to these choices. Yet, "the absence of community and the malady of political neglect are related" (193).

As has been demonstrated, the current mode of mobility lends itself more readily to dispersion and isolation than to cohesion, but this is not necessarily an inherent feature of automobility. "Capitalism . . . has favored the centrifugal, disintegrative tendencies of transportation" (Sawers [1978] 1984:227). Yet, "The automobile answers human needs (people have a taste for autos) only in a particular social, historical, and economic context. Reformers who wish to eliminate the auto must find a way to change the society which has called it forth" (236). And, as with many features of our landscape that we have come to take for granted, it is easy to confound a technology with its attendant modality. Sawers reminds us that it is not the inherent features of the automobile that "make" us use it in the ways that we currently do. He notes that nothing about a car mandates private ownership or free reign within cities, but rather the environment created for its use at the behest of capital interests "gave the automobile the specific social character that we now take for granted as the nature of the technology itself" (237).

Many of us have become too sophisticated and jaded to fall for utopian alternatives, and that is our loss. We are told every day (and tell ourselves and each other) in a million ways that we are happier, freer, more efficient and productive when we can get everywhere and anywhere in private vehicles. We recognize the disadvantages of sprawl, congestion, pollution, disease, and accidents to which the automobile makes enormous contributions, and even the uneven distribution of these negative effects throughout society. Most of us are nevertheless convinced that our lifestyles would be immeasurably diminished by its absence and that measures aimed at curtailing its use (increased gas prices, restrictions on usage, even pedestrian-friendly laws) are insufferable affronts on our personal freedom, as becomes crystal clear in chapter 4. We resent "big business" and even perhaps recognize that we are serving its interests over our own each time we buy a new overpriced vehicle or shun the bus because it would take us a few minutes longer to arrive at our destination. But for many of us this resentment does not hold a candle to the raging fire of indignation we experience at the idea of being told how we may and may not move about. Our consciences are somewhat mollified by the acknowledgment of our sophistication in seeing through the system. This is part of the seduction that keeps us believing that what we have is, while far from perfect, at least as good as it gets:

> We live and die rationally and productively. We know that destruction is the price of progress as death is the price of life, that renunciation and toil are the prerequisites for gratification and joy, that business must go on, and that the alternatives are Utopian. This ideology belongs to the established societal apparatus, it is a requisite for its continuous functioning and part of its rationality. (Marcuse 1964:145)

This discussion of equitable growth (with much focus on inequitable growth) has detailed the ways in which capitalism has created needs and then sweetly fulfilled them for some of us. The Green and Growth goals explicated above both shape and modify (often suppressing) concerns about social justice and transportation equity. The interplay between Growth, Green, and Equity goals is of central concern in this book, and to better understand this triangulated system I now turn to the urban regime literature, so central to the understanding of place.

Urban Regimes

Regime analysis was an attempt to reconcile the elite model (the Marxist and neo-Marxist analyses of the political economy) with the (for some) equally unsatisfactory pluralist model. On the one hand, the elite model appeared to rely too heavily on the "economy" side of the political economy equation, while the pluralist model proffered that power is more or less equally distributed among vying interested parties. Not content with either explanation—one overly deterministic and the other too cavalier regarding power differentials—Floyd Hunter (1953), Stephen Elkin (1987), and Clarence Stone (1989) were pioneers in the field of reexamining urban governing coalitions from a regime perspective. Following and extending upon their seminal examinations, a multitude of scholars have jumped into the fray (see for example John Mollenkopf 1989; Harvey Molotch 1993; Todd Swanstrom 1993; Manuel Castells 1999; Keith Dowding 2001; Jonathan Davies 2002; Peter Burns 2003; David Imbroscio 2004). Interestingly, two of the early scholars (Hunter 1953 and Stone 1989) chose Atlanta as the sites of their respective investigations.

Hunter (1953) focused on what he termed a "growth coalition." The essential features of this coalition were that decision-making power was concentrated in the hands of the business community and that issues were either framed for the public (or withheld from the public altogether) by those whose interests were primarily served by the decisions. It was Hunter's contention that by the time important urban policies came to the attention of the public, they were already "done deals." In his words:

> It has been evident to the writer for some years that policies on vital matters affecting community life seem to appear suddenly. They are acted upon, but with no precise knowledge on the part of the majority of citizens as to how these policies originated or by whom they are really sponsored. (1)

While much attention has been given in recent years to the importance of citizen participation in transportation and land-use policy, it will be shown through the examination of MARTA, GRTA, and the Beltline that this practice of projects appearing as faits accomplis has not been dramatically altered.

Stone (1989) extends on Hunter's notions of a growth coalition, defining an urban regime as "the informal arrangements by which public bodies and private interests function together to make and carry out governing decisions" (179). The question then becomes, What holds such a body together? Stone posits that "devotion to a common cause" is an unlikely basis for cooperation, because "[a] cause general enough to unite a sufficient body of actors to form a governing coalition is probably too general to guide the behavior of coalition members in a disciplined fashion" (180). Thus, Stone observes, governing coalitions rely on reciprocity, mutual loyalty, and a set of shared norms in order to maintain.

Stone's (1993) typology of urban regimes is particularly relevant to my discussion of transportation decision making in the current Atlanta context. He delineates four regime types that may emerge in a given urban center, and it is the interplay between the actors pressing for these distinct regime types that finally resolves in the dominance of one over the others. These regime types translate in my work into Growth, Green, and Equity Goals.

First, he speaks of Maintenance Regimes. This typology is essentially a status-quo regime: "Because maintenance regimes involve no effort to change established social and economic practice, no extensive mobilization of private resources is necessary and no substantial change in behavior is called for" (18). These "leave it alone" interests in the current context are best represented by the suburban actors who, as shall be demonstrated, would prefer that their local land use and transportation options would not be tampered with by regional policy makers.

The second of Stone's regimes are Development Regimes. This is the regime type Stone asserts has reigned in Atlanta for more than sixty years. Development regimes "are concerned primarily with changing land use in order to promote growth or counter decline" (18). It is the downtown business elite along with regional developers who are most influential and instrumental in this type of regime. As Stone notes, "Because they involve change and disruption, development projects are often controversial" (18). In light of this potential for controversy,

> [d]evelopment activities are often insulated from popular control . . . A set of actors must move in concert, but the number is small. It is not inherently difficult for them to frame a shared vision and inducements do not have to be spread widely. (18–19)

In other words, projects may become popular based on inducements for participation (what Stone calls "selective incentives") offered to key actors (such as minority contractors), and through media blasts hyping the positives of a particular venture (as will be well illustrated in chapter 5 on the Beltline). The political component of the regime is likely to broadly proclaim the benefits of such major development projects, but retain a safe distance from the minutia of enactment, "Mayors have tended to identify themselves more closely with the announcement of plans than with the details of implementation" (19). This is certainly evident with Mayor Franklin and the Beltline proposal. A further point that Stone makes in regards to Development Regimes is that they manage to garner a great deal of public support, financial as well as ideological, from the public, sometimes unwittingly as regards the fiscal side. These first two regime types, Maintenance and Development, correspond well to the interests that I refer to as Growth Goals.

Stone's third regime type is what he refers to as Middle Class Progressive Regimes. The neighborhood associations and environmental groups promoting what I refer to as Green Goals are akin to this regime type. Stone notes that "progressive regimes" need to be mindful of a variety of (sometimes competing) interests; including environmental concerns, affordability of homes, neighborhood preservation, and affirmative action. There is much pressure to develop but to do so in a way that balances "activity and restriction" (19). This imperative for Green groups to find common ground with the Growth coalition is profoundly illustrated in the GRTA discussion in chapter 4.

The fourth and final regime type that Stone speaks of is a regime devoted to lower-class opportunity expansion. This regime "would involve enriched education and job training, improved transportation access, and enlarged opportunities for business and home ownership" (20). While Stone notes that such regimes are "largely hypothetical" in the U.S. context, the influence of equity goals in regional transportation and land-use planning cannot be ignored and contribute—even if only for the purposes of appeasing and silencing those who clamor for social justice—to the ultimate regional practices. While Stone aptly notes that "[a] few individual opportunities or scattered chances to compete for a restricted set of positions are not enough [to constitute a regime devoted to lower class opportunity expansion]" (21), nevertheless, such mean and limited openings at the very least keep one small facet of the public gaze on these equity issues.

The debate surrounding what urban regime theory has been and should become has focused largely on three central issues: (1) agency versus structure, (2) how important framing, definitions, and ideations are in coalition formation and maintenance, and (3) whether the aims of urban regime theorizing are (or ought to be) descriptive or prescriptive. Examining each of these in turn provides a frame for sorting out the various positions and propositions that scholars have put forth.

Agency versus Structure

As noted, the balancing act between recognizing economic structures and yet giving credit to political agency in interpretations of urban governance has been a central concern of urban regime theory from its inception. In describing this negotiation, Stone (1993) explains that regime analysis acknowledges the centrality of private enterprise without becoming overly deterministic. Thus, he asserts, such analysis is able to expose a synthesis, in which the underdeveloped assumptions of equal spheres that pluralists hold, may be balanced against the views of structuralists, who, he maintains, see all the world through an economic lens (2). This balanced view has, however, been subject to criticism asserting that urban regime theory has gone too far in distancing itself from economic determinism. For instance, Davies (2002) problematizes Stone's (1991) assertion that more attention to agency is necessary by noting that, while attention to agency may help us recognize that changes in economics do not always bring about changes in regime, such attention fails to explain how economic conditions so often retard or prevent change. Further, looking at agency does not move us forward in shedding light on "why favorable conditions have proved difficult to sustain long enough for progressive coalitions to become sustainable" (14). Davies contends that more attention to structure, not more attention to agency, will further the goal of understanding, asking, "Given that social structures and political agency both matter, is it possible to achieve a more sophisticated understanding of the structural process?" (14). David Imbroscio (2003) echoes these sentiments, emphasizing that most scholars engaged in regime analysis have been political scientists and thus most concerned with the analysis of political processes, "As a result, regime theory scholarship has neglected in a relative sense a careful and rigorous examination of economic processes" (271).

On the other side of this debate, Todd Swanstrom (1993) argues that the changed world has blown a hole in the economy-centered perspective, which he asserts attempts to fit a template of global economic restructuring over all places, forcing a fit that simply is not there. Swanstrom argues that in order to understand the workings of the postmodern urban political economy we need to pay attention to changed realities and to distance ourselves from theories that view "economic interests . . . as fundamentally the same no matter what the politics, culture, language, or religion of a particular locality" (56). He avers that, among other things, new social movements cannot be explained in economic terms, noting that "these movements are motivated not by the politics of interest but by the politics of identity" (57). In response to Swanstrom and in defense of positioning economic forces as most salient in urban trajectories, despite the influences of globalization and the specificities of place, environmental concerns, and identity politics—asserting that such a positioning does not neglect the importance of human agency—Harvey Molotch (1993) asserts that the stickiness of social relations is inexorably intertwined with the tenacity of economic ones, and that place is created in the image of those who use it and have the power to name its functions, including and especially capitalizing on its use value. Thus, an understanding of the production of space in no way detracts from recognition of human agency. Rather, "[w]here there is similarity across places, it derives from shared institutional contexts and parallel patterns of volition, rather than iron-like determinisms of internal hidden hands or exogenous constraints" (31).

Thus, Molotch is reinforcing the notion that it is possible to recognize both the human hand and the structural forces that guide it.

Disentangling the balance of power between economic forces and political actors is the core of these scholars' endeavors. While often the focus is on the friction between urban governance and in-town economic interests, Peter Burns (2003) also cautions that the role of the state must not be neglected in the configuration. Through his study of the role of the state in urban education, Burns reminds us that state interests cannot be ignored when looking at local and regional policies.[3] This is relevant also to my study of transportation policies and procedures in the Atlanta metropolitan region, as state authority, as shall be seen in the ensuing chapters, often determines who plays and who triumphs. Burns says that one of his goals was to further regime theory through the inclusion of state political actors in the analysis. Urban regimes are deeply affected by state governments that can dictate practices and allocate resources. The role of the state can also create "a new set of policy winners and losers" (299). How states, cities, and business communities achieve domination is often at least as much a matter of persuasion as it is a matter of legislative or regulatory authority. Winning the definitional or issue-framing contest is frequently more than half the battle.

The Frame is the Thing

A new emphasis in regime theory in recent years is in paying attention to the role of definitions in urban regimes. What problems are put on the table, how these problems are presented, the range of possible solutions considered, and the actors perceived as playing a role in problem solving are to a large extent a matter of idea-manipulation. In 2001, Stone asserted that Atlanta's regime was losing "direction and vitality" (20). In posing the question of whether regime analysis is up to the task of explaining such a shift, Stone responds, "I will argue here that the regime concept can indeed address issues of political decline, but can do so most effectively by drawing on recent work on problem definition and issue framing" (20). Stone argues that the business community in Atlanta, long the backbone of agenda setting and project defining, largely because of regionalization, has weakened in its interests in, and capacity to frame policy initiatives for the city (29). This shift of focus to regional issues (which, interestingly, Stone contends resides particularly in a focus on transportation policy) leaves a space for local government to jump in to the fore as issue framers. But, Stone (2001) argues, despite its potential to develop a program aimed at redressing social ills associated with poverty, local government fails to do so because of fragmentation and frequent changes in structure and composition (27).

The Beltline project may well be Atlanta's new rallying point—bringing together business, political, and civic actors, all framing the Beltline as a potential salvation for many of the city's ills. This will be fleshed out in chapter 5. In arguing that the growth machine is alive and well (or, in my typology that Growth goals are likely to succeed) Molotch (1993) speaks of the significance of issue framing, noting, "Growth activism translates into influence over ideology and agenda setting" (33). He goes on to explain some of the ways in which Growth activists win the day against other actors (Green, Equity) through social capital that affords them the cultural cachet to define problems and solutions despite ideological opposition. He contends that savvy "growth activists," specifically developers, have incorporated "niceness" into their bag of tricks, giving them yet another advantage in negotiations, as against "sometimes strident and self-righteous community groups" (34). Having the "appropriate gestures, mannerisms, and architectural tastes" (34) affords developers greater entrée with policy makers, even environmentally conscious ones.

It is Molotch's contention that Growth goals are promoted and accepted by a broad range of actors, even when "rationally" they may not be in the best interests of all parties involved. In other words, the Growth coalition wins the framing war: "The wide acceptance of growth as a positive response to societal difficulties does not reflect an accurate appraisal of costs and benefits of development, but instead the ideological influence of growth coalitions" (36). Keith Dowding (2001) similarly posits that the formation of a new regime is dependent on ideas and persuasion: "[C]reating a new ideology . . . is a basis on which a new regime, rather than a simple winning coalition, may be created" (17). This attention to issue framing speaks to the agentive aspects of regime formation, yet allows for the possibility that such agency is embedded in a structural framework that privileges business interests over others. Stone contends that noting the importance of how and by whom issues are framed will aid us in further understanding the complexities of urban regimes. The question remains, Will such understanding advance us in our ability to bring about positive change?

Description or Prescription

Although Regime Theory seems to theoretically move us beyond pessimistic notions of iron cages and structural hamstringing, it has been unsuccessful in providing practical routes to get past such strictures in lived experience. Joel Rast (2005) laments, "[Yet] for all its seeming potential, regime theory has largely failed to deliver on its normative promises" (54). He maintains that regime theory has allowed us to better comprehend the relationships between corporations and governmental actors, but has not succeeded in providing meaningful alternate models.

While Rast (at least for the time being) contents himself with modest efforts to study, for instance, "how a corporate-centered regime was temporarily expanded to include a wider set of objectives,"[4] Imbroscio (2003) is more ambitious in his desire to extend the normative aims of Urban Regime Theory, which he believes can only be accomplished through a much more profound acknowledgment of economic processes. His extension of Regime Theory to include an "alternative economics" is posited as a starting point from which to "generate alternative political coalitions and institutional arrangements more consistent with vibrant forms of urban democracy" (280). Imbroscio further asserts that thus revised, Regime Theory may "make a substantial contribution to the struggle to both achieve economic justice in American cities and construct more democratic forms of urban governance" (282).

Similarly, Davies (2002) asserts that without a "return to Marx" (14), it may indeed prove difficult to move Regime Theory from the realm of the descriptive to that of the prescriptive, or to understand whether such a shift is indeed possible. He advises, "Regime theorists could usefully situate their work in a wider understanding of systemic trends and confront the implications of these trends for normative projects" (14). In so doing, Davies asserts, theorists would be better equipped to answer such questions as, "Is it possible to identify a trend toward more equitable regimes in the US or elsewhere? If not, is the commercial republic a realizable goal?" (14).

This notion, or perhaps oxymoron, of the "commercial republic" is one that occupies a central position in my own inquiry as well: Is it possible for growth-centered enterprises (commercial) to result in mobility patterns that are in the best interests of the most citizens (republican)? To further unravel this capitalist conundrum we turn to the literature dealing with the production of space.

SPACE NARRATIVES

The ever-increasing fluidity in capital and human movement, so much a function of the mode of mobility, has resulted in a "spatial turn" in social analysis (Soja [1989] 2003). The changed flows of people and capital have dramatically altered the landscapes we negotiate, which in turn refashions our identities and our interactions. The bent toward cultural geography has been more readily embraced by European scholars, but its influence on American sociology is not insignificant. Central to American concerns (as well as to global concerns), is the crisis of place rooted in both the movement of necessity (dislocations, diaspora, job chasing) and mobility fetishism[5]—enhanced by what Whitelegg (1997) refers to as the "status of distant things." These changes have created enormous alterations in identities and places.

The editor of The New Urbanism (Katz 1994) introduces the volume by taking a historical view on the notion of "true community." He speaks of the longtime needs of humans to group together for safety, and also for access to necessities—not only the life-sustaining ones (food and water), but also for the created ones, such as transportation sites and job centers. As has been oft noted, Katz also nods to the automobile as the life-changing mechanism allowing people to range further and further from these hubs. As time progressed, central cities were growing increasingly noxious so the impetus to flee was built in. Thus, suburban fever reached its zenith after World War II. Katz notes that the gains for suburbanites were many, but the down side was the loss of community—the sense of sterile isolation that has been so well documented (and analyzed) for suburban dwellers. Katz further asserts that our enormous gains in technological means of communication "are no substitute for true community" (xi).

Katz's disquisition is both problematic and emblematic. It idealizes a past that was a reality for a select few and generalizes an American experience and desire in ways that have been and remain detrimental to large segments of society, and in those ways it is problematic. Yet, I draw on it precisely because it is so representative of the New Urbanism movement and because it is so illustrative of the crisis of place as experienced by one influential sector of society—the elite. The reconfiguring of space, often at the behest of the elite, and sometimes against their will, simultaneously reconfigures time—and transportation policies and practices are at the heart of this time-space sea change. One articulation of this rearrangement is offered by Whitelegg (1997). He explains that the meanings of both time and place are profoundly (and in his view detrimentally) altered by ever faster modes of travel. For one, he says the meaning of home is attenuated because life is now spread across multiple spaces. Additionally, our experience of day to day routines is increasingly fragmented and experienced on the fly, in superficial and short-lived relationships with others similarly flitting by. Even when we are not on the move physically, Wolf points out, we can "consume large amounts of energy, food, entertainment or sex (or just go shopping)" before our "next bout of frantic time-filling at some distant location" (60), courtesy of modern conveniences, including the computer. It is his contention that this dramatic shift from local concentration of activities to distant ones is at the heart of our current planetary ills. "The intensified consumption of distance that is made possible by the destruction of time is fundamentally unsustainable" (60).

This scrutiny of the space-time connection in the social context is a crucial aspect of the spatial turn in the social sciences. Foucault ([1984] 1998) posits that the burning questions for nineteenth-century scholars focused on issues of time/history ("themes of development and arrest, themes of crisis and cycle, themes of accumulation of the past, a great overload of dead people . . .") (175). He asserts there has been a momentous shift of focus to issues of space and that "we are [now] in an age of the simultaneous, of juxtaposition, of the near and the far, of the side-by-side, of the scattered" (175).

Globalization of the Local

The drive-in homogeneity of our national landscape, as we see, think, and feel it, cannot easily be overstated. From Walmartsville to Burgerurbia, we are one nation, under Coca-Cola, with freeways and hamburgers for all. I would argue that transportation policies and infrastructure are axial in the configuration of space.

Putnam (2000) observed that "one inevitable consequence of how we have come to organize our lives spatially is that we spend measurably more of every day shuttling alone in metal boxes among the vertices of our private triangles" (212). He was struck by the statistic that Americans (on average) spend significantly more time in cars than cooking or eating and twice as much time in these vehicles than the average parent spends with their children. Perhaps most telling of all, from Putnam's view, is that overwhelmingly and increasingly, this time is spent all by oneself (212).

The "spatial practice" (Lefebvre [1974]1991) of large numbers of people spending inordinate amounts of time alone in cars arriving at various destinations at the expense of other human activities, is a practice that has been forged over time. Yet structures that came before have not been fully eradicated, but rather interwoven into the new fabric, not always in a way that allows a smooth transition for users. For instance, "The walking landscape has been overlain with one ordered around conduits of speed and continuous movement, often justified in economic terms and time saving . . . People not equipped for the motorized landscape are . . . in a constant state of negotiation between the old and the new interpretations of time and space" (Jain and Guiver 2001: 575).

And yet the car, with its appropriation of space and manipulation of time and mobility's meanings, has engaged both the national imagination and the lived experience of Americans in a way that little else has. Having both a mythological power on us, embodying, as the automobile so readily does, the American ethos of freedom and adventure, and a practical application of both retreating from and moving toward others rapidly and relatively comfortably, the car is the quintessential embodiment of Lefebvre's conception of the production of space.

The automobile's potential for destruction is deeply informative in our relationship to it as well, both symbolically and materially. In Car Crash Culture, Brottman (2001) draws out the connection in the Western consciousness between the ethos of individualism, freedom, and democracy, and the automobile. Most especially, he notes that in keeping with the quintessentially American fascination with mobility for its own sake, the car in America represents arrival and autonomy. For all its flash and freedom, however, the other side of that shiny coin bares a darker face. Brottman reminds us that "no other civilian invention has such an enormous degree of carnage associated with its everyday use" (xxxvi). Uniquely, much of the United States was constructed for the automobile, which has, consequently "become as iconic to U.S. culture as the gun" (xxxvi). He implies that our love of cars and guns is hardly coincidental, in that the flip side of the American maverick spirit is the American wild man one—on a crash course to self-destruction. In his words, "If the car is the symbol of America, then the car wreck is the nation's bloodstained sarcophagus" (xxxvi).

Throughout this discussion I have been treating automobiles as spaces in themselves as well as objects within space. This is important because spatial theorists caution us to be aware that redistributing objects in space is not sufficient to change social relations fundamentally—space itself must be (re)appropriated and reconfigured. This points to the controversy regarding transportation planning versus land-use planning. I focus so largely on the automobile because so much space has been configured at its behest—with those concerned with Representations of Space (urban planners, architects, and conservationists) using automobile space as the starting point for their efforts, whether those be in opposition to or conformity with its hegemony. Lefebvre points out that the U.S. tax on gasoline contributes enormously to highway construction, which in turn contributes to the automotive and oil industries. Each scratches the other's back and increases both the need for and the profits of the other. "Goodman calls this 'asphalt's magic circle.' It is almost as though automobiles and motorways occupied the entirety of space" (Lefebvre [1974] 2004:374).

And yet, they do not. People (along with much else) also inhabit space, and the privileging of automobile space circumscribes their negotiations within it. As we have noted, this circumscription is modulated by class, age, race, gender, physical ability, and more. Representations of Space, most especially transportation-related representations, have dramatically altered the face of cities—both in terms of practical use and in imagery (or we could say, use value and exchange value). Regarding practical use, many inner-city residents have become increasingly disengaged from the economic and cultural life surrounding them through the encapsulation of their physical and social space. Some argue that this has resulted in a "new" ghetto, distinct from the old by virtue of its economic isolation. Marcuse and van Kempen (2000) draw the distinction this way; both varieties of ghetto are highly concentrated areas where people are placed through no will of their own based on race, religion, or ethnic identity and are perceived and treated poorly as compared to the dominant group. The added element in a new ghetto is that those in the ghetto do not participate in the economic activities of those outside the ghetto, and the dominant group also does not profit (in direct economic form) from the ghetto's existence (19).

The creation of these "new" ghettos and other inequities already enumerated are best understood in the context of the divide between the private and the public. This divide in the American context is well illuminated in transit space, because, as Caesar (2000) notes, "Transit space reveals cultural specificity like few other kinds, because such space consists in peculiar negotiations among the resources of both public and private social interaction" (3). While Caesar's remarks were addressed to the micro level—how, for instance, when we move through space in a car we are in a private place negotiating public (and publicly subsidized) space—they may also be applied on the macro level of interaction. As Jain and Guiver (2001) point out, "Individuals can solve their own mobility problems with more car use, and remove their individual social inequalities through access to a wider set of destinations, employment opportunities and services, but this can only extend the collective problems" (583). Public/private partnerships, often looked to as a means of salvation, frequently tragically backfire for the sector most in need of respite. As Harvey (1989) notes, despite rhetoric to the contrary, public/private partnerships in the United States have largely resulted in redistributing wealth upward. They have accomplished this by further increasing the assets of the wealthy and powerful by making it possible for their power bases to remain in cities, putting an added burden on "local collective consumption for the working class and poor" (14).

The fetishism of mobility and its attendant image-based depiction and distribution of the built and natural environments speaks to issues of exchange value. And in this context, exchange can take on a double meaning, first, its customary economic implications, and secondly, the notion that one place may readily be exchanged for another. We are at once in place and out of place in our surroundings, the landscape must increasingly be configured to be read while whizzing by at high speeds. Therefore, substance is often substituted by symbol such that passers-by will know where and how to spend their dollars. "The term 'placelessness,' which has been used to refer to the creation of standardized, homogenized landscapes that diminish the differences among places, signifies one aspect of the loss of meaning in late capitalist cities" (Greif and Cruz 1999:4). The metamorphosis of cities, so extensively studied and written about, is steeped in mobility's powers of transformation. The whirl-by of scenery on a ribbon of highway increasingly incorporates a virtual highway as well. The move toward information technology as the dominant form does not obliterate spatial relations but does sometimes obscure them. Bayer (1999) points out that one means of effectively hiding the collateral consequences of highway construction has been through "the metaphoric translation of superhighways into the 'information highway' " (53). The paving of America, courtesy of enormous governmental highway subsidies and postwar automobile production and consumption gluttony came at a high price; "fossil fuel production, neglect of public transit, environmental degradation, and community destruction" (53). But, she asserts, all of this is facilely made invisible through the device of symbolic representation—it has been made to appear that we are smoothly transitioning from a world of physical travel to one of virtual travel with no damages along the way. The possible benefits and burdens of virtual movement will be addressed more fully in the concluding chapter. For now, suffice it to say that unequal access within mobility patterns of people, goods, and information becomes hidden behind notions of science, rationality, efficiency, and progress. For a solution to, or at least a reprieve from, these homogenizing, crippling and blatantly unjust transportation and land-use patterns, some look toward local responses to these global issues.

Localizing the Global

Some scholars (Sachs 1992, Janelle 2004) despite the overwhelming evidence that the current road, paved with whatever variety of intentions is leading away from anywhere most of us would like to be, nonetheless retain a guarded optimism. Some hope for the transformative powers of information technology, believing that there is the potential for our use of it to act as a corrective to mobility's present inequities. That is to say, rather than using it as an extension of the current mode of virtual and extremely unequal control of space, we may yet find ways to resituate the global in a local context, revitalizing our selves and our cities in the process.

Lefebvre, perhaps partly because he lived and wrote mostly before information technologies dominated the landscape, concerned himself more directly with spatial transformations and the impossibility of changing anything if we do not change space:

> So long as everyday life remains in thrall to abstract space, with its very concrete constraints; so long as the only improvements to occur are technical improvements of detail (for example, the frequency and speed of transportation, or relatively better amenities); so long, in short, as the only connection between work spaces, leisure spaces and living spaces is supplied by the agencies of political power and by their mechanisms of control—so long must the project of "changing life" remain no more than a political rallying-cry to be taken up or abandoned according to the mood of the moment. (59–60)

There are many ways to address this notion of reconfiguring space, attempting to work with, and perhaps move beyond these "technical improvements of detail" that Lefebvre denounced to a more profoundly space-altering use of the environment. People have and do engage with all of them—graffiti to (re)claim public space; a dial-a-llama service in Alaska as a transportation alternative (Alaska 1998); features added or removed to make communities more bicycle, pedestrian, and transit friendly; and so on. Whyte (1980) in The Social Life of Small Urban Spaces, recommended what he called the celebration of randomness (e.g. replacing row seating with casual seating for intimate shows), creative use of public space, suggesting that "odds and ends of spaces may be put to good use"; the idea is "not to escape the city but to partake of it" (100).

Changing the world, as Lefebvre asserted, is contingent on a vision that has perhaps not yet appeared on the landscape, or perhaps is partially embodied in the principles of New Urbanism—a revisioned architecture of community. Some have no doubt that the blueprints for such an architecture are etched in transportation (and land-use) policies. Many have become convinced that the "freedoms to" (unrestricted mobility, efficiency, timesaving) for some are coming at too great a price of "freedoms from" (from pollution, noise, congestion, unequal access) for all. A more public transit, bicycling, and pedestrian-friendly society—while perhaps not Utopian in scope—speaks for many to a richer and deeper way of life, embedded in a sense of local community. The sticking point, as noted earlier, is that the trade-offs are often either neglected or rejected. Yet for some, these trade-offs are well worth the rewards. Speaking of a space reconfigured for people over cars, Sachs (1992) evokes notions of sacrifice and compromise, but worthy ones. He remarks that changing the way in which we "do" space is anathema to our furtive lifestyle. But, he admonishes, we need to relinquish this cherished movement, "minimizing the resistance of distance and making space more penetrable" (220). He advises that we need to reframe our vision in such a way as to privilege locality over fetishism with distance and that the only way to accomplish this is through "sovereign self-limitation" (221). If we both slow down and stay closer to home, Sachs suggests, we may enjoy our lives more while harming the earth less.

To address this tension, Marshall (2000) suggests that a city's transportation system is the key to its residents' sense of community and much else. He asserts that questions regarding transportation system choices are the most fundamental in the creation of place. Such considerations largely determine the nature of a city. "Do we pave roads or lay down tracks? Do we fund buses or subsidize cars? Do we lay down bike paths or more highway lanes? Do we build airports or high-speed train lines?"(211). The answers to these questions are not simple. Within the context of a space fundamentally configured around automobility, an underconceptualized turn toward public transit (especially trains over buses) can, as we have demonstrated and shall discuss further in the coming chapters, often make things worse. Allen (1996) addresses how this played out in Atlanta. As elsewhere, the car was paramount in directing Atlanta's development. Efforts at governmental control were largely fruitless. Allen reminds us that as MARTA incrementally added rail to the North line in an effort to draw in white riders from north side neighborhoods, "They spurned it in vast numbers" (224). By the mid-1980s, nearly two billion dollars and better than a decade of effort had gone into MARTA and ridership remained depressingly low and overwhelmingly African American. "A survey by the *Journal-Constitution* in 1985 found MARTA's prospects 'cool' in Clayton County, 'chilly' in Gwinnett, and 'icy' in Cobb" (225).

Allen goes on to explain that MARTA hurt several communities by disrupting neighborhoods and putting small businesses out of commission. He also notes that in response to MARTA's failure, GDOT (and later the Atlanta Regional Commission) reverted to the tried and true practice of creating more roads in an attempt to build Atlanta out of the problems of sprawl. Quick, or even painstakingly slow, fixes often prove ineffective. This does not necessarily imply that Atlanta would be better off had MARTA never been built; that is impossible to discern, as we cannot guess what other turns it might have taken had MARTA not been chosen as a transportation alternative (there is more on this point in chapter 3). It does, however, demonstrate that the Spatial Practices that the automobile society requires and recreates are stubbornly trenchant.

In comprehending this intractability, it may be conceptually useful to apply the notion of McDonaldization to issues of mobility. In his 1996 book, The McDonaldization of Society, George Ritzer draws on Weber's notions of rationality to explain how the McDonald's-like system of doing business (and life overall) has become so dominant and resistant to change. The concepts of efficiency, calculability, predictability, and control—offered by Weber in the context of rationalization and refined by Ritzer speaking of McDonaldization (as the epitome of rationalization)—certainly help us to understand how space is currently created and used in general, and in regard to transportation options in particular. Taking Ritzer's definitions, it is easy to apply this formula to the automobile society.

If, as Ritzer states, efficiency is the optimum method for getting from one point to another, then clearly the car and the environment built to its specification fit this formulation to a tee. Ritzer conceptualizes calculability as an emphasis on the quantitative aspects of products sold (portion size, cost) and service offered (the time it takes to get the product). Not only the automobile but also the mobility it affords have been packaged with calculability in mind. Thus, automobiles are readily available in various sizes, colors, shapes, and costs, and likewise, distances are apportioned and packaged for the ease and convenience of the car. In this formulation, predictability is the assurance that products and services will be the same over time and in all locales. Both the automotive industry and the landscape it serves (and that serves it) homogenize space to ensure predictability. And finally in regards to control, Ritzer speaks of control over how the product is both produced and consumed, noting how both consumers and producers are manipulated or constrained by the spatial system to behave in certain ways. Automotive hegemony perfectly exemplifies this reading of control (9–10).

The relevance of all of this to the mode of transportation is that when seeking alternatives to the current mode, the architects of radically new transportation and land-use planning must bear in mind that they are proposing nothing less than an escape from the iron cage of rationality and that such transgressive and ambitious propositions will certainly be met with forceful resistance, both conscious and unconscious. Revisioning community is hardly a new enterprise, and acknowledgment that external and internal forms must dramatically change for that to take shape is also not nascent. Marx ([1846] 1978), though from a different time with a different set of signs and symbols, foreshadowed the hopes for renewed community that much of the scholarship I have been invoking is aimed toward producing. He noted that the experience of freedom (freedom to be fully human and to "cultivate [one's] gifts in all directions") is only possible in community with others. Furthermore, he maintained, community is only possible when it is not class-structured and contentious. In this true community, it is through our associations that we surprisingly find autonomy (197).

Heeding these lessons and applying them to transportation policies means both listening to all voices and negotiating solutions that promote growth, green, and equity goals alike. This involves, among other things, being willing to imagine, together, new landscapes that do not privilege some at the deep expense of others. My position is neither "antimobility" nor "antichoice," as framed by free-market advocates. Rather, I seek to engage with a society that is thoughtful, judicious, and above all conscious. We need to recognize those practices that have put a stranglehold on meanings of and access to mobility, sometimes resulting in believing that we are moving faster than ever before when in fact we are approaching a total standstill. To disentangle and weed out trenchant policies and procedures that have become both invisible and obsolete is serious work. It is my hope that this book will serve as a beacon in that endeavor.

THREE

MARTA

Much Ado Regarding Topographical Arrangements

In this chapter I will situate the Metropolitan Rapid Transit Authority (MARTA) in the greater arena of mobility options and practices in the Atlanta region. From its inception, MARTA has been a primary site of contestation and power negotiations among the various area stakeholders. It has ever been a scapegoat for white animosity toward poor blacks as well as a locale in which African American resentment of white mobility privilege has been situated. Alternately framed as the city's crowning glory and its embarrassing dirty secret, MARTA's defining moments have been fraught with struggle and strife.

I here examine the ways in which MARTA has been unable to live up to its potential from nearly everyone's perspective. It has been variously envisioned as a vehicle for transforming Atlanta into a world-class city; as a reducer of both traffic congestion and air pollution; as a means for those with no other options to have decent mobility opportunities; and as the hub of a regional transportation system linking the region in a seamless manner. Yet, from its failure to deliver adequate services to the transit-dependent to its inability to attract choice riders, MARTA has been received at best as a disappointment and at worst as a blight on the city. Interviewing twenty transportation experts (including planners, transportation agency board members and employees, activists, and lobbyists) and interrogating the available information base, I expose MARTA's social location in the region. MARTA is space and symbol, actor and acted upon, engine and caboose. In these pages I disentangle the causes of MARTA's inadequacies and explore ideas about correcting them. Concomitantly, I expose MARTA's symbolic role as host of the city's deep-seated racial and spatial divides.

A SLOW START FOR RAPID TRANSIT—A THUMBNAIL SKETCH OF MARTA'S HISTORY

To begin, let us look at MARTA's raison d'être. According to Keating (2001), MARTA's creation was more about appearances and less about rationalizing time and space than one might presume. He notes that when the rail portion of MARTA was conceived (in the early 1960s) and got underway (in the early 1970s) these efforts were notably far more geared toward image enhancement than toward truly addressing the already dire transportation needs of the region (113).

In light of the fact that most other major metropolitan cities have subway systems, in order to compete in the world market, it was posited that Atlanta should likewise have such a system. Because other transit options were known to be more likely to achieve the twin goals of cost effectiveness and mobility enhancement, it is possible to read the insistence upon the rail portion of MARTA as fundamentally expressive of the desire to bolster the city's image, rather than improve its mobility. For instance, studies conducted in 1967 and 1969 both demonstrated that expanded bus service would be less expensive and more efficient than rail service. Further, Keating asserts that a retrospective analysis performed in 1997 concurred that MARTA had in fact done little or nothing that additional bus service could not have accomplished. Similarly, regarding MARTA's influence on growth, Giuliano (2004) cites a 1997 study by Bollinger and Ihlandfeldt in which "the authors concluded that MARTA had neither a positive nor a negative impact on population and employment growth," attributing these findings to, "(1) MARTA's insignificant impact on accessibility, (2) the absence of a significant increase in transit use, and (3) public policy efforts limited to rezoning" (267).

It is not possible to reconstruct a consensus on MARTA's purposes any more than we can today find consensus on its next steps. Certainly, in addition to being in keeping with many Atlanta efforts to endow the city with a cosmopolitan air, it was framed by some proponents as a means to "increase transit use, reduce private vehicle use, revitalize the downtown, and promote growth within the rail corridors" (Giuliano 2004:267). Notably, four sets of actors with distinct agendas influenced MARTA's inception and subsequent path: the downtown overwhelmingly white business elite; suburban whites; the black middle-class leadership community; and the poor and mostly black residents with least access to mobility.

For the business elite (embodied in the Atlanta Chamber of Commerce), the rail portion of MARTA was largely about image and an effort to reinvigorate the central business district. For instance, in 1961, Ivan Allen Jr. (president of the Chamber of Commerce) campaigned for mayor on a "Forward Atlanta II" program aimed at infusing new life into the city. This included a specific call for a large-scale rapid-transit system for Atlanta

(Roth and Ambrose 1996:188). Suburban whites were skeptical regarding what a rail system would do for them, and feared that it would result in masses of poor African Americans pouring into their neighborhoods. For African American political leaders, it appeared to present the possibility of gains for middle-class blacks in terms of contracts and job opportunities and the potential for greater mobility for impoverished African American citizens. Conversely, there was the well-founded fear that MARTA would result in business as usual, with more opportunities for white Atlantans and fewer for blacks. For those with least access, MARTA held out the promise of improving their lot, but also the threat of adding insult to injury by reducing bus service and replacing it with a mode and routes that favored anyone but them.

These disparate concerns kept the MARTA referendum of 1968 from passing. In November of that year, City of Atlanta, Fulton County, and Dekalb County residents voted on the bond referendum for MARTA and it was not approved. Just under half (48.9 percent) of DeKalb county residents were in favor of the bond, but well under half (41.9 percent) of City of Atlanta voters (ninety thousand of them) voted for it. Interestingly, white voters, especially the business elite, were considerably more likely to vote in favor of the MARTA bond than black voters, more than half of whom voted no (Keating 2001:122). On the MARTA Web site (www.itsmarta.com/about/history01.htm) the explanation for this defeat is the lack of solid financial backing going in. The plan was that local ad valorem taxes would cover the expenses of the system with a hoped-for, but completely unconfirmed, 50 percent subsidy from the federal government. The only group at the time with unequivocal support for MARTA was the business elite. They refused to accept the negative outcome of the 1968 referendum as a final defeat and it became their mission to rally others to the cause. In order to do so it became necessary to ensure that others' interests would be met—or at least that they would appear to be met. This campaign to create MARTA involved some compromises and some covenants.

In the early 1960s the Chamber of Commerce had "recommended a sixty-mile, fixed-rail system that would connect the city proper with five metro-area counties: Fulton, DeKalb, Cobb, Gwinnett, and Clayton" (Keating 2001:115). In a 1965[1] referendum vote, "the referendum passed in every jurisdiction except Cobb County" (118). This established that Cobb County had opted out of MARTA, both in terms of representation on the board and in terms of having the system extended to its borders. Gwinnett and Clayton, on the other hand, were still participants. But the nature of their participation was very unclear. Their continued support for MARTA was contingent upon guarantees that it would not be a financial burden to their constituents; issues of how MARTA would be funded had to be addressed.

As for the African American community, assurances about job opportunities, reasonable fares, and access to largely poor and black neighborhoods were central to their concerns. Efforts were made to please as many palates as possible. Keating (2001) informs us that, for obvious reasons, suburbanites favored a sales tax over an income tax as the mode for financing MARTA. Yet, this would clearly not be in the best interest of the inner-city poor (and their advocates). The Action Forum decided to add a penny to the sales tax set aside to support MARTA, but as a concession to those fearing its detrimental effects on those in poverty, they suggested a low fare (fifteen cents) and an assurance that this fare be locked in for seven years (Keating 2001:126).

The need to court both black and white voters to get MARTA up and running was evident to all. The penny sales tax proposal and the promises to set and keep fares low were in anticipation of the 1971 referendum vote that would finally and firmly establish MARTA as a working system. In further efforts to address African American concerns, "the MARTA board agreed to support an affirmative action plan, training programs, and minority representation in companies doing business with the Authority" (Bayor 1996:194). Additionally, there were pledges that lines favoring poor black neighborhoods would be the first to go in and that "final route plans would pay attention to the needs of those traveling from residential sections to work, hospitals, and shopping areas, and crosstown service would be improved" (Bayor:194).

Historical evidence had made many African Americans leery of promises from the white elite. Too many times, projects had been presented as considering or even centering the concerns of blacks, yet "once the goals of the White community have been realized, no further consideration is given to the needs, desires, and interests of the Black community."[2] In this context, then, fear and distrust were evident for both whites and blacks. Bayor (1996) explains that many white voters suspected MARTA would hasten the spread of black residents to suburban locations, speeding up the dreaded school desegregation process. On the other hand, some black voters still feared, promises aside, that MARTA would largely benefit white residents (194). The then mayor, Sam Massell, was not helping the cause much. In October 1971 he spoke at a YMCA weekly luncheon. These meetings were the primary forum in which Atlanta's black and white leaders convened to hammer out portentous issues.

> With a live TV audience watching, the mayor lit into the black leadership for making too many demands. Rapid transit, he told them, was too important to risk losing. In a fateful choice of words, he urged them to "think white." The phrase was greeted with a few gasps and then an icy silence. A handful of members of the audience stood up, turned their backs, and walked out. (Allen 1996:175)

Such public faux pas on the part of politicians simply meant that the business elite had to redouble their efforts to win friends and influence people. In further efforts to court the black vote, "blacks were added to both the MARTA Board of Directors and its staff, and MARTA hired a young black executive as community relations director with primary responsibility for selling the proposition to black voters" (Jones 1978:103). The framing of dissenters as backward and anti-progress also went far in influencing the black community. Jones suggests that the mutually beneficial but tenuous and unequal relationship between the business community and black leadership required African American politicians to get behind the referendum once MARTA made its pact with the coalition. Because of the way in which MARTA was positioned, for a black politician to voice opposition to the referendum was tantamount to opposing development and advancement for the city as a whole. To allow oneself to be saddled with such a perception would be political suicide (103).

These promises of inclusion for blacks and fiscal comfort for whites paid off. The 1971 referendum passed. The black vote was most influential in its passage, and consequently it was DeKalb, City of Atlanta, and Fulton (those counties with the largest African American constituencies) that bought into the one penny sales tax while Gwinnett and Clayton counties (predominantly white) opted out. This meant that MARTA would serve only those areas that paid in, and yet, because of earlier referendums,

> The two counties [Gwinnett and Clayton] were given representation on MARTA's board of directors. Even state officials were given representation on the MARTA board, even though the state provides no funds to MARTA. Many black leaders and community activists in Atlanta and Fulton and DeKalb counties condemned this practice as "representation without taxation." (Bullard et al. 2004:54–55)

Several efforts have been made to redress this seemed imbalance but none have been successful to date. As an area transportation authority board member told me:

> Well, through the years there's been several attempts to amend the MARTA Act—to take them—their representation [Gwinnett and Clayton] off. As recently as last year [2004] the then Chairman of the MARTOC[3]— . . . dropped a bill in the hopper that would change—that would take them off—however, the bill never got out of committee. It never got to full vote, just never got anywhere in the legislature. There've been several attempts over the years, and none of them have ever been able to be passed.

This disjuncture between who is served and who has power to determine MARTA's course has been partially responsible for many of the problems that continue to plague the organization.

Despite its myriad difficulties, to be detailed below, currently MARTA is the ninth-largest transit system in North America. It carries more than 450,000 passengers a day, using 556 buses, 338 rail cars, and 110 passenger vans, as well as 15 small buses. The budget is approximately $725 million (operating and capital) and it operates forty-eight miles of track. Regionally, it outperforms all other area transit systems combined and is the backbone for all metro transit operations.[4] Let us review the most prominent complaints against MARTA and some of the efforts to redress them.

HOW DO YOU SOLVE A PROBLEM LIKE MARTA?

Foremost among MARTA's difficulties are the unsettled questions of whom it is primarily meant to serve and what its fundamental purpose ought to be. In this section I will examine the reception, interpretation, and critique of MARTA's mission from various perspectives. A second critical issue for MARTA has been its struggle with the delivery of quality service to riders. MARTA's inability to attract and retain ridership is often linked to lack of amenities and to potentially correctable inconveniences. Consequently, service delivery will also be explored. Underlying mission and service is MARTA's most profound impediment—its nearly constant financial crises. The relationship between these three is recursive, with lack of funding resulting in inadequate service and inability to expand its mission, and with perceptions about goals and execution effecting funding decisions. Thus, I will speak to MARTA's fiscal predicament in this section as well.

MARTA's Mission

The question here is whom (or what) does, and perhaps even more importantly should MARTA serve? There seem to be three basic answers to that question, tying in to a central theme of this book, namely, that mobility polices and practices are hammered out in the struggle between equity, growth, and green goals. Let us look at each in turn: (1) MARTA as provider of mobility to those with no other means and as employer of those most in need of decent employment (equity); (2) MARTA as servant of downtown business interests, which includes notions of MARTA as image enhancer, as suburban commuters' means of entering and exiting the city, and as a perk for tourists, conventioneers, and airport users (growth); and (3) MARTA as facilitator of air quality improvements, sustainable and less congested movement, and land-use practices favoring those goals (green).

EQUITY: SERVING THE POOR OR POOR SERVICE?

In the 1960s, when MARTA was in its nascent stages, it was Atlanta's white business elite that was most interested in its formation. Ironically, this is the very group that is currently most interested in its demise. A Chamber of Commerce respondent told me that MARTA is plagued by an Afrocentric bent, corruption, systems of kickbacks, and unreasonable wages for employees. He noted that he heard about a bus driver making more than $100,000 a year, adding that we should all quit our jobs and go work for MARTA. He believes that MARTA is beyond redemption and should be dismantled and replaced by a less "tainted" and "broken" authority. This and other respondents (as well as many others in the community at large) are of the opinion that MARTA is too single-mindedly focused on serving the needs of its employees and the largely African American transit-dependent. For instance, MARTA has been given the not-so-secret local appellation of "Moving African Americans Rapidly through Atlanta."

MARTA is also still the recipient of the opposite claim, that it does not adequately address the needs of its largely black and poor riders. Thus, MARTA gets it from both sides, in terms of being accused of paying too much attention to and neglecting the same population. For instance, Anita Beaty, a homeless advocate, told me:

> I care about people's ability to get to work and to housing and to schools for their children around the city. I care about the cost of MARTA for poor people. We've cared for a long time about MARTA's—it seems intentional—exclusion of poor people.

Many echo this sentiment that MARTA has not kept all its promises to Atlanta's poor and African American community. In particular, a long-pledged line to a predominantly black neighborhood was never fully installed.[5] Also, as initially framed, MARTA was going to keep fares low and routes and buses plentiful (at an early planning stage it was even once proposed that MARTA's rail would be free of charge to riders). Over the last several years there have been numerous fare hikes and reductions in service. As of 2008 the fare was $1.75. The bus routes that have been reduced or eliminated disproportionately affect the poor and people of color. Social justice and transit advocates have shown a strong presence at public meetings and have been extremely vocal in their objections to these fare increases and service changes.

In December of 2001, there was a series of four public meetings, allowing the public to respond to the proposed fare hike and service reductions on various MARTA routes.[6] I had the privilege of attending three of the four meetings. I say privilege, because the atmosphere at these meetings was very exciting. The electric feel of democracy in the air was palpable. Participants were feeling the heady sense of power and exhilaration that is born of the belief that you are involved in a righteous and crucial battle, and that you are not alone and your collective voice may be heard. MARTA was accused of being racist, anti-church (because of proposed cuts to Sunday bus service), anti-poor, anti-disabled, and anti-American. The energy was intense and the crowd noise almost deafening at times in response to such proposals as starting up independent transit service, and, at one point in one meeting, a chant of "Boycott! Boycott!!" got underway. There was also much concern voiced over the lack of adequate Board representation at these hearings.

The participants at the meeting were not insensitive to Marta's difficulties. Much of the political rallying centered on calls for the state to bail MARTA out, but the primary concern on the ground was to preserve routes and maintain reasonable fares (already believed to be too high). The result of MARTA negotiations and these dazzling public input sessions resulted in some compromises and concessions, which are summarized in a communiqué that MARTA sent to community leaders on February 12, 2002. It read, in part:

> As you are aware, the MARTA Board of Directors held four public hearings in December 2001 to consider service modifications for bus and rail and reduced bulk discounts for the Employer/University Pass Sales Program. These were three elements in a package of options to help MARTA address a $20 million shortfall in revenues due to the recent economic downturn. The public spoke and we listened!
>
> Approximately 1,800 people attended these hearings, 400 people spoke, 1,600 written comments were received, including 74 petitions. Staff analyzed comments and reviewed suggestions and recommendations from these hearings and offered a revised proposal for consideration by the Board . . . Under the original proposal, 14 Weekday routes were to be eliminated. However, only eight weekday routes will be eliminated and six weekday routes will be modified . . . Under the original plan, 34 Saturday routes were to be eliminated. However, only seven Saturday routes will be eliminated and 21 routes will be modified and five routes will remain unchanged. Under the original proposal, 65 Sunday/Holiday routes were to be eliminated. However, only 19 Sunday/Holiday routes will be eliminated and 35 Sunday routes will be modified and 11 routes will remain unchanged. (Ford 2002)

As for rail service, MARTA determined that a two minute increase in off-peak service would go into effect; fare discounts would be slightly reduced; and some paratransit service would be eliminated (noting that "the new service schedule will impact fewer than 100 paratransit customers").

From the perspective of MARTA, as the COO informed me in a retrospective discussion of his attempts to save the Authority money, these service reductions were only a small piece of their greater attempts at frugality and were long overdue. As part of this discussion he noted:

> Per capita, we provide a lot more service on the street than some of our peer transit systems. So, you know, while we built and expanded the rail system, we never really contracted the bus system to fit—you know, to shrink it down. It just literally stayed there, almost at the same levels of service that it had been—prior to the rail service coming in . . . The year after nine-eleven and the year after that year, were the two worst years in MARTA's sales tax history. We had a negative six percent growth, and a negative five percent growth. Never in the history had there been higher than a negative four percent growth—and that was the year after the Olympics. And there never was two consecutive years of negative sales tax growth . . . So that pushed us into a very aggressive cost containment process. In that cost containment process we reduced literally two hundred million dollars in expenses between that time frame and Two Thousand Eight . . . We've done a service modification, which, truth be told, that service modification was necessary in any case—because these were very, very, inefficient routes and it forced us to really take a look at the entire system and repackage it.

Who lost or won this round is open to interpretation, like so much of MARTA's history. What can be gleaned from it, however, is that separating MARTA's interests from those it primarily serves is not finally possible. A further way in which it would appear that MARTA harms the poor is through neighborhood dislocations, and those dislocations fell disproportionately on black residents. By March 1994, about 1,650 households had been relocated to make way for MARTA and almost 85 percent of those were impoverished African American households (Davis 1997:85). The one area in which promises have been kept is regarding contracts and employment. MARTA has a good record in hiring minority contractors and also in hiring African American employees at all levels (its record is not so impressive with women).[7] This positive track record with minority hiring has been largely due to early affirmative action, labor unions, and requirements by the federal government that tie minority representation in these areas to federal dollars for MARTA. This promise fulfilled is the site of much current criticism of MARTA from various quarters. For instance, the commissioner of the Georgia Department of Transportation (GDOT) in reference to MARTA's problems in general and labor issues in particular, recently averred, "I hate unions—kick 'em out" (2/21/05 Urban Fellows meeting).

To hear a MARTA representative tell it, "MARTA's primary mission is providing service for people within the two-county area that have no other means of transporting themselves." If this is the case, they are apparently not doing a very good job of it. Transit-dependent people and their advocates do not think MARTA is putting their concerns first, while ironically, other actors believe they are doing so at too great a cost. In its quintessentially American efforts to befriend too many, perhaps MARTA has merely succeeded in fashioning a bond between unlikely groups for whom enmity toward MARTA is the common glue. This brings us to the next set of actors vying for MARTA's loyalty.

Growth: Business Interests

MARTA was largely created to benefit downtown Atlanta business interests. As Roth and Ambrose (1996) point out, Atlanta has long been known for its marriage between business leadership and local government officials. In keeping with this tradition, the original City of Atlanta MARTA board members were four business executives—"three whites (including department store owner Richard Rich, who became MARTA chairman) and one African American (L. D. Milton, president of Citizens Trust Company)" (195). It was widely assumed that MARTA would bring shoppers to Rich's and other downtown businesses (with the Five Points Station as MARTA's centerpiece) and that by easing the flow of traffic more merchandise would be moved. In the present context, the business community looks to public transportation to provide relief from gridlock that prevents sales representatives and other workers from getting quickly to downtown destinations, thus reducing productivity.

In this vein, a Chamber of Commerce respondent posited that MARTA's goals ought to be (but are not) about "traffic congestion reduction" and "maximizing ridership." He expressed that the best ways to accomplish these goals are through travel-time reductions, free parking, and the perception of a special right-of-way.[8] In February 2005, at the strong recommendation of an influential lobbying group, several actors formed the Congestion Mitigation Task Force. The leader of this lobbying group, Mike Kenn, frames transportation priorities in this way: "We're of the opinion that congestion relief should be the primary driver in addressing our transportation needs, because everything else is a positive by-product of it—it's not the other way around." In other words, Kenn believes that mobility patterns are not dependent on land use and public transit use, but rather:

> Congestion relief—everything is a by-product of congestion relief—whether its air quality or safety—if you reduce congestion, you reduce emissions, you improve air quality—you reduce congestion, you reduce traffic incidents and you improve safety, and, uh, you reduce congestion, you improve people's quality of life because you've reduced their overall commute. We made a recommendation to the Department of Transportation, and actually today [February 17, 2005] it happened. What we recommended to GDOT and to GRTA, and to the ARC and to SRTA [State Road and Tollways

> Authority] is that we need to set a congestion relief goal and then develop a plan that achieves that goal . . . So they passed a joint resolution which actually became a directive by the governor today called the Congestion Mitigation Task Force—to develop benchmark strategies and goals to look at the cost benefit methodology in evaluating projects and then apply them to the state transportation plan within the metro-Atlanta attainment area . . . Something historical happened! For the first time in the history of the state, you have four entities agreeing to develop a plan . . . It's a huge leap! It's monumental!

According to Kenn and the Congestion Mitigation Task Force, coordination among the regional players is key to getting transportation "right." Yet once again MARTA has not been invited to the table. In my interview with a MARTA representative, he made reference to a task force that he was a part of at one point. I mistakenly assumed he was referring to the Congestion Mitigation Task Force, and when I asked him to clarify, he said, "No. And I'm not—I'm not a member of that, and that is a sore subject to me right now [laughs]—it's not even—I shouldn't open my mouth about that!"

MARTA's exclusion from this conversation may be read as emblematic of its position in the regional transportation hierarchy. Granted, the "Metropolitan" piece of MARTA is largely lip service, as it is only allowed to serve two counties of the twenty that comprise metro-Atlanta. Nevertheless, MARTA is the largest and most utilized public transportation provider in the region. As such, it seems astonishing that it would not be invited to the table for a discussion of such import regarding transportation decisions. This is especially so in light of the fact that it receives criticism for not positioning congestion mitigation as its primary goal.

If MARTA is perceived by some as not paying enough attention to those things that make a transportation system a central piece of the metropolitan area's economic fabric, others criticize it for catering too much to those very forces. Anita Beaty (the executive director of the Task Force for the Homeless) spoke of the ways in which MARTA policies are in keeping with its historical tendency to pander to the downtown business elite interests, illustrating with these examples:

> It was right before the Olympics when we found out all kinds of information about the number of tokens that were being sent out as gifts to hotels and you know, around the city for rich people. And during the Democratic convention in Eighty-Eight—that's when it started—we found out that X number of dollars were spent out of MARTA's marketing budget for free tokens to market to the people they wanted. You know, the rich folks, Buckhead—you know, the tourists—and we said, well, you know, good! Now use some of those

> marketing tokens and dollars to reduce the fare for people who can't—who have no other option!

It is worth noting, however, that the MARTA union, and the drivers in particular, came out the heroes in this tale:

> Anyway, MARTA's always making the money without accommodating poor people and people who have to get to work. Well, the union, to make a long story short, the MARTA union was aware of our attempt to sensitize the Board to the plight and to get some half-price fares and to be held accountable to distributing them. We got a "no" for years! The union called us in, and they said, "Here!" And they gave us bags and bags of tokens that the bus drivers had bought on their own at retail . . . over the years they've done fund raisers to get tokens too!!

Despite these transit-dependent-oriented actions of the union members, homeless advocates perceive the MARTA administration as pandering to the elite. From the perspective of some of the elite, MARTA is too focused on urban actors. Still others fault MARTA for being too suburban in its orientation. This also speaks to the rail versus bus functions of MARTA. Sally Flocks, an influential pedestrian advocate, explained:

> I thought MARTA was better before they put the train in, because I could get a direct ride downtown. And I think one of the worst things—or just dumbest—was that they built a transit system that serves the suburbs and the suburbs aren't paying for it . . . Before the train went in, I could get a bus on Peachtree Circle a few doors down from my house . . . Once they put the train in, I could [still] take a bus until I realized what a waste of time that was, and so I had a ten minute walk to get to the train—I had to go down two or three escalators, in a hugely overbuilt station—wait ten minutes, come downtown, walk another tem to fifteen minutes, depending on where I was going—it's just a very inefficient system! And ninety-eight percent of MARTA's buses feed into the train system—which—it's very suburban!

Flocks is bemoaning the fact that the bus/train configuration favors suburbanites and tourists because the buses largely feed into the train system. In an urban-centered bus system, the buses would run primarily on routes not attended to by the trains. Once again, we see that MARTA's role is regionally contested. Is MARTA meant to be a people mover for the city; a centerpiece for the region; or a catalyst for sustainable development?

Green: Sustainability or Social Engineering?

Public transportation in general and MARTA in particular have been looked toward as potential air pollution reducers and sustainability promoters. In 1993, a MARTA advertisement ran in the *AJC* illustrating the dangers of pollution, the potential impact on the business community, and MARTA's promise to address those problems. The heading read: "What Metro Atlanta's well-dressed executives may soon be wearing." It depicted two male and two female business-attired individuals sporting gas masks. The text spoke to the growing pollution in the area, the threat of an EPA mandate and its potential impact on the business community in terms of restrictions and penalties, and offered a partial way out of these problems: company-subsidized MARTA passes for employees. The ad further noted that several area businesses (including Coca-Cola and Georgia Power) were already on board with the program.

This ad demonstrates the impact air quality problems were beginning to have on the region. The degradation in air quality caused in large measure by automobile emissions was plaguing the area. MARTA was attempting to position itself as a partial solution. The Chamber of Commerce was becoming concerned that businesses would not come to the area because of pollution problems. Shortly thereafter (see chapter 4 on GRTA) transportation funding for the area was severely threatened, deepening these concerns. An intensive public relations campaign by the Chamber in conjunction with MARTA was aimed at stemming the tide of negative perceptions regarding air quality issues.

The May 17, 1993, *AJC* ran several articles addressing these misgivings. Hugh Chapman, chairman of the Atlanta Chamber of Commerce, published an article that day detailing an initiative called Clean Commute Day—an effort by the Chamber to promote "green" travel practices. In the article, Chapman both commodifies Atlanta and calls for sustainability:

> How does Clean Commute Day enhance the product we market as Atlanta? First, the habits begun through Clean Commute Day will help relieve congestion on our region's roadways . . . Second, clean commuters help maintain the environmental quality that keeps companies coming. Our motto at the Chamber is "Where you live better . . . you work better," and clean commuting can protect our irreplaceable environmental assets. Third, clean commuting makes economic sense, Employees are more satisfied, costs of travel are lower, and we can maximize our investment in transit and roadway facilities through efficient use (*AJC* 5/17).

Chapman goes on to call for all chamber members to participate through car pooling, using transit, telecommuting, biking, and/or walking. That same day (and throughout that week) several articles were in the *AJC* addressing issues of smog, congestion, alternative fuels, telecommuting, and—not least – promoting the use of public transportation. One of the articles spoke of the alliance between MARTA and the Atlanta Gas Light Company aimed at the addition of natural gas buses to MARTA's fleet (a complete conversion is only now underway in 2006). Over the years MARTA has worn many hats. Alongside access provider for affluent downtown venue goers, means of transport for those with no other avenue, and controversial employer of many union workers, MARTA has also worn the hat (or at least tried it on) of environmental superhero.

MARTA has always borne criticism from the Right and the Left. From the Right, MARTA's actions have often been seen as too concerned with the needs of the poor, too riddled with union contract problems and corruption, and too easily manipulated by land use and sustainability "fanatics." From the Left, MARTA is accused of catering to the wealthy, ignoring the needs of the poor, and contributing to environmental racism through such actions as leaving the most polluting buses on routes that service poorer neighborhoods (not to mention being riddled with union contract problems and corruption).

Thus, MARTA has been and remains a major player in the Growth, Green, and Equity tug-of-wars that so characterize the metropolitan Atlanta landscape. For growth-oriented actors, MARTA and its promoters need to stay out of both the social justice and the environmental arenas. Addressing MARTA's role in the region, Jim Wooten opines in an op-ed piece that appeared in the *Atlanta Journal-Constitution* on June 14, 2005:

> Grow the private sector and, in the process, create a regional transportation system with one mission: transportation. When advocates veer off into other agendas—land use, density, or anything that has the word "justice" connected to economic or environmental policies—be wary. We're no longer talking about solving a transportation problem. We're into social engineering.

In many critiques, often not so explicitly linked to social justice issues, this concept of "social engineering" has become synonymous in the minds of many free market champions with Smart Growth. There is a deeply negative connotation attached to its use, as though such a proposition is fundamentally coercive and against the American principles of freedom of choice. In a 2001 online blog from Demographia, in a section entitled "From Social Engineering to Freedom," the author comments, "The smart growth movement has identified no problem of sufficient magnitude to justify its draconian proposals" (www.demographia.com). And frequently, any sort of public transportation, particularly if it involves, as MARTA does, Transit Oriented Developments, is linked to smart growth.

In a thirty-plus page diatribe, O'Toole (1997), writing for the CATO Institute, decried the Intermodal Surface Transportation Efficiency Act (ISTEA), asserting that it might better be named "the Urban Immobility and Pork-Barrel Act." He further states:

> Given a clear choice, few Americans would be willing to give up their cars and the lifestyles they make possible. Yet an extreme anti-auto view has become the dominant paradigm behind ISTEA. That has happened because the supporters of immobility have stolen the terms of the debate by claiming to want to reduce congestion and pollution whereas, in fact, they want to increase congestion and, in effect, pollution. In truth, ISTEA
>
> - mandates for transportation a comprehensive central planning process that has been captured by the New Urbanists in many cities;
> - gives cities huge incentives to build rail lines and other expensive but practically useless transportation projects;
> - creates perverse incentives for cities to increase congestion, making them less likely to meet federal air quality standards; and
> - hands out billions of federal dollars for mass transit, roads, and other projects that satisfy political agendas rather than local transportation needs. (2)

As for the transit-dependent, Cox (2004) of the Heartland Institute recommends that we buy them all cars. He asserts that it would be cheaper and more efficient than subsidizing public transit. He notes that this proposal is merely a "thought experiment"; it is

> not an actual proposal for converting transit subsidy programs into automobile options for low-income transit riders. But it demonstrates the extremely high cost, limited success, and unfair distribution of benefits of the current transit subsidy scheme. It is time to start considering alternatives that would provide greater value for taxpayers and more choices for transit riders. (2)

The perception from such automobile champions is that transit advocates are car haters, out to limit choices and push for draconian measures to remake the world in their left-leaning image through "social engineering." Yet, I believe we would be hard pressed to find the piece of physical engineering that is not also social engineering. This is the point of view expressed in an online Sierra Club article called "Is Smart Growth Social Engineering? Or is Sprawl?" In it, the author, Holtzclaw (2000) asserts that:

The dysfunctionalism of Post WWII social engineering includes:

- The bulldozing of highways through urban areas.
- Federal housing loan policies that redlined urban neighborhoods.
- Massive demolition of housing in urban neighborhoods.
- Single-use zoning that separated housing from shopping, work and schools.
- Migration of federal and state agencies . . . from urban centers to the sprawling suburbs.
- Huge subsidies for driving, equivalent to $3 to $5 per gallon of gas. (www.sierraclub.org/sprawl/articles/social_engineering.asp)

For most people in decision-making positions, however, it seems much more difficult to make the connection between these long-standing practices and social engineering. Legislators and lobbyists are far more likely to perceive smart growth initiatives as a kind of social engineering. In this context, support for public transit may be perceived as a piece of a greater agenda toward environmental and/or equity consciousness. In Atlanta, this perception is often linked to MARTA in particular. Coupled with perceptions of inefficiency, corruption, and general mismanagement, this leaves MARTA in a very vulnerable position. As a MARTA insider told me:

> We are a very unpopular entity . . . I'm not a conspiracist . . . I don't think there is a conspiracy and an actual plan to see us go under—I think a lot of individuals who are in a position of holding our fate in their hands, would just as soon see us go under—or in some cases would actually like to see us go under.

In response to my question as to whether this was based on general anti-transit sentiment or hatred of MARTA specifically, he was silent for a moment. I said, "I mean, if you understand the distinction I'm making." He replied:

> No, I understand the distinction; I'm just trying to decide how frank I should be in answering. I think if they—I think that they—that they—there is a general—there is a general lack of understanding of public transportation—in a broad and general way. I mean, I don't think that people would not support—I mean, there are people who would support no public transportation 'cause they just don't understand how it fits, or what its role is, or why it's needed—uh, and—then beyond that there is particular dislike in some quarters of MARTA because of what we are and who we serve!

This quote demonstrates that we cannot easily disentangle the growth, green, and equity meanings embedded in MARTA's mission. From this respondent's perspective, "what MARTA is and who it serves" are repugnant to "some people." He is alluding in particular, I believe, to some Chamber of Commerce representatives who also voiced to me (as previously noted) their disdain for what they perceive to be MARTA's mission. In this context, "what MARTA is," is an agency that provides employment to a largely African American workforce for what is thought to be too much compensation for too little work. "Who MARTA serves," is seen as the poor and primarily minority transit-dependent inner-city Atlantans.

Nathaniel Ford (COO of MARTA) was far more circumspect in his responses regarding perceptions of MARTA by the business community. He was hesitant to voice perceptions of prejudice or mistreatment, but was unable to disguise his frustration when speaking of MARTA's often unrecognized central role in the provision of area service and support. So while MARTA is believed by many to provide too much service to poor, black riders, it is also criticized for providing inadequate service all around.

MARTA's Incompetence

The quality of service that MARTA provides (or fails to provide) is widely critiqued. Some of its inadequacies have already been delineated, for instance: its paucity of routes and inability to get people where they need to go; the perception that it serves too narrow a constituency; and its costs to the public. MARTA service is also often charged with being slow, unsafe, not running on time, not providing reasonable comforts (benches, shelters, and so on), and not attending to aesthetics. A MARTA executive himself noted:

> The frequency of the buses and that sort of thing is that it's a real disincentive for riders of choice. You know? And so it sort of creates this downward spiral . . . I had this conversation with somebody the other day. I live downtown . . . earlier in my life I lived over on Morningside . . . for years I would bus down in the morning, and I would run home in the afternoon . . . and that was a very viable thing for me to do . . . I had two choices I could take the Sixteen Noble or the Thirty-One—I lived about equidistant between the two, so just whichever . . . It was never more than a ten minute wait, you know, and I didn't ever have a ten minute wait because you knew when the buses ran . . . and knowing that I could—and then not having the hassle of parking—both of them put me off right in front of my office—not having the hassle of parking—it was very little difference in the commute time, very little—maybe five minutes. Uh, and those buses would fill up—there were mornings I'd have to wait, you know—I mean not HAVE to wait, but I would make

> the choice, you know, knowing there's another one coming along in five minutes I'm not going to get on this crowded one here. Stand here and read the paper for another ten minutes. Uh, now they run something like every forty minutes—nobody rides them.

John Sibley, a leading conservationist, also voiced concerns about MARTA's paltry service:

> I ride MARTA every day, I rode MARTA here just now to come back to this meeting from the Capitol—I've been on MARTA four times today—so I'm a rider of MARTA—I'm a lover of MARTA. Its—from just a customer point of view, MARTA's been slipping. You can see it in the deferred maintenance that's just plain to the eye, you can see it in . . . just the interface with the customer, you can tell that MARTA hasn't been able to fund some stuff that it needs . . . to provide a first class customer experience.

In both these accounts poor service contributes to a decrease in ridership, which contributes to further financial woes, which contribute to less ability to correct the problem and so on and on in a vicious cycle. In order to attract anyone other than the transit-dependent it is seen as imperative to provide the best possible service. A private sector transportation planner noted in this regard:

> You know we do have to recognize that personal mobility is now ubiquitous. Everybody's got a car. That's one of MARTA's big problems is they can't rely upon a captive market anymore because even, you know, people of very limited means end up having cars. And if they're not treated well by the system and if it doesn't serve their needs well they just get behind the wheel of a car.

This notion that "everyone has a car" is of course incorrect, yet his greater point is not: insufficient service leads to insufficient usage. In early November 2005 about a dozen of the *Atlanta Journal-Constitution* op-ed staff experimented with getting to work by any means other than a car for one week. Their experiences culminated in an online blog relating their impressions. They also invited comment from the general public, resulting in hundreds of responses. On November 13, the *AJC* printed a special section entitled "Commutants Come Home," sharing a number of the comments that both staff and readers had posted regarding non-auto travel. Many of these remarks were specifically about MARTA. The responses covered a wide range, from racialized diatribes to thoughtful social commentary. I will share a smattering of them here because they embody many of the points

I make about the distance between growth goals, green goals, and equity goals. They also speak to (or in some cases scream out!) the social distance between urbanites and suburbanites.

For some suburban residents, living outside the city means not having to be plagued by buses and the riffraff that, in their minds, rides them. It also means freedom from social engineering:

> Hey, if you people want to ride a bus to work, live in DeKalb or Fulton counties and quit your whining about lack of buses. Don't you get it? We don't want buses in Gwinnett County no matter how much the government tries to ram 'em down our throat.

Additionally, many white respondents expressed distrust and distaste for the "blackness" of MARTA. MARTA becomes a site in which:

White privilege is challenged:

> I ran up the stairs at Doraville and when I got to the train door, the driver shut the door in my face and yelled out, "Sorry, whitey" and took off. I happily drive myself to work now and don't have to be subjected to perverts and racists. I'll sit in traffic any day.

Sense of security is threatened:

> Ever since being accosted on a MARTA south rail by a gang of punks on the way to the airport, I have decided to drive my self and Park'n Ride. MARTA's police are a joke, especially if you happen to be a white male. No, thanks. I'll stay way outside the Perimeter with regards to any public transportation.

Automobile dependency is justified:

> I am not giving up the comfort of my vehicle to ride on a smelly, nasty bus or train and sit next to someone who looks like they'd kill me for a quarter.

The urban/suburban rift is vindicated:

> Of course there's an overriding feeling among the white constituency that [MARTA is] not very safe, regardless if that's true or not. In the more than 12 years I've lived here, the "hate whitey" culture of Atlanta has been demonstrated almost daily. It's the biggest reason so many of us suburbanites avoid the city.

Some black riders responded to the unevenness of the system and its racist distribution:

> The level of service you receive does depend on your area. The North Springs trains are always air-conditioned and, for the most part, always on time. MARTA tries to cater to the white people in Alpharetta way more than the black folks in Decatur. I ride MARTA because I want to and because it is convenient. But if MARTA continues to see white people's money as more valuable than mine, I will start driving to work.
>
> If all the scared white people in the suburbs would realize they are more likely to get killed in an SUV rollover than by some criminal on public transit, maybe things would start to improve. Our daily rush-hour clogs are nothing more than a continuation of segregation for the new millennium: Separate and horribly unequal. Until transportation is integrated, every new highway interchange should be named "The Jim Crow Interchange" to show them what they really are.

These comments speak volumes about how MARTA is created through race and space conceptions. They also demonstrate that Atlantans are seriously concerned about transportation issues and willing to spend considerable time and energy on either avoiding, participating in, or working to correct the problems. As far as solutions are concerned, several citizens were more than willing to offer advice, often complex and explicit. I reproduce one section of these offerings below as it tells us much about how the issues are framed and received by and for the public:

Quick answers:

1. Gov. Sonny Perdue needs to declare an immediate state of emergency and take over MARTA.
2. Fire all union employees of MARTA and merge it into GRTA; if you have to, lay them off and give severance. MARTA is going downhill quick.
3. Require GRTA, CCT, and GCT to offer service from 4:30 a.m. to 9:30 p.m. on an hourly basis.
4. Develop hub-and-spoke networks off rail stations.
5. Require all metro counties to participate [in MARTA] or lose all state funding on all projects. You have to have a carrot and a baseball bat.
6. Provide bus-only lanes on all interstate corridors; if this means taking a lane from regular traffic, so be it.

7. Limit truck travel in metro area to 9 p.m. to 6 a.m. and 9 a.m. to 3 p.m. Issue $5,000 fines for each violation with revocation of commercial driver's license on third offense.
8. Raise gas prices significantly to force mass transit solutions. Keep gas at $3 a gallon.

This sophisticated reading of the area transportation troubles and possible solutions neglects only one thing: politics. The highway lobby, of which the Congestion Mitigation Task Force is a strong arm, would take exception to many of these proposals, especially number 5. Number 1 and number 2, which speak to the dissolution of MARTA, on the other hand, are probably well under way in some form. The COO of MARTA, whom I interviewed and who has been disparagingly referenced by Chamber of Commerce respondents, resigned in November 2005. He has taken a position in San Francisco, perhaps wisely fleeing a sinking ship. Central to and interwoven with all other problems are MARTA's financial woes, which the COO found to be insurmountable. To be understood, these must be situated in politics and prejudice—or, in other words, in the context of race and place.

The Best Things in Life Are Free—MARTA Is Clearly Not among Them

The federal government provides most of the capital funding for MARTA. The controversial funding issues begin to come into play when we look at its operational side. As the COO noted, "We're the only transit system of our size—multi-modal transit system of our size in the country that doesn't receive state operating dollars." This fact is so well known and frequently repeated that it has taken on almost mythic proportions. As a conservationist reported:

> Well, you know, MARTA is—this is the kind of factoid that we all repeat and I can't vouch for its absolute truth, but you know, it's regularly said that MARTA is the only similar system in the country without some form of ongoing state funding.

Robert Bullard, a prominent environmental justice scholar, told me, "You know, we're the only major transit system in the country that doesn't get any earmarked state funding. You know, that's scandalous! That's ridiculous!" Funding for MARTA's operations is one of the most politicized transportation issues in the region. The current operating funding sources are best described by the COO of MARTA who explained:

> Our primary source of funding is the one penny sales tax that is assessed in DeKalb, Fulton, and City of Atlanta. That makes up about sixty-five percent of our funding [operating].[9] The fare box

> receipts represent about another thirty percent of our funding, and the remainder of our funding we try to make up with advertising, leasing coming from some of our transit-oriented developments and things of that nature. The gap is never made up—I mean, you know, in good years, when the sales tax revenues are very good, we put monies in reserve and hold those monies for, sort of like a rainy day fund. We hold those reserves for leaner times, like we're going through now—and those reserves make up the difference between our operating expenses and our revenues.[10]

While MARTA ostensibly serves a limited area, its impact on the region goes well beyond those boundaries. Likewise, decisions and policies set and carried out, outside the MARTA ridership region, leave an imprint on MARTA. The question of subsidization is a major point of contention when it comes to transit, both in general and in Atlanta in particular. Accusations regarding who carries the bulk of the weight when it comes to subsidies are thrown in multiple directions: rail versus bus, city versus suburb, rich versus poor. In general, in that the poor contribute considerably less overall to the tax base, they consequently foot less of the public transit bill. On the other hand, if we consider sales taxes as well as income taxes, which are sometimes used also to subsidize transit, "the poor contribute the same proportion of their consumption expenditure as the rich, but a greater proportion of their income "(Deka 2004:340).

In Atlanta, the one penny sales tax is the major source of MARTA funding. Consequently, it is true in Atlanta that the poor pay proportionally more of their income toward transit. Similarly, if we look at an urban/suburban split, another complex piece of the subsidization picture revolves around fares and distance traveled. Those who reside within cities and with low incomes usually travel shorter distances than prosperous suburban travelers. Consequently, if the transit system's fare schedule is not distance-based, those traveling shorter distances will actually be largely footing the bill for those who go farther. "For a particular transit system, Wachs (1989) noted that a user who travels 1 mile pays more than twice the true cost of the trip, whereas a user who travels 20 miles pays only 20% of the cost" (Deka:340).

Although in the Atlanta region there are currently separate systems for the city and the suburbs, the affluent within the city tend to make longer trips. For instance, one of the most common usages of MARTA for well-off users is riding from relatively distant parts of the city to the Atlanta airport. A final aspect of ridership that speaks to who is paying more of the costs of transit relates to peak versus off-peak usage. Since systems must be designed with the capacity to handle peak volumes, Deka suggests that this is another way in which the poor are subsidizing the affluent, in that the poor are more likely to travel during off-peak hours, thus defraying the costs for those requiring the peak volume capability.

The ways in which federal monies are dispersed for transit also disproportionately favor the non-poor. The federal government pays nationally 54.2 percent of transits' capital expenses, but only 3.4 percent of operating expenses. This speaks to the rail versus bus issue in this way: for rail most monies required are on the capital side (intensive construction costs) but for bus the greater financial needs are for operations (labor, upkeep, and so forth). Buses are the piece of public transit most heavily used by the poor. In terms of federal subsidies, "[w]hen only bus and rail modes are considered, bus receives only 31% of the capital funds, although it carries more than 60% of the trips made by transit" (Deka:342–43). In Atlanta, "revenues from bus fares generated $5 million more than that taken in by rail in 1997" (Bullard et al. 2000:58). This demonstrates that bus is the predominant mode in Atlanta as well.

In the minds of suburbanites, and for some city dwellers also, it appears as though public transportation spending, particularly on buses, is a form of "welfare on wheels" or a subsidization for a mode of transportation that they are not likely to utilize themselves, being far more disposed to get on the train than on the bus. Yet, it is political choices, however disguised, that determine the landscape and in the deepest sense "subsidize" automobility. Marshall (2000) speaks of the American infatuation with the notion of a free market: "We tend to think that places and economies just happen, built by the invisible hand of Adam Smith if by anyone" (134). Thus, if we think about it at all, we tend to think that the built environment develops in response to our needs and wants coupled with sound financial decision making. "We tend not to see the government's prior decision to build an Interstate through the area that made the whole thing possible. The intersection of place and economics is often in transportation" (134).

There are (at least) two additional ways in which subsidization may be hidden; one is through parking practices and the other via maintenance and operational procedures. To clarify, in regard to MARTA and parking issues, a 1997 survey revealed that about 44 percent of the cars parked at MARTA stations' ample free parking spaces were from outside the two-county area that pays the one penny sales tax. In other words, "it appears that Fulton and DeKalb county tax payers are subsidizing people who live in outlying counties who park their cars at the park-and-ride lots and ride on MARTA trains into the city and to the airport" (Bullard et al. 2000:59). As for the maintenance and operational issues, the COO of MARTA explained to me that none of the additional suburban transit systems that are currently in operation could function without the "expertise and experience" of MARTA, not to mention the salience of economies of scale. For instance, he explained:

> We encode all of the cards for every transit system in the region. We purchase buses in the hundreds; our prices are a lot different

> than somebody who's purchasing twenty buses. So we—in both Gwinnett County's case and Clayton County's case, they bought their buses on option underneath our bus procurements. Georgia Tech Shuttle, the Buck in Buckhead, and Emory University—they all fuel at our natural gas fueling facility.

He tried valiantly to cling to the notion that MARTA's indispensability would ensure its viability as a central player in area transit solutions, noting:

> For example, coordination of buses over multi-jurisdictional lines, over a twenty county area is no small feat! Infrastructure-wise, we have a bus communications center that's currently doing over five hundred square miles. We have a communications center, as it relates to customer information, schedule information, things of that nature that's right in this building and houses about twenty people just to do MARTA—I mean in terms of our size . . . So when we start talking about expanding transit in this region, along with it comes those kinds of support and administrative issues that has to be the backup—has to support the operation, and we have it in place . . . So, whether we're operating or not, we're sort of the backbone and the foundation underneath the success of the other transit systems.

MARTA's fate is not so certain in the minds of others. For instance, John Sibley (president of the Georgia Conservancy) expressed concern. While he himself is sympathetic to MARTA he is not so certain about how it may play out:

> I'm very supportive of MARTA. We've got to preserve MARTA in all of its functions as the heart of the regional transit system. There is so much baggage, political baggage around MARTA, and MARTA being more regional in scope and all of those issues, that we frankly might have to find some other accommodation. I don't want, personally, any one that would hurt MARTA or the functions that MARTA performs—but we're going to have to fashion that solution over time in the real world—in the world of real politics—and it may not be that MARTA will be the best way to do that.

He then went on to speak of the need to stand behind MARTA. Yet his words make it clear that he is uncertain as to whether others share his commitment to ensuring that MARTA continues as the primary area operator:

> MARTA cannot be allowed to collapse. I mean, it is too important to the overall transportation system of this region, and I'm absolutely convinced it won't be allowed to collapse. I mean, it just can't—it can't happen! It would be an absolute disaster . . . I think there are enough people who understand that MARTA is so essential to our transportation system and the future of this region that it simply can't be allowed to collapse—and I don't think it will be allowed to collapse . . . I just—I can't see—it's just unimaginable to me that anybody really believes that for MARTA to somehow go away or collapse would be a good thing—I just don't think anybody believes that. But I'm not sure—there are some people—basically anti-transit people, who believe that, but I don't think anybody in a responsible decision-making position believes that.

In light of these kinds of speculations from all quarters, the question becomes not only one of MARTA's survival but also of area transit solutions in general. Will the "best" for the region spell doom for MARTA? This begs the question of how "best" is defined and implemented. Will solutions be fashioned in terms of sustainable mobility, equitable distribution of the benefits and burdens, or maximum growth for the region regardless of side effects? For those whose distaste, distrust, and scorn for urban bias, Afrocentric practices, and bleeding-heart overemphasis on the undeserving poor is housed in MARTA—any transformation may not seem like enough of a departure.

MARTA'S FUTURE: REVISE OR DEMISE

Early perceptions of the benefits and burdens that MARTA was likely to afford have fundamentally shaped those very advantages and impediments. Currently, financial hardship born of these perceptions and their consequences, coupled with deeply entrenched image problems resistant to face-lifts and other superficial measures, leave MARTA teetering on the brink of ruin. Race and regionalism are at the heart of both MARTA's existence and the controversy surrounding it.

The current conversation at the decision-making level, primarily through the Atlanta Regional Commission (ARC) is around how to best manage expanding and coordinating transit in the region. There is much discussion as to who should handle operations and who should handle oversight. There is fairly widespread agreement that these two pieces should be separated. Many proposals are on the table, several of which include the notion of splitting not only operation and oversight of transit in general, but also of somehow dividing rail and bus and thus creating a new configuration—perhaps leaving bus to MARTA and giving rail to another entity.[11] If that particular option is chosen, it will most probably spell doom for MARTA, whose struggles are already so great that it can barely keep its head above water. As noted earlier in this chapter, bus service is operations-intensive, and it is the operating budget that has historically proven most problematic.

The ARC conversation is being received and framed by some transit advocates as a hostile takeover. The Atlanta Jobs with Justice coalition posted a "call to action" and a meeting announcement on the Web on September 19, 2005. In it, they speak to issues of MARTA union contracts and service cuts in regards to ARC's current proposals under discussion. They note, "MARTA riders and rank and file employees are the most affected by what happens with public transit, yet the ARC/State Take Over would eliminate their voice in the decision making process." They assert that the "ARC/State Take Over" would take away the people's voice and result in worse service as well as being anti-union and bad for workers. Their position is that "This InJustice Is Not Acceptable!" They further suggest that ARC's actions would result in greater harms to the poor and disenfranchised, and that "fare increases and cuts will continue to transfer the financial burden to the people who can least afford it—the poor, workers, immigrants, the elderly and disabled." Invoking the oft-chanted mantra, "MARTA is the 9th largest transit system in the Nation . . . It is the only one of these systems of such size that doesn't receive ongoing support from its state for operating costs," they further pronounce that "[t]his is an extreme injustice, especially when we realize that MARTA has brought businesses, workers, and prosperity to Atlanta, the region and the state," citing the 1996 Olympics as a case in point. It is their contention that "[b]ecause of its experience, infrastructure, and workforce, MARTA must be designated as the Region's sole provider and planner of Transit!"

It is possible that theirs is not a detailed or sophisticated analysis of the ARC proposals and it may be that what they fear is not in fact taking place. On the other hand, their passion and defensiveness may well be justified, in that whatever results from ARC's negotiations is likely to be less than perfect from a social justice perspective. Much maligned and long left to fend for itself on too meager a budget, MARTA may disappear or become something quite different through semi-hostile "rescue." If the outcome of this latest round is—or even appears to be—further denigration of MARTA, such a result will likely turn MARTA from villain to martyr for some champions of mobility equity. Despite MARTA's checkered history, as outlined above, with evidently racist and anti-poor practices, it is, in the final analysis, the only game in town for the transit-dependent. Any attempt at last-minute salvation at this crucial juncture may appear instead as assassination.

A MARTA official spoke quite directly to the reorganization efforts that are currently underway through the Atlanta Regional Commission, although he did not invoke the name of that organization. I spoke with him in late March 2005, and the slightly more public discussion of ARC's plans did not begin until September, yet clearly rumors had been circulating for some time. My informant told me:

> Like I say, there's no conspiracy out there, there's no master plan, you know, of how to deal with MARTA. But I think there's some people out there, I know, because they've expressed it, that have the misconception that MARTA could be reorganized, and through the reorganization they could get out from the legal obligation that they have collective bargaining in MARTA.

I inquired as to what way this reorganization might take place and he answered:

> You name it—I've heard all kinds of—I mean, a legislator just the other day suggested that the MARTA board should be reconstituted to be a thirteen member board with a member from each of the thirteen counties . . . and that the thirteen counties should all have one vote on the MARTA board . . . I just mention that because it is one of the more absurd things, but this was actually said by a member of the legislature, and obviously all these questions you just asked, they never asked themselves! You know, they're just out there running their mouths! But still, you know, with certain people running their mouths, because of who they are, it gets listened to! But, uh, no, I think there are some other people who would like to see the rail system split off—and have the state support the rail system, but not—and leave the buses, you know, to fend for themselves.

He went on to speak for some time of the dire financial straits that MARTA was currently experiencing. He spoke about the other area transit systems and how their operating funding, which is currently Congestion Mitigation and Air Quality (CMAQ) money, would soon run out and so a regional solution would have to be fashioned for all area transit systems. He also spoke of grassroots efforts and local support for public transit and how he had some hopes for that influencing business and political actors. However, the reality uppermost in his mind, which he confided was coloring both his mood and the tenor of the interview, was, "We had a couple of spending bills that didn't get out of MARTOC today—this week—They are going to require—it will end up necessitating further service cuts." When I noted how discouraged he seemed, he offered:

> Well, best case scenario we had before these spending bills failed—and the fact that they failed worsens our situation considerably—but

> the best case scenario we had there was that without significant service cuts and/or—in combination, you know, with fare increase—we would be through our reserves and broke by fiscal Two Thousand Eight. And we were trying to hold out until fiscal Two Thousand Eight, you know, fairly—without a fare increase and with only moderate service cuts . . . [but due to the current defeat of the spending bills] I mean, we can't! You know, it was absolutely dependent upon having that money! So . . . we'll either have to cut service, raise fares, or go broke sooner!

As for eleventh-hour hopes for MARTA, there are three possibilities on the horizon. First, MARTA has been in the process since the spring of 2003, of performing what is called the Atlanta Inner Core Feasibility Study. This is a study of a transit loop within the city of Atlanta. It engages the Beltline notion (which will be fully detailed in chapter 5) and also some possible alternative transit stretches, including what is called the C-Loop.[12] This study, which has been quite extensive—engaging experts, community input, and statistical analysis—is often taken by the public as a Beltline study. It does, as I noted, include the Beltline as envisioned by Ryan Gravel and lately the Belt Line Partnership as one possibility, but it differs from the Beltline study in two important ways. First, that twenty-two-mile loop is one of four scenarios under study, meaning that MARTA is not emotionally or structurally attached to one version over another. Second, the MARTA study consists of transit only—unlike the Beltline study, which also includes a major greenspace component. Neither mode (light rail, heavy rail, bus rapid transit), nor operator (not to mention operating funds) has yet been identified, but MARTA owns the study. While not likely to pull MARTA out of the fire, playing a central role in managing and/or providing transit service along the Beltline would certainly enhance both its visibility and their credibility.

A second possible hope for MARTA's salvation would be its Transit Oriented Developments (TODs). TODs potentially please both growth and green advocates, representing new urbanism at its finest. MARTA's TOD efforts involve partnering with business and residential developers to create spaces for people close to transit. MARTA then receives proceeds from rents as well as an increase in fare revenues from the addition of riders produced by the TOD. MARTA has plans for several such nodules in the future (and the Beltline is hoped to inspire many more).[13] The TOD that is currently under construction is The Lindbergh City Center, (with Carter and Associates as developer) a forty-seven-acre site "which includes BellSouth office towers, a multi-tenant office building, new parking decks and a Main Street retail promenade, apartments and condominiums" (History of MARTA: www.itsmarta.com).

When the BellSouth/MARTA partnership was announced in 1999, The Atlanta Business Chronicle touted the Lindbergh TOD project as the "Best Mixed-Use (Real Estate) Deal of the Year" (History of MARTA: www.itsmarta.com). The business community has been delighted with this smart growth initiative. An online area business publication, AllBusiness, noted: "It is one of those 'live, work, play' communities that urban planners say is exactly the right medicine for Atlanta's air quality, suburban sprawl and traffic ills" (www.allbusiness.com/periodicals). Like everything else associated with MARTA, the Lindbergh TOD has detractors on all sides. First of all, it is not without neighborhood opposition:

> Peggy Whitaker, a residential architect who has worked in the area for 25 years and lives in the nearby Peachtree Heights East neighborhood, thinks MARTA has "overstepped its bounds as stewards of our money . . ." Although Whitaker says she supports the idea of dense, multi-purpose development at Lindbergh, she thinks a project with 10,461 parking spaces is too big. "The first design was a fabulous urban village with small shops and apartments above them. It was wonderful." But this design, she says, has too much office space and too much parking. "They've spent a fortune to tag this as a TOD, but in reality it's a Bell South office park." (www.allbusiness.com/periodicals)

Neighborhood interests, as we see throughout this book, are often at odds with pure growth goals. Neighborhood actors tend to have "green" concerns that include livability, walkability, neighborhood preservation, parking, and density issues. From the "growth" perspective, the MARTA oversight committee, MARTOC, is apprehensive that the Lindbergh City Center will not generate revenue adequate to justify its outlay. In a January 5 article regarding MARTOC's misgivings about MARTA's financial status, the author notes:

> [B]udget items that raised concern on the 14-member joint committee were [among others]:
>
> The Lindbergh Center, a mixed-use development on MARTA property for which MARTA has spent $80 million of their capital funds. Chambers [chair of MARTOC] said MARTA expects a return of less than as million a year after the center is completed. (Swint 2006:2)

Evidently, Green and Growth actors have their reservations about MARTA's TOD forays. Equity advocates also express concerns that the Lindbergh City Center will be business as usual in terms of distribution of benefits and burdens. There is particular uneasiness about the probability that it will negatively impact the Latino population that is overrepresented in that area of town. In 2001, when plans for the development were just getting under way, an article in the Environmental Justice Resource Center newsletter expressed grave concerns about the Lindbergh City Center's probable effects on the surrounding Latino community. The author feared that the plan to "tear down the 379,230-square-foot shopping center at Lindbergh Plaza and build about 800,000 square feet of retail and 250 apartment units" would likely result in dislocations and severe disruption of the neighborhood. Most especially, the fear was that it would sever the tenuous ties that the Lindbergh area has long held with the oft-hidden Atlanta Latino community (www.ejrc.cau.edu). The hopes for and misgivings about MARTA's TOD involvement, illustrated through the example of the Lindbergh City Center, once again demonstrate how truly difficult it is to seamlessly link growth, green, and equity goals in area transportation planning. There is widespread agreement that MARTA cannot (and does not) function in a vacuum. Consequently, its fate is linked to regional decision making.

Thus, the third and final piece of conceivably good news for MARTA resides in the same ARC conversation that could spell its doom. Some MARTA personnel are optimistic that the fact that all area transit systems are struggling financially could be auspicious for MARTA. Since a regional solution will have to be fashioned, it could be that MARTA will be the beneficiary of part of that resolution. Nathaniel Ford (the COO of MARTA) spoke on this point at length. He informed me:

> The strategy that we have right now in terms of looking at additional funding is really to look at transit in its entirety—not just MARTA—and funding. I think far too often the discussion in terms of funding for transit has just—just touched upon MARTA. However, now you have transit systems in Cobb, Clayton, Gwinnett, and then you have the GRTA express bus system. And right now, at least in the Clayton and GRTA express bus system case, there's not a clear understanding of where they're going to get their future funding from. Right now they're using demonstration dollars—they're using CMAQ dollars—they're demonstration dollars for only a three year period and they have not clearly identified what will be the funding mechanism when that three year period ends. So, our effort will be to right now, one—operate within our current funding structure using our reserves to make up the difference, but over the next year or two to start developing a transit coalition that's not just focused on MARTA but focused on mass transit—or public transit, for the entire region. And, to take it one step further, there's over ninety urban and suburban or rural transit operations in the state. They're suffering with financial or funding

> challenges, as much as, say, MARTA is—so there's maybe even a bigger coalition than just metropolitan Atlanta. Colleagues and I, we talk quite often, you know, when we talk about transit funding everybody automatically looks at MARTA. Well, there's other systems out here that are going through similar challenges.

The discussions under way at ARC are similarly targeted toward fashioning a regional solution. There is general recognition that transit needs subsidy and that the state has a role to play in that respect. However, there is major disagreement about MARTA's future role in area transit solutions. Indications from all quarters are that MARTA's financial woes cannot be disconnected from its reputational ones. Splitting rail and bus, changing the structure of the board, reorganizing the labor structure, or any combination of these moves, will likely not solve MARTA's misfortunes. As long as the name MARTA continues to be associated with any piece of area public transportation, it is likely to persist in being the site of racial and spatial conflict.

FOUR

GRTA

Old Whines in New Bottlenecks

GRTA COMES INTO BEING, NOW WHAT TO DO WITH IT? THE DOG THAT CAUGHT THE BUS

In 1996, thirteen Atlanta metropolitan region counties were in serious violation of the National Air Quality Standards as designated by the Environmental Protection Agency (EPA). As a consequence, federal monies for transportation projects were withheld until serious efforts to redress this noncompliance were demonstrated. In 1998 a group of business leaders formed the Metropolitan Atlanta Transportation Initiative (MATI) and began in earnest to analyze the reasons for the noncompliance and to formulate suggestions for correction of those factors. They determined that crucial to the solution would be an intensive effort to curtail automobile usage in the region, and the provision of alternatives to make such a reduction possible. In large part due to MATI's suggestions, Governor Roy Barnes created and named the Georgia Regional Transportation Authority (GRTA) in 1999.

According to its remarkably concise mission statement, "It is the mission of GRTA to improve Georgia's mobility, air quality and land use practices" (from GRTA Web site). Its intended purposes, the degree to which it has carried these out to date, and where it may be headed are the substance of this chapter's inquiry, with a particular focus on the ways in which competing understandings of its roles and responsibilities have carved out GRTA's path. The GRTA statute, contrived under the administration of Governor Roy Barnes, endowed GRTA with monumental breadth and depth of powers.

In this chapter I demonstrate that GRTA has been unable to tap into this expansive authority precisely because of Atlanta's political economy (or urban regime) and the ways in which power is distributed. I will further demonstrate that a central piece of this power struggle involves the invisible and seductive aspects of hegemonic ideology, in which battles are often won by means of dissenters discovering that their own competing goals dictate a different desired outcome than that which they may have initially believed they wanted. For instance, while some green groups may start out as staunch supporters of greater densities for the sake of transportation alternatives, they may discover that the kinds of dwelling units proposed to be developed as corresponding to that level of density (such as high rise developments) in some neighborhoods, are unappealing and even run counter to other cherished goals, such as neighborhood preservation and current sense of community. To begin, we will look at a brief history of GRTA.

Several other entities, some with considerable authority over transportation matters in the region, were already in existence at the time of GRTA's creation. The Georgia Department of Transportation's (GDOT) primary roles and responsibilities are over state roads and bridges; the Atlanta Regional Commission (ARC), the area's Metropolitan Planning Organization (MPO), has wide-ranging authority over transportation planning for the area; and the Metropolitan Atlanta Rapid Transit Authority's (MARTA) role is implementation of public transportation (trains and buses) for Fulton County, DeKalb County, and City of Atlanta.

Each of these authorities had reason to be at best perplexed and at worst threatened by GRTA's creation. Similarly, each metro county has a stake in the outcomes for their own reasons. The counties have some authority over some of their roads and considerable authority over land uses that are affected by transportation decisions and were thus quite leery of GRTA's possible powers. The federal government was also uncertain as to what to do with GRTA. As Jeff Rader, one-time executive director of the Regional Business Coalition and a former transportation manager for GRTA, told me:

> The agency [GRTA] was neither fish nor fowl, it was a very unique agency—and quite frankly I think that's one of the things that slowed it down a lot at the beginning. The federal government didn't have a place to plug into an organization like that. You know they have a federally prescribed planning process that includes the Metropolitan Planning Organization and the state DOT, and, those are the two entities that they end up dealing with—they didn't have this third wheel in their model, and they didn't know what to do with the third wheel.

From its inception GRTA has been grappling with an identity crisis due to the breadth of its scope, its relatively recent entry on the transportation landscape (two respondents referred to it as "the new kid on the block"), the selectivity of its use of possible tools, and its uncertain relationships with other authorities. The fears of its potential powers, discussed at length later in this chapter, were initially fueled by notions that GRTA had the capacity to place the Atlanta region under "sprawl martial law." Jim Wooten, an *Atlanta Journal* editor, raised concerns about GRTA being antisuburban and perhaps dictatorial (Jaret 2002:184, 189). The contestation over GRTA's definitions and meanings, eased by the variability of interpretation of the statute and fueled by the competing interests in its outcomes, has resulted in the shaping of GRTA. In order to illuminate this process and understand its transformations, I interviewed key players from the groups of interested parties in the region, in addition to reading broadly on the topic and attending various relevant meetings and lectures.

As we shall see through the course of this analysis, GRTA's route has been directed and redirected throughout by reception and perception from other actors in the transportation arena. GRTA was granted an enormous amount of power and what it was meant to do with this power was very uncertain. As one respondent put it: "It's like the dog that caught the bus—what do you do with it now?"

GODZILLA OR JOLLY "GREEN" GIANT?

GRTA's potential was conceived differently by different actors. From the growth proponents' window, particularly the exurban actors, the Godzilla image meant that GRTA might well be an out-of-control, oversized, dictatorial monster, about to stomp on local authority and impose unwanted regulation on regional decision making. The Jolly Green Giant image is twofold: from the business view it could mean turning the faucets back on for the flow of federal "green" (money) back into the Atlanta metropolitan area; and from the environmentalists' perspective, GRTA could be a friendly "green" influence in terms of cleaning up pollution and offering transportation alternatives to the automobile.

Let us begin with a bullet point summation of the most salient items from the GRTA Statute (1999, Title 50: Chapter 32):

- All board members including the chair shall be appointed by the governor.
- Its jurisdiction includes all counties that fall under nonattainment of the Clean Air Act, at the time of inception thirteen counties,[1] and any reasonably expected by the EPD to fall under that within the next seven years from August 1999.
- Duration of its authority—each county will remain under its authority either:
  —for twenty years from attainment (USEPA determined) under Clean Air Act, or,
  —twenty years from when such designation is no longer made by the USEPA.

- GRTA will have no power over airports.
- Notable among its myriad powers:

  Section 50-32-11 a. 33: States in essence that the Authority can limit or deny access for any local roads to the state highway system, either new or existing, "to the extent necessary to achieve the purposes of the authority." Meaning, it may exercise this power for any reason GRTA deems appropriate or necessary to aid in the accomplishment of its land transportation betterment and air quality goals.

  Section 50-32-13 a. and b. 1–4: This section grants GRTA the authority to approve or disapprove (but not "tweak") both the Regional Transportation Plan and the Transportation Improvement Plans of the area MPO (ARC).

  Section 50-32-13 c.: Describes the mandate to measure and report air quality standards annually—both in terms of efforts applied and progress made.

  Section 30-52-14: This section stipulates that any Development of Regional Impact (DRI) must be approved by GRTA in order to take place and to withhold funding for such projects if the plans do not meet with the approval of the agency (GRTA).

  Section 50-32-17: GRTA shall have powers of eminent domain over some lands, "as necessary," provided it is property that is already owned by, or for the purposes of, GDOT.

Overall, as described in Section 50-32-11 (3 and 4)—GRTA's purpose is to "plan, design, acquire, construct, add to, extend, improve, equip, operate, and maintain or cause to be operated and maintained land public transportation systems and other land transportation projects, and all facilities and appurtenances necessary or beneficial thereto . . ." and ditto for "air quality control installations" (not defined) for its specified jurisdiction and by and through contracting with others (agencies, governments, etc.) as necessary.

This truncated glimpse into the GRTA statute demonstrates both the breadth of the powers granted to it and the wide interpretability of the language used in its creation. In its early days, GRTA's potential powers struck fear into the hearts of many. Jeff Rader (an area transportation consultant) noted "when enacted, you know, you could take a look at that legislation and you could write "Godzilla" on the front of it because it really was pervasive in its authority." These sentiments were echoed by Rebecca Serna, a local transit activist, "I mean there were all sorts of fears when it was formed that it was going to be this huge—just monster power and authority that was going to steal all the authority for itself."

Some local governments were also quite vocal in their expressions of distrust and trepidation about GRTA's possible demands and actions. In June 2000, Fayette County Commissioners sent letters to GRTA in response to a communication "informing local elected officials that GRTA plans to activate jurisdiction over the 13 counties that have failed to meet air quality standards set by the federal Environmental Protection Agency" (Hamrick 2000: 1). In a letter penned by commissioner Greg Dunn, the commissioners asserted that they "will never agree that our elected governments are under the jurisdiction of an appointed board. To do so would equate to us transferring to you the responsibilities and authorities bestowed upon us by our citizens" (Hamrick 2000:2). The following September, the Fayette County Commissioners met with then Executive Director of GRTA Catherine Ross, at which time Commissioner Dunn informed her, "We will not allow anybody outside of Fayette County to make land use decisions in Fayette County" (Hamrick 2000:2). In response to assurances from Ross that GRTA would make no nonnegotiated decisions for counties, Commissioner Linda Wells asked, "How do you negotiate with someone you've taken jurisdiction over?" and Dunn added, "The bill clearly states that if you decide we aren't cooperating you can punish us" (Hamrick 2000:2).

The unusual power with which GRTA was endowed made it unique not only locally but on the national landscape as well. In 2001 the Southern California Association of Governments (SCAG) did a study of ten regions in the United States and included a section on Atlanta. They had this to say about GRTA:

> Atlanta has received a fair amount of national attention because of the formation of the Georgia Regional Transportation Authority (GRTA) which provides unprecedented power to a regional agency over transportation and land use . . . This arrangement has, frankly, scared many cities fearing that level of State-level "intervention." And certainly GRTA has been controversial in Atlanta . . . It took an extraordinary level of gubernatorial power—and the fact that they were being penalized by the feds—to make GRTA come about. It remains unlikely that, wise or unwise, this model will be replicated very widely. (11)

GRTA's renown even became international. In 2003 a Berkeley professor of City and Regional Planning presented a paper at the 2nd International Conference on the Future of Urban Transport in Goteborg, Sweden, in which he remarked on the unusual authority vested in GRTA, noting that "the state of Georgia has made a bold departure," and commenting that GRTA is "an all-powerful regional transportation authority" (Cervero 2003:17). He went on to emphasize that not only does this entity have veto power over all fiscal and planning transportation decisions for the region, but further,

GRTA has the authority to regulate land use. It can, if its officers so choose, extend its tentacles into decisions regarding malls, office parks and sports arenas. If development and transportation decisions are not in line with GRTA's vision, it has the authority to withhold state monies for projects (17). As is apparent from the respective tones of these various quotes, some were hopeful and some were fearful, but all were convinced that GRTA could and probably would exercise considerable control in the region.

Evidence suggests that this lion has been effectively transformed into a kitten, to the chagrin of some and the relief of others. This transformation was in large measure due to an administrative change. When Governor Sonny Perdue took over the helm (the first Republican governor of Georgia in more than a century) GRTA's mission began a not-so-subtle shift. GRTA representatives began to speak more about notions of congestion mitigation (highway expansion and commuter bus systems) and less about public transportation. Rebecca Serna, a regional transit advocate notes: "Well, GRTA as it was originally formulated I think was a lot more ambitious than what it is now. I mean, now it seems like they're an express bus service. I don't see them taking the leadership role that they were meant to take." The impression from an authority at GDOT is that "GRTA has some modest authority over land use, but mostly that is left to local governments." A private sector transportation planner instrumental in many local projects of import remarked:

> I think GRTA was an attempt to make changes . . . in our bureaucratic structure [more quickly] than [you could] if you worked through the system. I think there was always this thought that GRTA could control MARTA, and to a certain extent control ARC, and to an even greater extent control DOT. And by creating GRTA you could avoid having to do the hard work that would take a long time dealing with all three of those groups. And it sort of blew up!

The governor under whose administration GRTA was formed (Roy Barnes), said that at one point ARC was almost folded into GRTA. He said that GRTA's creation was about having enforcement powers but he noted that state legislators are too jealous of power to relinquish it without a major battle (Urban Fellows Meeting 1/20/05).

ROAD BLOCKS, STOP SIGNS, AND YIELDING THE RIGHT OF WAY

The notion that transportation planning must be tied to land-use issues in order to have a genuine impact on an area is becoming increasingly pervasive, especially among smart growth advocates sometimes referred to as New Urbanists. Regionality is a major aspect of this re-visioning of use of space:

> The city, its suburbs and their natural environment should be treated as a whole—socially, economically, and ecologically. Treating them separately is endemic to many of the problems we now face, and our lack of governance at this scale is a direct manifestation of this disaggregation . . . Developing such an architecture of the region creates the context for a healthy urbanism in neighborhoods, districts and at the city center. (Calthorpe 1994:xi–xii)

As written, the GRTA statute imbues it with the ability to be instrumental in such a regional approach to planning for transportation and land use. GRTA has powers allowing it to tie transportation dollars to land use and it also has the authority to regionalize transit systems. From this perspective then, the creation of GRTA was a remarkably progressive and forward-thinking act, giving Atlanta the opportunity to begin to escape its reputation as "Sprawlanta," air, water, and land offender of the first magnitude, which it has garnered over the last several years. So the question becomes, what has prevented GRTA from achieving even a modicum of its potential thus far?

Road Blocks

As already touched upon in this chapter, much of the opposition to GRTA's utilization of its powers seems to be fear-driven. Fears that GRTA would be undemocratic, anti-road, and apt to overstep its authority abounded. Let us scrutinize both what drove these fears and how such concerns came to be privileged over equally pressing worries about "fixing" both Atlanta's transportation reputation and its measurable mobility constraints. Regarding Atlanta's transportation reputation, a Chamber of Commerce informant told me:

> Our polling of voters and businesses shows that everyone—no one needs convincing that we've got terrible traffic . . . like seventy-nine percent of voters think that traffic is either a major or a minor problem in their day-to-day lives—eighty-six percent have seen it get worse since they've been here—sixty-six percent of businesses consider transportation their biggest impediment to doing business in Metro Atlanta.

And as to the growing gridlock, the same respondent noted:

> With another two-point-three million residents coming by Twenty Thirty and the current plans, we'll see traffic up by twenty-three percent by Twenty Twenty, up somewhere around forty-six percent by Twenty Thirty. Instead of spending about one and a half work

weeks stuck in traffic if you're a commuter, you'll be looking at eighty to one hundred hours stuck in traffic a year.

The business community and the transportation agencies (GRTA, MARTA, GDOT, and ARC) are all in accord that the number one roadblock to implementing transportation procedures that would meaningfully improve the landscape is lack of funding (especially for public transport projects). It is broadly reiterated that it is a zero sum game in which limited funds are already spread too thin. To use some of the motor fuel tax for transit, for example, according to the GDOT commissioner, would be constitutionally prohibited. Moreover, when transit advocates suggest that such prohibitions can be changed, GDOT representatives and similar parties (such as members of the Association County Commissioners of Georgia and Georgians for Better Transportation) contend that this would constitute stealing money from necessary road and highway projects that are already receiving less money than they require.

The roads versus transit debate can also be understood in the context of the urban versus suburban dilemma that plagues the area. Here I refer to the divisions between the city of Atlanta and the counties in metro Atlanta outside the perimeter highway (I-285) with respect to their needs, priorities, and funding. Additionally, there is a further rift between the metro region as a whole and the balance of Georgia counties. This rupture, and the fears, suspicions, and rivalries associated with it, is sometimes framed as the Atlanta region versus the rest of Georgia (or the "other" Georgia as some locals refer to it). These perceptional splits are at the heart of much of the debate around transportation issues in Georgia (and I have touched on the intra-metro cleft already in the discussion of suburban fears of GRTA's powers). The metro Atlanta versus the rest of Georgia controversy is well illustrated in the controversy surrounding Congressional Balancing.

The Congressional Balancing law went into effect around the time of GRTA's creation in 1999. This state law stipulated that after certain exemptions and exceptions (up to 15 percent) for GRTA, MARTA, the Governor's Road Improvement Program, and the Georgia Ports Authority, the remaining 85 percent of federal transportation money was to be divided equally among all congressional districts in the state. There have been several attempts to exempt highway projects from this balancing formula. Many believed the balancing distribution did a disservice to the Atlanta region; as Sally Flocks (executive director of PEDS) put it, "The congressional balancing act has been very unfair to Atlanta." But suburban and rural residents felt that changing it would disproportionately benefit metro Atlanta and shortchange rural projects. A sometimes heated and much negotiated debate resulted in a radically different bill concerning the distribution of federal transportation funds being proposed and finally signed into law by Governor Perdue in May 2005.

Matthew Hicks, of Association County Commissioners of Georgia (ACCG), privy to many of these negotiations, explained the final result as follows:

> The legislators in the House Transportation Committee began asking many questions and proposed returning to a form of congressional balancing that would require eighty percent of the federal funds allocated to Georgia be distributed evenly across the state's thirteen congressional districts, without exception. The remaining twenty percent would be distributed according to the discretion of the State Transportation Board, with the idea that the money would go to the areas of highest need. Financial analysis conducted by GDOT and ARC showed that the alternative would indeed benefit all districts and increase the amount of federal funds they see . . . The only exemption to the balancing formula is for money specifically earmarked for a project in a congressional district. An example would be if Congressman John Lewis obtained a twenty-five million dollar earmark for the Atlanta Belt Line; instead of the money having to be divided across the thirteen districts, the funds would remain in District Five for the project intended.

According to Mr. Hicks, all stakeholders were satisfied with this compromise. Be that as it may, the hot and heavy journey to this outcome merits a deeper look. As suggested, the new congressional balancing bill was perceived by many people in other parts of the state as a pro-Atlanta/anti-the-rest-of-Georgia piece of legislation as originally proposed. In an online publication called the Cracker Squire, in an article entitled "The Lord giveth and the Lord taketh away—The Other Georgia gave to the metro. Will the metro now take it away?" the author notes:

> The "congressional balancing" bill, which would exempt interstate highway improvements from the state [law] requiring equal transportation spending in each of Georgia's 13 congressional districts, has yet to win statewide support. The Association County Commissioners of Georgia doesn't support the bill because rural leaders fear it would take away transportation dollars. (Frankston 2005:1)

And in a far more adamant and extreme tone, the Southern Party of Georgia, in response to the fact that the bill was strongly supported by the Metro Atlanta Chamber of Commerce, posted this inflammatory statement on the Internet:

> Legislative Alert-SB4—why are they changing highway fund allocation?

> Is this a less roads in Georgia and more in Atlanta bill? The title is "balancing of federal/state funds" but the bill exempts the Georgia Interstate System from balancing . . . Note the following from the Metro Atlanta Issues List for 2005 Legislature:
>
> > "The Metro Atlanta Chamber supports modifying this formula [balancing] by exempting the amount spent on interstate projects. Interstates should be exempted since they are critical to the movement of people and goods statewide. Additionally, interstate projects can consume an entire district's transportation allocation leaving little money for other road or transit projects."
> >
> > In other words spend more of your tax dollars in Atlanta! The Chamber greed never ends does it? Are you ready to give up YOUR roads to bail out MARTA? (Southern Party of Georgia: www.spofga.org)

The controversy around congressional balancing highlights fears and suspicions that the Atlanta region is trying to force its agenda on all of Georgia. These misgivings are also shared by some metro counties outside the city of Atlanta (such as Fayette and Cherokee), which are squeezed between urban and rural concerns. Exacerbating some of these fears is the notion that Atlanta might export its "problems" to the suburbs via land-use regulations and through Metro-style public transportation expansion carried out by GRTA.

Stop Signs

A great deal of suburban resistance to regional transit seems to be about race, according to many of the respondents with whom I spoke. In fact, some believe that all area transportation issues have deep ties to racial concerns. Radically changed economic conditions in the South since the end of the Civil War did (and do) not necessarily connote corresponding cultural changes for some white Southerners. As a Southern scholar pointed out, some post–Civil War white political actors, "intended to pour the old cultural wine of planter rule and white supremacy into [those] new economic and demographic bottles" (Reed 1991:226). For some that may still hold true today. As a business leader and long-time transportation expert expressed it:

> Our racial problem is our biggest transportation problem in Atlanta! And we don't talk about it! We speak in—we talk in code sometimes—but we don't talk about it directly! And I've said that to groups, and I've had audible gasps come from the audience,

> 'cause you're not supposed to say things like that in Atlanta—it's just not right! If we have a problem, we don't want to talk about it as a problem because that's insulting somebody—and so we're not honest about that.

While "pollution does not stop at the border" (as a GRTA informant told me) apparently some people are meant to—not all places are intended to be linked by accessible transportation lines. The resistance to regional transportation options seems to remain firmly rooted in the soil of racism. However, most of my informants posit that this entrenched system is slowly eroding for three reasons: (1) dramatically shifting demographics carrying more people of color to previously predominantly white areas, and the back to the city movement bringing more middle and upper-class whites back into the center; (2) ecological concerns, which force people to make changes despite color lines; and (3) financial shifts (such as an infusion of in-town money) tied to the first two that necessitate the breakdown of these well-guarded boundaries.

Robert Bullard noted in regard to the expansion of public transit buses to more suburban counties:

> It has taken thirty years to even get to the point of saying we need to have transit in areas where people have cars and not just where people are transit-dependent—and I think the driver behind getting people to that realization is the fact that there's no black air, there's no brown air, there's no Hispanic air—there's AIR—everybody breathes, and it's dirty! If you have a car, you're stuck in traffic whether you drive a Mercedes or whether you drive a Ford Pinto . . . The lawsuits forced a lot of these agencies to say, hey, if you're going to tie up millions of dollars, or even billions of dollars because of not conforming to air quality standards . . . when they start feeling the money crunch . . . they start to do something!

Yet this willingness to do "something," apparently did not go so far as to allow GRTA to fully regionalize transit. Instead, what GRTA has implemented thus far (along with some other carriers) is distinct, disconnected, and unlinked bus services for various locations that, according to some, do little to mitigate the problems of disconnectivity and in fact merely serve to inflame them. Mike Kenn, an influential lobbyist, remarked, perhaps slightly overstating the lack of coordination:

> You've got MARTA, you've got the Gwinnett system, the Cobb system, the GRTA express bus system, the Buckhead Shuttle, you've got the trolley line being considered on Peachtree, you've got the

new BRT [Bus Rapid Transit] system that doesn't have an operator identified yet, and is there any coordination between all those different operators? No, there's not!

As we saw in the previous chapter, it is not possible to speak of race, Atlanta, and resistance to regional transit without speaking of MARTA. Regional perceptions of what transit is (and is not) are intimately intertwined with notions about this entity. While much of MARTA's role in Atlanta mobility patterns was explicated in chapter 3, it is necessary to highlight a few points about it in regard to regional issues influencing GRTA's role. Anti-MARTA sentiment is rampant and many believe this is based on race and class perceptions that are inseparable from anti-urban sentiments. Some informants contend that MARTA should be at least the regional operator, if not the regional coordinator of transit, since it has the experience, mechanisms in place, equipment, technology, etc. to get the job done. In addition to the logistical impediments to this solution (such as fleet size and jurisdiction), there are also powerful ideological ones. Robert Bullard tells us:

> It's race based, it has continued to be race based . . . the mere fact that Atlanta would continue to somehow drive . . . Fulton, DeKalb, and Atlanta—would drive a regional transit system, and it would be MARTA-dominated, or MARTA-emphasized, that sticks in the craws of a lot of people. And there are people in the suburbs who would say, you know, we're proud to have a transit system that's not MARTA. I mean they'll almost brag! But none of these bus systems could be functional without having MARTA—they would close! You know, what would they feed into? One express bus in here, and where do you go? So, you know, GRTA in my mind has not done a whole lot to move towards linked, coordinated, and seamless, what it has done is to facilitate these suburban systems and has really not done anything to strengthen MARTA . . . all these other transit systems that feed into—and we like to say feed off MARTA—they're not paying their fair share.

In response to my question as to whether MARTA might take a greater role in regionalizing transit (either as an operator or as a coordinator), a prominent and influential member of the business community responded:

> No . . . MARTA has tainted their image so badly that if they cleaned their act up and then went on a PR campaign . . . Ten years from now we might be having the conversation that MARTA should expand. But in its current form MARTA is broken . . . It is the board that has driven this agency into its current state through their policies,

> mandates, and . . . senior staff selection. If you ask MARTA what their mission is—and what their mission really is—their mission is about employee jobs and moving the transit dependent to work. That's it!!! . . . And what's not in their mission is traffic congestion reduction or maximizing ridership . . . that shift started happening in the eighties and then after that it's just all been a bunch of, uh, boy—that's the wrong term—there always was a healthy balance between business interests and civic interests, or—and . . . that has definitely—the preponderance has shifted towards – more towards the civil rights advocacy, um—the interests of the poor and the transit-dependent, that has been the focus of the board for at least fifteen years!

A bit startled by the naked racism expressed in this response and the venom with which it was iterated, I asked "And—do you feel there is a place for issues of equity in transportation planning?" The reply, "Yes. Absolutely! It just can't be the only one!"

Perhaps those who believe that some people would be delighted to see MARTA disappear have legitimate reasons for this impression. A MARTA official remarked:

> I think historically racism is a huge piece of it [anti-MARTA sentiment] . . . less of a driving force than in the past and maybe it's a little more subtle—definitely it's more subtle—but I think it still plays a substantial role.

Racial tensions have loosened their grip on the area's transportation planning and procedures for the above stated reasons. Yet clearly they have not entirely lost hold. Addressing suburban resistance to bus service in some locations my GRTA informant had this to say:

> Some of it's racial, I'll be honest with you, some of it's racial, a lot of it is racial. And I don't mean just race, it's economics—it's everything. You know, we don't want your poor, we don't want your minorities, we don't—it's a little bit of every—it runs the gamut . . . it's disabled—it's every way that a person doesn't want to see their community, becomes the reason why. So it's a lot of ignorance!

It's also about a deep philosophical, political, and moral objection to having policies imposed on local jurisdictions (such as suburban counties) from the "outside"—a robust American sensibility regarding how decisions ought to be made and who ought to make them.

Yielding the Right-of-Way

I posited at the outset of this chapter that GRTA has accomplished (and failed to accomplish) its various missions to date based in large part on problem definition and issue framing. Attention to the contestation over issue framing allows us to "consider how issue concerns come to be specified as purposes, and how they are linked, enlarged and refined for action" (Stone 2001:20). As explained in chapter 2, Stone's typology of urban regimes (1993) corresponds neatly to the growth, green, and equity actors in the Atlanta region who compete for authority over definitions and actions. The Maintenance and Development regimes are two aspects of the pro-growth perspective—local (suburban) governments and residents represent the Maintenance regime, with the downtown business interests and developers embodying the Development regime. Some of the influential in-town neighborhood groups with green and preservationist goals, along with agencies and actors such as the Sierra Club and the Georgia Conservancy, stand for what Stone refers to as middle-class progressive regimes. As for the equity piece, Stone (1993) speaks of "regimes devoted to lower class opportunity expansion" but notes, "In the US, such regimes are largely hypothetical" (20). In this study, such aims are represented by actors such as the Environmental Justice Resource Center and Jobs for Justice. I contend that none of these "regimes" currently has full dominance in the region, and that it is the interplay between these disparate interests and the contestation over framing of transportation issues that determines policy outcomes.

In relation to GRTA's (in)ability to fulfill its stated mission, it seems clear that the growth coalition, most especially the maintenance branch, has won the definitional battle, transforming an entity that had the potential to be a radical transformer for the area into little more than a glorified express bus service. While clearly contested by various influential and salient groups, the challenges have not yet achieved the level of social resonance necessary for transformation. Deeply ingrained precepts of the American ethos are at the heart of this victory. Perhaps foremost among these is the idea that "distant" government entities should not dictate how local residents live. Closely related to that principle is the idea that public policies that require altering existing urban or suburban forms (land uses and lifestyles) is "social engineering," which is an anathema to the cherished value of individual freedom. Taken together these strongly held precepts can generate enormous fear and resistance to GRTA, when GRTA is framed as an entity with the power to impose limits on automobile usage, enact policies requiring greater housing densities, and impose mixed-use and other "smart growth" initiatives.

One question that this analysis raises is whether these fears and noncooperation represent a form of "Southern exceptionalism," or whether they are a more generalizable reaction to land-use innovations. Resistance to smart growth principles in transportation planning is certainly not unique to the South (see examples regarding Pittsburgh, Buffalo, Los Angeles, and Washington, D.C., in Just Transportation [Bullard 1997]). It is possible that arguments and understandings about these issues in the South may have a particular flavor distinct from other locations. As Reed (1991) notes, Southerners "reflect an anti-institutional ethic that says: In the last analysis, you are on your own—and should be" (230). Reed grants that the cultural and attitudinal divides between the North and the South are diminishing for all the obvious reasons, "urban life, education, by travel and residence outside the South, by exposure to the mass media" and, of course massive "migration to the South" (229). Nonetheless, he posits that one of the last strongholds of Southern ideology is housed in notions of "economic libertarianism," reflected, he notes, most tellingly in attitudes toward land-use legislation (230–31). However, I contend that the ideological frame represents a broader American sensibility, rather than a uniquely Southern mindset. This position seems to be based on the shared and widely broadcast notions of liberty and resistance to a "planning regime" (so dubbed on a California-based Libertarian Web site) that GRTA represents to those who fear its powers.

Even those respondents who were in favor (some very adamantly in favor) of GRTA taking a more aggressive role in both regionalizing transit and in land-use planning are ever mindful of these basic assumptions about how politics proceed and recognized in many cases the need to go slow or retreat altogether. A large-scale area planner told me:

> I believe it's desirable, but may not be possible, to invest our transportation dollars in ways that encourage people to take shorter trips . . . It's hard! I've had folks say to me that, that's just not American! I had one politician one time say to me, he said, "I just don't like that kind of talk at all!" He said, "I just don't think it's right!" He said, "My family had umpteen acres in Cherokee County for three generations, I want to be able to sell it for what I want!"

Mike Kenn of Georgians for Better Transportation, who is more politically and ideologically aligned with the cited Cherokee politician, epitomizes the essence of this free-choice ideology in the following statement:

> I believe people have a right to live where they live, and how they want to live—and if they want to live in an area that's got a higher density and has a walking community after they're done with their work commute, then there's plenty of choices and places for them to do that—as there are for people who want to live in a more rural setting and have a one-acre backyard, and still have to get to their car to drive to the grocery store. Those are choices and we should never try to legislate, uh, that type of lifestyle on people.

These two quotes highlight the power of allegiance to ideals and notions of freedom of choice in transportation planning. But there are others who do not believe that the current system allows for meaningful choice. It must be remembered that all physical engineering is to some degree also social engineering. The placement and layout of schools, places of commerce, entertainment, housing developments, and those systems that link and/or separate them (roads, trains, and so on) dictate how we live. To assert, for example, that policies which privilege transit accessibility over auto-centered development are coercive in terms of lifestyle choices borders on the absurd in light of the fact that current policies are so dramatically skewed in the opposite direction, now forcing people to drive everywhere and to eat up time and space in our daily practices. As one respondent noted: "You've got to realize that every time you spend a transportation dollar you influence development. You're already doing it! It's not a matter of if—it's a matter of how!" In Critical Mass (1997), Whitelegg speaks of the ways in which the built environment and ideology link to create policies that continue to favor hyper-automobility. He opines that despite widespread belief that transportation demand is driven by natural law, in reality the ever-increasing desire for automobiles and highways is fueled by consumption patterns and lifestyle choices. These choices are in turn shaped by market-driven decisions about where to place centers of commerce and by modes of stimulating the public appetite for distant products. He further avers that the public willingness to buy the notion that cars and roads spring up because we need and want them to is very convenient for policy makers. Such a position allows those in power "to extol the virtues of freedom and choice, and to pour scorn on those who suggest different arrangements which would reduce the demand for transport" (34). Thus, he concludes, any hint of government intervention into where and how we move about is rejected.

Fears of social engineering blind us to how our "unfettered" mobility has already so deeply constrained us. Yet changes in transportation patterns are widely and increasingly recognized as inescapable and already underway due to issues of sustainability and to the evident demographic changes taking place nationwide. The urban/suburban tensions around these changes are hardly unique to the Atlanta region. Cervero (2003) speaks of the ways in which the financial costs of sprawl coupled with its ecological ones have placed concerns about smart growth at the center of national conversations in the United States. At the same time however, he notes that especially in this country the road to smart growth is a complex and circuitous one, "obstructed by messy institutional landscapes and political detours" (12). He suggests that one of the distinctly American stumbling blocks impeding tying land-use practices to transportation policies lies in the disjuncture between where policies are formulated and where the results of such decisions are experienced. Policies are arrived at locally, the impact is regional. "Travel, of course, knows no boundaries" (12).

So change is a reality for transportation planning as for all else—as already quoted regarding the distribution of transportation dollars, it is not a matter of if, it is a matter of how. There are many visionaries, both local and national, who would be both qualified and delighted to help guide these changes. GRTA was created to be a part of this transformation—and yet, despite the ripeness and the readiness, one perspective seems to have won out in framing GRTA's role. In the change in administration from Governor Roy Barnes (Democrat) to Governor Sonny Perdue (Republican), GRTA's transportation policies have been reduced and reframed, emphasizing suburban commuter transit and staying safely away from its powers to restructure land uses via its authority over Developments of Regional Impact (DRIs) and its ability to determine road access.

By limiting GRTA's role to that of commuter bus service provider from suburban counties to downtown Atlanta, its role as land-use coordinator and smart growth proponent has been effectively eviscerated. This leaves the landscape with its requisite demand for hyperautomobility virtually unchanged. In fact, GRTA's actions (and most especially its inactions) reinforce the existing arrangements through enabling suburbanites to have their cake (a distant auto-centric satellite city) and eat it too (access to the amenities of downtown Atlanta without paying the costs of participation). The Maintenance Regime thus wins this battle, ensuring that road capacity, not inner-city public transportation, will once again be privileged. Whitelegg (1997) notes that it is not so simple to determine which came first; millions of people clamoring for more transport or a select few "steer[ing] the development of the space economy and the market for transport services" (50). He points out that it is one of the inherent contradictions of so-called free markets that their course is largely set by stakeholders. In this context, "[w]ithout exception, they work in the direction of increasing the demand for transport and the growth of the matching infrastructure" (50).

Technically, ARC and other regional authorities already had the power to do what GRTA was created to do, but they have been unable to do so because of the hegemonic tacit proscriptions against such action. GRTA has not overcome those proscriptions. As Jeff Rader told me:

> Georgia has, I think, a little bit of a habit of . . . legislatively addressing a difficult issue over and over again from a statutory perspective but then won't follow through in the implementation of those statutes because they represent political difficulties. So just because you can do it with another entity has not precluded us from setting up a new agency to reinvent the wheel, we do it over and over again . . . We have the authority and the enabling legislation to do it [tie transportation dollars to land use], we just don't have the guts to push it through on people!

This reluctance to follow through on environmentally (and often economically) sound policies tying land use to transport planning is in large measure due to the shift, or more precisely expansion, of power in Atlanta from the CBD elite to the suburban elite. Morcol, Zimmermann, and Stich (2003), in their article on GRTA, draw this point vividly in explaining that Stone's conception of an urban regime worked well in describing Atlanta from the mid-1940s to the late 1980s. They go on to say (noting Stone's own acknowledgment) that there have been dramatic shifts since that time. The advent of increased financial and political power in the suburbs changed the location and character of Atlanta's business elite. It is no longer possible to speak solely of a downtown bloc, it is imperative to recognize that understanding area development now "necessitates the adoption of a regional perspective in economic growth issues" (491).

This suburban influence, as discussed regarding the MARTA board composition, is particularly important with regard to GRTA and represents a double-edged sword. On one side, we have the increased wariness and influence of suburban constituents who perceive GRTA's powers as potentially harmful and intrusive, violating rights of home rule. On the other, there is the push for regionalism guided by the growth-oriented goals of actors who recognize the potential for profit and expansion. "Enlightened self-interest" of business leaders gives some a bias toward the precepts of smart growth and regionalism. Morcol et al. (2003) note that, interestingly, it is the business community, before politicians or other area actors, who by the nature of their interests are forced to think regionally. Private enterprise has an incentive to read the larger landscape and heed the messages received because profits depend upon it. This is true because "human capital problems created by the fragmentation of local governments, such as the education of the workforce and moving welfare recipients to work, are important for the profitability of businesses" (493).

Thus, some seeking change, or at least recognizing its inevitability (and recognizing its potential profitability), turn to discourses concerning market forces as the logical, efficient, and best way to allow (rather than force) that change. Many from the business community and some conservationists (erstwhile enemies) are lauding the Metro Chamber of Commerce for initiating changes (including being instrumental in the creation of GRTA) that will lead Atlanta in the right direction as far as land use and transit issues are concerned. In general, there is widespread agreement that the market (endowed with its capitalistic reified personality) will result in more equitable distributions of benefits and force land use more in keeping with smart growth precepts. Several quotes from respondents drive this point home:

> The fundamental relationships are not ideological, you know, they're physics and they're economics.

> We believe firmly in a market-based response to that [both land-use decisions and transit options]. But the demographic shifts that have happened and will continue to happen are going to drive the growth rate of single family housing down considerably. And the demand for mixed-use, high amenity, low-maintenance communities will actually skyrocket . . . so there is a role for transit to play—we believe it should be market-based.
>
> We need thousands and thousands of multifamily units that people who are baby boomers might actually desire to live in. I mean, between the baby boomers and the young people who are waiting longer to have children, there's a huge potential for people to live closer to where they work. And that's the secret in Atlanta—it's not people riding MARTA!

These ideas and contentions resonate with a broad audience—relying on the "invisible hand" of consumer demand and supplier response to steer development in the right direction. Environmental concerns, as long as they do not dramatically disrupt these "sacred" forces, are also increasingly considered legitimate, and some conservationists are in turn becoming more versed in the language of free-market ideology. John Sibley (president of the Georgia Conservancy) noted:

> The market can actually drive a lot of this . . . I don't think the political world is going to let GRTA be heavy handed, but I think GRTA can do an intervention that will make sense to people . . . there is an opportunity in our region to have a wonderful urban place . . . if we create that wonderful urban place and let the market—help the market respond to that . . . The market is already moving so much in that direction that if you help communities get out of the market's way, a lot can happen that's good for the ultimate ends that I'm aiming for.

Despite this general reliance on the market to allow for positive changes, many environmentalists and some planners recognize that it needs a helping hand (if not a kick in the pants) if meaningful changes are to be realized. John Sibley asserted that that is in fact why GRTA was created; to serve that function of "helping" the market along.

However, while smart growth—laissez-faire style—is gaining broader currency, other challenges to current transportation policies meet with greater resistance. In doing this research, I have observed that two usually overlapping positions are looked at with strong suspicion by legislators and politicians and are least likely to receive high priority in policy considerations. The first of these centers on issues of race (and to some extent class) and is espoused by people who suggest that we implement policies emphasizing fairness—even if it's not what the market dictates. In this regard, Robert Bullard cautions us to speak of "fair growth" rather than "smart growth" and "equitable development" in lieu of "sustainable." The principles of justice are not wholly quantifiable and thus challenge the market-driven paradigm. This position corresponds to what Stone referred to as "regimes devoted to lower class opportunity expansion."

The second challenge meeting with powerful resistance is linked to the first. This is the idea that government could and should guide us in enacting policies and procedures that are fair and equitable to all citizens and that the "market" is inadequate to do so; in fact, it is the wrong mechanism to rely on. Doing so leads to accumulation of wealth and privileges for some, and burdens and hardship for others. To put forth this challenge is to risk social sanctions, marginalization, and the "socialist" brand. This position extends beyond Stone's typologies, in that it poses a challenge to the basic precepts of capitalism itself. Many moderates are viewed by conservative ideologues and politicians as ideologically aligned with this camp, or at the very least invidiously compared in public forums to impress this connection in the minds of the public by those who oppose them, and thus labeled "tree-huggers," "social engineers," "planning dictators," and the like.

But it is not the name calling that is most deeply troubling or influential. It is, rather, the more subtle and acceptable language of the reasoned "average" citizen that persuades through logic and mass appeal to presumed shared values of individuality and autonomy, as demonstrated above in the discussion of market-driven approaches as the only truly plausible basis for transportation and land-use planning. This discourse is not uncontested and there is much debate as to the merits of market-centered land use and transportation policies versus ethically (in the interests of social justice) based ones. There is an online forum provided by the Reason Institute, which describes itself as follows: "Reason Public Policy Institute is a public policy think tank promoting choice, competition, and a dynamic market economy as the foundation for human dignity and progress." In an ongoing conversation on this site between self-proclaimed Libertarians and New Urbanists some of this often unspoken background antagonism is well explicated. Samuel R. Staley of The Buckeye Institute for Public Policy Solutions jumps into a conversation about reducing the philosophical/ideological distance between New Urbanists and Libertarians, noting among other things that

> [t]he market-oriented folks, for the most part, do not view Smart Growth through the prism of urban design. They see it through the prism of politics. Smart Growth is a political movement. As such, most are objecting to the coercive components of Smart Growth, not New Urbanist design per se. Many of those on the market-oriented

> side of the debate aren't objecting to New Urbanism as a design philosophy, but object to the New Urbanist design being imposed on those that don't like it or want it . . . So, why so much rancor about New Urbanism in the market-oriented movement? Because many of the design recommendations of New Urbanism have been incorporated into policy prescriptions that are seen as highly prescriptive and coercive. (4)

He goes on to note that (as I have detailed above) market-oriented and smart growth advocates can have a cozy and mutual beneficial relationship if the latter keep their hands off policies. Several responses from both Libertarians and New Urbanists (the renowned Andres Duany among the latter) go on to say that while there are convergences, to be true to their own beliefs, they must also highlight the distances between the two positions. Duany at one point quotes his associate Philip Bess in an articulation of the New Urbanist position. Relevant here is this point: "New Urbanists think that persons should have as much freedom as justice allows" (9). It is precisely this qualification that leads to the need for policy implementations and it is this need that is abhorrent to free market proponents. Staley (2003) further tells us that for free market proponents, it is not the job of the government to dictate either minimums or maximums when it comes to density. Similarly, policies aimed at controlling, or even guiding land-use practices at the neighborhood level are considered "coercive." In essence, he maintains, "[p]rescriptive policy recommendations work against a view of the urban development that is organic and evolutionary, the intuitive framework from which the libertarians/free market people operate" (4).

The suburban interpretation of the GRTA statute as fundamentally coercive, prescriptive, counterintuitive, and un-American has shaped what GRTA has thus far become. Rather than utilize the "blunt instrument" or "gross mechanism" (as my respondents variously referred to it) to vote the Transportation Improvement Program (TIP) up or down (without wiggle room to tweak it instead, thus, "burning everyone") or to use their power over Developments of Regional Impact (DRIs) and curb-cuts to manage land-use decisions in the region—GRTA has for the most part chosen instead to take some small measures that are in themselves controversial. The two I will address here are the GRTA Express Bus and the Bus Rapid Transit (BRT) options.

WHEN IS A BUS NOT A BUS?

The GRTA Express provides a regional system of buses bringing people from the suburban counties into the city of Atlanta (and back again). The following is a description from the XPRESS Homepage:

> Xpress is the clean, comfortable, convenient express commuter service in the Atlanta region. Connecting home, work, school and play, Xpress luxury coaches carry riders throughout the region each weekday, freeing them from the costs and worries of driving alone. Xpress coaches operate as part of the CCT [Cobb County Transit] and Gwinnett Transit services in Cobb and Gwinnett counties, and under agreement with the Georgia Regional Transportation Authority (GRTA) in the other nine counties Xpress serves. So Xpress yourself! Ride Xpress today and see how comfortable commuting really can be. Xpress is open to the public. All coaches are ADA-compliant and wheelchair lift equipped.

While Express buses do not as yet operate on designated lanes, the Bus Rapid Transit (BRT) option involves running rubber-tired buses in (shared) HOV lanes from various suburban locations to midtown and downtown Atlanta. Both of these proposals and subsequent implementations (still in progress) are the subject of controversy for several reasons. Some smart growth advocates object to the ways in which GRTA is implementing these projects because they believe they are counterproductive to the goals of increased density in land-use planning, in that it facilitates the shrinking of distances thus supporting existing residential patterns. Brian Hager of the Sierra Club said of BRT as proposed for the region:

> When you put high capacity transit on the interstate it has almost no positive impact on growth and development. What it does is it enables people to live long distances from work . . . and then commute thirty to fifty miles to Cumberland or midtown—and it makes it easier for them to commute these long distances and then live in these monoculture residential subdivisions out in the exurban areas.

Similarly, Sally Flocks, of Pedestrians Educating Drivers on Safety (PEDS) expressed frustration regarding GRTA's transit decisions:

> I think it's really ironic that GRTA is creating a suburban bus system with direct route where they don't even feed into the train systems, and they want to clog up the main street [Peachtree Street] with these buses that don't serve the people who live there . . . I think the stupidest thing in the Regional Plan is the I-Seventy-Five Project—the north-west connectivity thing—that should not be located on the interstate, that's an incredible waste of money. Because all it is, is basically an express bus—when you want to put transit in you want to do it in a way that will influence development to support transit. . . . we favor transit, we just want the right kind of transit!

> We don't want transit that ends up on the freeway and you get to a park-and-ride lot or you get to a station on I-Seventy-Five, and now what?

Others object to the notion of GRTA being an area operator at all, believing that this role detracts from GRTA's potential to make a meaningful impact on transportation practices in the region. John Sibley said:

> GRTA should not try to be the regional transit operator . . . the essential role for GRTA to perform is this kind of CEO or coordinator of good transportation and land-use planning in the region. And that would be plenty for GRTA to accomplish to get that done well—and if GRTA is at the same time trying to be the operator of a regional transit system, I don't think that role will get done.

To hear at least one local business leader tell it, it would seem that how GRTA got into operations in the first place was circumstantial:

> Then there's this regional bus system and this regional transit action plan and all of these sort of transportation services that GRTA has now come to implement. And as I said, one of the reasons for that was to actually get some stuff going, another reason was so they would have these streams of operating funds that would come directly to GRTA as an operator that would somewhat insulate them from the legislature when it came to operating money and allow them to build their staff and the extent of the organization. I think right now that's being rethought a little bit—you know, GRTA as an operator.

And the final objection, as alluded to earlier, revolves around the issue of racial inequity. Robert Bullard pointed out that the distribution of "old, dirty polluting buses," as compared to that of the newer Compressed Natural Gas (CNG) buses, demonstrates "built-in discrimination," in that "suburban choice riders" get the new buses and inner-city (largely black) residents get the old ones. He noted that this uneven distribution of benefits and burdens once again exemplifies a "two-tiered system."

All of these expressions emphasize the persistence of and conflict between growth, green, and equity goals in transportation planning. The balance among them determines policy and procedure. It is often not a particular mode that is objected to, but rather the means of its implementation. For instance, some transit advocates believe the express bus service and the BRT are fine innovations, or at least could be if done properly. Rebecca Serna (a transit advocate) expressed it like this:

> Well, there's not a dedicated lane for it right now [BRT]—and I just don't think putting a bus in is going to do a whole lot . . . transit works best in higher densities, and I think you need to make sure you're taking care of that first, and when that's all squared away—then it's a great idea. I don't have any problem with commuter buses . . . I just don't think that's the priority. Especially if they're not going to have a dedicated lane—but on the other hand the Cobb County and Gwinnett County buses have worked out pretty well, many people say it gives them an hour or two of their life back!

More sympathetically, Matthew Hicks (ACCG) remarked:

> The Bus Rapid Transit that's out there right now—that GRTA's doing—seems to be extremely popular . . . I'm hearing really good things by the people that ride, it reduces their stress and allows them time to do their work on their way to work.

The different lenses produce different views: From an ecological perspective, attentiveness to triage is needed—that is to say that while Express Bus and BRT would be fine additions to a landscape with sufficient public transportation options, given that we have limited financial resources in the region and woefully inadequate public transit, this must be attended to first. From a growth perspective, more is better (more modes, more mobility, more cost effectiveness). A Metro Atlanta Chamber of Commerce respondent was not only very positive about BRT, but also expressed that the Chamber was instrumental in its development:

> Some of the things that we have seen change that we have advocated [for include] sort of the transition in transit policy or programming away from heavy rail towards Bus Rapid Transit or what we try to coin as flex-trolley as a more cost effective means of providing for a city that has developed the way Metro Atlanta has.

Of the perceived choices—GRTA as transit operator, GRTA as transit oversight, or GRTA as national leader in innovative land-use transformation—it would appear that GRTA to date has opted for the first choice. I have demonstrated in the course of this chapter that this "choice" has been hashed out on a public and private political, moral, and philosophical—that is to say, ideological—battleground. Despite growing national and regional recognition that getting land use right means greater densities with work, school, and play in reasonable proximity to one another and that issues of economic and racial equity must take precedence over purely economic concerns—nevertheless, in the contest over issue framing regarding GRTA's role, the status quo seems to have won the day. How long this timid approach to transportation issues in the region will be allowed to prevail remains to be seen. When I asked one respondent what GRTA has in fact become, he aptly pointed out that a better question would be, What is it becoming?

WHAT WILL GRTA BE?

As previously indicated, many believe that GRTA either should or will become an oversight body for a "rational regionalized system." As John Sibley (conservationist) asserted:

> That made GRTA essential—that you really needed somebody—some agency that was not driven as much by local politics as ARC ultimately is—to rationalize the system. And I think GRTA has all the tools necessary to do that, and that's the role GRTA has to play.

Some do not think that is possible. An informant intimately acquainted with GRTA's inner workings noted that while GRTA's role as a regional transit authority was certainly within the realm of its possible powers, she doubted that GRTA would ever take on that responsibility, "for political and economic reasons." Many believe it will remain part operator and part facilitator, offering additional transit services to the area. In the capacity it was originally created to serve (that is, as an oversight body), GRTA could perhaps fulfill its stated mission of improving land transportation and air quality in the region—but only if it utilizes all the tools at its disposal in that oversight. But in its current state, as a transit operator and facilitator, it is likely that it will have little impact on either, and that eventually yet another entity will have to be brought into existence to address the pressing concerns of hypermobility.

As GRTA is an entity largely at the beck and call of the governor, some speculate as to what it might have become had Governor Barnes remained in office. Others suggest that perhaps with future changing governors GRTA too will change. Several transportation planners and agency administrators indicated a need for a charismatic leader (one respondent referred to the need for a "visionary" and another for a "transportation Czar!") or a committed, incorruptible institution that is not swayed by time or changing administrations and is steadfastly devoted to improving transportation in the region. Whether GRTA will be that entity remains to be seen.

Regardless of GRTA's ultimate fate, its path to this point can teach us much about the ways in which the mode of mobility is produced and reproduced in the Atlanta region. It is not simply competing goals, but rather different lenses through which transportation options are viewed and interpreted that determine outcomes. The divisiveness and lack of shared interests among counties and other local jurisdictions in the Atlanta region is particularly salient in the GRTA case, and it is through this regional fragmentation that we can read the irreconcilable imprints of mobility fetishism, traditionalism, racism, and innovation on the landscape.

POSTSCRIPT: ON BEYOND GRTA: DÉJÀ VU ALL OVER AGAIN

Several months after my research was completed, a new Atlanta regional transportation planning entity, the Transit Planning Board (TPB), was created. In January 2006, the ARC's Regional Transit Institutional Task Force chaired by Sam Olens (ARC chairman) created the new planning body, composed of representatives from ARC, GRTA, MARTA, GDOT, the city of Atlanta, and the counties of Cherokee, Clayton, Cobb, DeKalb, Douglas, Fayette, Fulton, Gwinnett, Henry, and Rockdale. The mission of the board is to spend the next two years evaluating the transit needs of the metro area. At the conclusion of that study period, it may transform into an oversight agency. According to Donsky (2005):

> The planning board then would give way to a new transit super agency that ultimately could govern all the area's buses and trains—from Gwinnett County's local bus system to MARTA's 48-mile rail network and 556-bus fleet. The regional agency could orchestrate expansion and funding for metro Atlanta's transit network, perhaps even levying a regional tax to pay for projects. ("Officials enforce new transit planning board," www.cobbrides.com)

The driving force behind the creation of this board is financial. MARTA will exhaust its reserves by 2009 (best-case scenario) and the other area providers also have uncertain futures in terms of funding. While proponents argue that it is a win/win proposition, there are already mounting fears, especially in social justice quarters, that this will amount to a state takeover (and demise) of MARTA, and a disservice to transit-dependent riders in the city of Atlanta. While Mayor Franklin hails the creation of the TPB as "a major win for our region" (www.bizjournals.com/atlanta/stories/2006/01/23.html), state senator Vincent Fort worries, "I don't have any assurances that this new state agency will be receptive to the needs of MARTA riders" (www.cobbrides.com).

In August 2008 the TPB adopted the Atlanta Regional Transit Concept Plan (Concept 3). This plan consists of plans for expansion and addition of various transport modes in the region including MARTA heavy rail extensions; light rail or streetcar lines; commuter rail lines; BRT lines; as well as expanded local central city and suburb to suburb bus options for much of the metro region. The capital costs are estimated at about sixteen billion dollars and operation and maintenance costs are estimated at approximately 650 billion dollars. Neither time frames nor operators are specified in the overview of the plan, but presumed benefits are explicated. These potential benefits once again reflect the Green and Growth goals discussed throughout this book. Notably, none specifically reference Equity concerns. The benefits specifically cited include:

Providing a viable travel choice to the automobile
Providing greater flexibility for the region's work force to choose housing and lifestyle
Providing travel transit times that are competitive to the automobile
Expanding the region's overall transit capacity
Connecting the region's activity centers
An increase in the percent of regional trips taken by transit (mode choice)
A reduction in Vehicle Miles of Travel (VMT) by automobile resulting in improved regional air quality
Improved overall regional mobility by providing congestion relief
An increase in overall system efficiencies
Improved competitiveness for the region in attracting national and international businesses to the region
Improved regional competitiveness for federal funding for projects
Economic development opportunities within transit corridors (http:/tpb.ga.gov/)

More voices seem to have been invited to the table in forming this board and formulating this plan than has been the case with any other Atlanta area transportation planning agency to date. It remains to be seen whether this fact will be enough to prevent it from becoming yet another in a long line of failed efforts to regionalize transit and coalesce the various factions jockeying for position in the transportation issue-framing arena.

FIVE

THE BELTLINE

Great Green Hope

> Well, it's been said of it that it could have the impact that the airport had and I think that that's not an exaggeration . . . I'd say the Beltline may be the biggest, best idea we've seen here in thirty, forty years!
>
> —Bill Bolling, Executive Director Atlanta Community Food Bank

As we have seen in the preceding chapters, transportation projects are frequently the vehicle for trying to address large-scale social and economic problems in the Atlanta region. As has been demonstrated with MARTA and GRTA such efforts often stall or backfire. In this chapter, we will closely examine the latest of such efforts—the Atlanta Beltline—to see if it may fare better. The Beltline project (described in detail below), while still in its early stages, has already engaged multiple actors from both the public and private sectors. It has garnered much enthusiasm, expectation, and jockeying for position. More recently (and predictably) it has begun to also invite some criticism and concern, which I shall address later in the chapter. The transportation experts, advocates, and planners with whom I spoke had much to say on the topic of the Beltline. It is an excellent site from which to view conflict and coalition building in action and to investigate power dynamics in the mobility arena in the region.

WHAT IS THE BELTLINE?

In 1999 a Georgia Tech graduate student, Ryan Gravel, wrote his master's thesis based on the observation that there existed

> a loose network of four historic 'Beltline' railroads that form a rough loop around the central city. These lines were built after the Civil

> War to expand the industrial base of the City, and for the most part, predated the adjacent neighborhoods . . . Gravel's thesis [links] mixed-use redevelopment of the industrial land along the way to a new transit line that has sufficient stops to become useful not just for tourists but for daily use as well. The transit line is extended to include intown neighborhoods to the south and west and to connect into the MARTA system at the four compass points. Parallel bicycle and walking paths are added to create a 22-mile linear park—an "emerald necklace" around Atlanta. (from the Friends of the Beltline Web site, http://beltline.org/)

This concept, while not entirely unique, was so well developed and articulated by this young man that it resonated with a broad audience and snowballed into a coherent development plan that has been met with abundant eagerness.

Since its inception as the brainchild of Ryan Gravel, the Beltline has had a complex journey toward its realization. First, Cathy Woolard, then a city council member, realized its potential and strongly promoted it and advocated for it. From there, various actors became involved. Gravel and Woolard formed a Friends of the Beltline organization working to bring the concept to the attention of potential allies—particularly the neighborhoods that would be most affected by it. A Yale Urban Planning professor, Alexander Garvin, became deeply involved through the Trust for Public Land. He used the Atlanta Beltline concept as a template for urban development done right, and wrote a book entitled The Beltline Emerald Necklace: Atlanta's New Public Realm (2004), which has received national attention. Mayor Franklin got on board and in the summer of 2005, through the city's Atlanta Development Authority, formed the Beltline Partnership with Ray Weeks, an area developer, as the chair of the Beltline committee. The key actors and their roles as outlined on the Beltline Partnership Web site are reproduced below:

> Atlanta Development Authority: Manage redevelopment plan; manage economic impact study; manage transit panel; present TAD [tax allocation district] to City Council and Atlanta Public Schools Board, and Fulton County Commission
>
> Friends of the Beltline: Lead community outreach/grassroots efforts
>
> Park Pride: Advocate for parks and adequate park maintenance funding
>
> Atlanta Committee for Progress: Provide general business community support; assist with community bond fund raising; provide business support for TAD
>
> Trust for Public Land: Raise capital for parkland/right of way acquisition; acquire property to sell to city when TAD funds available; advocate for park component

PATH Foundation: Raise capital for building trails; assist in design of trails; assist in leveraging federal money for trails and managing trail development; advocate for trails component

MARTA: Complete Alternatives Analysis/EIS [Environmental Impact Statement] to select locally preferred transit route; advocate for transit component. (www.beltlinepartnership.org)

In addition to these actors with official connections, several other players are intimately involved. Notably, Wayne Mason (and his newly formed NorthEast Atlanta Beltline Group), an area developer (who had heretofore focused almost exclusively on suburban development),[1] bought 4.6 miles on the Beltline in the Northeast section, running from DeKalb Avenue to Piedmont Park to I-85. He paid about $24 million for close to seventy acres of land, purchased from the Norfolk and Southern Railroad, in some of Atlanta's most sought-after neighborhoods, including Inman Park, Virginia Highland, Morningside, and Ansley Park. His development plans (specifically, two high-rise towers, thirty-eight and thirty-nine stories tall, on the corner of 10th Street and Monroe Drive, between Piedmont Park and the Virginia Highland neighborhood) have sparked some controversy and have inspired the creation of the Beltline Neighbors Coalition in direct opposition to his strategy. This group of determined citizens wishes to help birth a Beltline that holds protection and preservation of neighborhoods as a primary goal. This conflict will be fleshed out as the chapter proceeds.

Other salient actors include the Sierra Club, which has become deeply involved in the effort to create the TAD, engaging in a telephone and door-to-door campaign to garner support; the *Atlanta Journal-Constitution* and other news media, which have both aided in the popularization of the Beltline concept and brought forth critiques and cautions; and neighborhoods and individuals who have a stake in the outcomes, represented, for instance, by ongoing on-line conversations about the possibilities of the Beltline (e.g., halfass.com/blah/2002/05/13/atlanta-beltline).

From the Beltline Partnership's perspective, the key issue at this point is funding, and the fundamental source of start-up funds would be the TAD. In this regard, the mayor announced in April that the TAD "is the most realistic and expeditious way to raise the significant capital needed to complete the BeltLine without tax increases or other City financial obligations" (www.beltlinepartnership.org). The TAD would pay for capital costs only and would work, according to the Beltline Partnership Web site, as paraphrased below:

> Properties in the potential BeltLine TAD generate tax revenues for the City of Atlanta, Fulton County, and the Atlanta Public Schools (APS). Once the TAD is adopted, the existing base would be frozen, i.e. the local governments would continue to collect taxes at the current rates. As property values rise within the TAD, any

> incremental tax overage would be used to repay the bonds issued by the city to pay for BeltLine capital infrastructure (transit, property for parks, etc.) for 25 years. This is not a tax increase, but rather revenue from increased property values within the TAD. Unlike most conventional TADs, this one is not primarily focused on developer incentives—rather most TAD funds will go to greenspace acquisition, park development, transit, and affordable housing. This will then attract development and property value increases that will fund further TAD investments. After TAD expiration and repayment of all bonds, all additional property tax revenue from properties within the TAD will be available to the City of Atlanta, Fulton County, and APS. (www.beltlinepartnership.org)

The Beltline proposition had a lengthy voyage before it got to this point of awaiting funding. Backing up a bit, let's take a look at its remarkable conceptual journey to this point.

WHAT'S BLACK AND WHITE AND GREEN ALL OVER? A BELTLINE TO PLEASE ALL PALATES

A flyer sent out by the Beltline Partnership announcing a public hearing well illustrates the Beltline's appeal to multiple actors offering multiple functions. Among its myriad virtues, the flyer references "trails, workforce housing, jobs, parks, historic preservation, streetscapes, environmental cleanup," and, last but not least, a "20 billion dollar boost to our economy" (www.beltlinepartnership.org).

A sampling of news clips on its potential speak to the Beltline's road to its current acclaim:

> Anticipating another 2 million people in the Atlanta region by 2025, many officials, activists, developers, and residents see a new potential for its long-term prosperity in the proposed 22-mile trolley Beltline built upon old rail beds around intown neighborhoods, with City Council President Cathy Woolard stressing that the project "has more constituencies" than any other she has ever done, Atlanta Housing Authority officer Tony Picket saying the vacant industrial land along the line can seat "mixed-income, mixed-use development," and developer Kim King calling it "a jewel of an opportunity." (Hairston 2003)

> It's [the Beltline] loved by number-crunching transportation planners who see it reducing car trips by the several thousands, as well as by developers who are licking their lips over the intown development it could spur. (Wall 2004)

> "We've set a very aggressive timetable for moving it [the Beltline] forward," says Greg Giornelli, president of the Atlanta Development Authority, the city's development agency. "This is a huge priority for the city." (Pendered 2004)

> "In short, the Beltline has the potential to define Atlanta for the next generation," Atlanta Mayor Shirley Franklin said in May. (Woods 2004)

> Civic leaders and city officials Tuesday hailed a proposed intown loop of transit and green space as a potential economic catalyst as important as Hartsfield-Jackson International Airport. (Hairston 2005)

> The Beltline "is probably the single most important project in terms of shaping Atlanta's growth in the future," said Greg Giornelli, president of the Atlanta Development Authority. (Donsky 2005)

From executives to transit activists, nearly everyone I spoke with had little but praise for the Beltline notion. A transit authority executive remarked, "I think the community's excited about it! I've never seen a project that has so much universal support, and it . . . it truly does!" The alleged benefits of the Beltline are quite exhaustive and touch on tangible and intangible benefits. As enumerated on the Beltline Partnership Web site, they include:

> The BeltLine can change the way we think about Atlanta. It can provide a unique framework for economic development and new amenities that will greatly improve our quality of life. By redeveloping the 22-mile corridor of largely unused railroad tracks that encircle downtown and Midtown Atlanta, the BeltLine will:
>
> increase parks, trails and greenspace
>
> enhance mobility
>
> stimulate economic growth.
>
> This is just the tip of the iceberg. The BeltLine's rich benefits will be meaningful to different people in different ways. Its impact will be felt in every corner of Atlanta and throughout the region, not just in the neighborhoods within walking distance of the actual BeltLine route. Help us understand why the BeltLine will be important to you.
>
> As for the intangibles:

Atlanta has a stellar opportunity to connect existing parks with new ones in a first-class parks system, highlighted by trails for walking, cycling, jogging, roller blading, and relaxing outdoors.
We will have a compelling alternative to driving once the BeltLine trail connects neighborhoods directly to new and existing parks and BeltLine transit connects riders directly to MARTA lines.
The BeltLine can function like a new hybrid of the town square . . . the place where people connect with each other, while also connecting with favorite places and parks around Atlanta.
We can offer developers incentives and a strategic framework for . . . growth to happen on the BeltLine. (www.beltlinepartnership.org)

And the expectations for growth and development are phenomenal. A recent study projects that the Beltline "will spur more than $20 billion in development and increased property values over the next 25 years," and create about 37,000 permanent and 48,000 temporary jobs, as well as about 28,000 new housing units, with one-fifth of those (5,600 units) "dedicated to workforce housing"[2] (www.beltlinepartnership.org).

The Beltline, then, is clearly not "one thing." Pedestrian advocates envision it as a haven for walkers and bikers, developers see it as a potential gold mine, some environmentalists see it as a saver of greenspace and air quality, and new urbanists love the potential for mixed-use, high density land use. Ryan Gravel told me:

> I'm a designer, not a transportation planner or anything like that, so what I was always interested in was how you can design infrastructure to accomplish multiple goals. So one goal is mobility, of course, but also better air quality, water quality, access to cars, better economic redevelopment in neighborhoods that haven't seen it in a while. Recreation . . . all kinds of different . . . you can pull all kinds of things into the Beltline project, which I think is one of the reasons that people really like it so much. I think everybody likes it for a different reason.

From the greenspace perspective, Jeff Rader remarked:

> The primary organizing feature of the Beltline will be its role as a continuous belt of greenspace that is connecting park amenities, and the development of amenities within the Beltline, not so much the transportation aspect of it.

As to the public transportation aspects, Rebecca Serna, president of the advocacy group Citizens for Progressive Transit, opined:

> Well, I'm worried that the transit aspect is kind of being shafted a little bit. I think the great thing about it is that it combines, you know several things—I mean greenspace, and economic development, and connected communities—but if you don't have the transit . . . I mean, greenspace would be nice, but the thing that makes it unique is the transit.

For some it remains a vague and nebulous, but nonetheless worthy pursuit. As one area planner put it in response to a question concerning the utility of the Beltline:

> I don't know! All I do know though is that if we add as many people to the city of Atlanta as projections say, we're going to be—we're going to find some difficulties in terms of congestion—and if we get something like the Beltline in place early enough it could influence development so that it will allow us to add these folks without just locking everything up. That's not very scientific and it may not even be correct—but it's the best I've got!

Representative of those who love it because it is clearly linked in their minds to smart growth principles, John Sibley noted:

> I personally am just as much for the Beltline as I was against the Northern Arc[3]—but for exactly the same reason. Because the Northern Arc was something that needed to be stopped to keep the worst of sprawling development from happening—the Beltline is something you can be for as an example of the best opportunities of developing in this region in a way that will both maximize transportation potential and save natural resources.

Different actors believe the Beltline will transform the city in different ways. But the perception that it will be transformative is widely shared. The different understandings and perceptions about the Beltline (as with MARTA and GRTA) may turn out to play a central role in determining what it in fact becomes. As a transportation planner noted, "The Beltline is an exciting project—it just may not be what people think it is!"

POWER AND POLITICS

That this modest proposal by a graduate student has metamorphosed into such a tantalizing possibility for revisioning of a city's flavor speaks to the salience of smart growth principles in our current national conversation. Tying land use to transportation planning is at the heart of this discourse. Cervero (2003) highlights the back and forth play between land-use planning and transportation issues. Smart growth planning, he asserts, depends on the recognition of this link. He speaks of " 'derived demand'—derived by the need to get to and from places or activities" (12). Since, he asserts, land use is at the end of the road (literally and figuratively) of transport, he recommends we privilege that piece of planning (i.e., that relating to land use) rather than focusing first on transportation options per se. He does caution, however, that it must be remembered "that transport infrastructure can be a powerful tool for shaping land-use visions" (13). The Beltline's appeal is most certainly tied to its land-use implications, yet what it will turn out to be and the logistics of its creation, as noted, are still up in the air. An area planner remarked:

> I think the Beltline is the most amazing project I've seen in thirty-three years! People love it—and they don't know how much it's going to cost, what it's going to look like, or what the technology is going to be! [Laughs] But they love it!!!

This tendency in Atlanta to jump on board before fully knowing how a project will take shape is not unique to the Beltline concept, nor is it exclusively limited to transportation projects. Stone's (1989) retrospective remarks about the building of the Atlanta Stadium (although referring to a very different kind of enterprise) are remarkably similar to the above respondent's comments about the Beltline:

> The building of Atlanta Stadium is itself a remarkable event. Later, Atlantans were to remember how the city had built a stadium for a team not yet signed, with money it did not have, on land it did not own. (63)

Unbridled growth, accompanied by enhancing the city's image on the world stage, sometimes by appearing to address those very issues that such unrestrained growth creates, has long been the key to the popularity of major projects in the area. They have also frequently floundered or backfired. Such has been the case with MARTA, the Omni International, and Underground Atlanta.[4] Widespread and energetic enthusiasm for projects such as the Stadium and the Beltline is perhaps in part a measure of how desperate Atlantans are for solutions to multiple problems that such big-ticket items promise to address. Here again the needs may be best read through the tripod of growth, green, and equity goals. Greater greenspace, transit access, safety, sustainability, and flavor are all at least hinted at via the Beltline vision, in addition, of course, to enormous growth potential.

As to the amorphous notion of "flavor," some cities are noted for this elusive characteristic—such as New York City—while others are notorious for their especial lack of it—such as Atlanta. Allen (1996), in support of this sentiment, goes so far as to wittily assert that "[t]he old cliché about New

York, that it was a fine place to visit but you wouldn't want to live there, could be neatly reversed and applied to Atlanta. Atlanta was a wonderful place to live, not so great to visit" (223). Marshall (2000) also captures this idea in the phrase "too much space, and too little place" (209). In discussing what he refers to as the "End of Place," he speaks of our collective nostalgia for a sense of community provided, he asserts, by cityscapes founded on a built environment oriented toward walking and public transportation. The current landscape, created almost exclusively for the automobile, has deprived us of this unique sense of place. He bemoans this loss that has accompanied the proliferation of big box stores and car dealerships in our towns and cities. He specifically notes the change at the street level, noting that streets used to be the site of sense of place. But, he offers, "The car changed all that. The parking lot and the tire, not the street and the foot, became the baseline of a city" (42). He further exclaims that no matter how well planned or appointed, a shopping mall cannot evoke a sense of place (42).

Marshall shares the widespread notion (quoting another scholar in his illustration) that Atlanta epitomizes this trend, and at the same time points the finger at transport policy (or lack thereof) as largely responsible for this pattern:

> Spiro Kostof observes in his masterful book The City Shaped that some American cities, like Atlanta, grew up simply around the sum of decisions by independent developers, resulting in "an uncoordinated patchwork of grids." But it's also true that such cities are the worst cities. Atlanta's urban history relates directly to its nature today as a fragmented, sprawling suburb that provides little sense of identity or place to its region. (146)

That the Beltline is meant in part to create this savory city-feel, at least from some perspectives, is clear in the choice of words used by many to describe some aspects of it. For instance, the greenspace piece of it is alternately referred to as "an emerald necklace," "a band of green," or an "oasis in the city." This elusive but salient notion of urban flavor is spoken of in reference to the Beltline in more general terms as well. For example, the initiator of the Beltline concept averred, "It sort of changes the way Atlanta thinks about itself." So one aspect of its appeal is the idea that it will help to turn Atlanta into a world-class city while promoting sustainability at the same time. Another has to do with inertia.

Once a major project becomes popular with influential proponents, two things seem to happen. One, they convince themselves and each other more and more of the rightness and importance of the project. And two, opposition is increasingly marginalized and silenced. These tendencies seem to have a long history in Atlanta. In his 1953 seminal work, Floyd Hunter spoke of both of them. In regard to the former, he noted, regarding his investigation of the power structure, "that many of the men who, in the early stages of a campaign, may know that propaganda tells only a part of the truth, begin to believe their own propaganda as it unfolds" (181). And as to the second point, he notes that when leaders at last agree upon what policies to implement, "there is an immediate demand on their part for strict conformity of opinion . . . Pressures are put upon dissenters and the project is under way" (181).

An otherwise cautious and skeptical official, representing MARTA, provided this rather grandiose image of the Beltline's potential in the course of our interview:

> I like to think not so much of what it [the Beltline] would do for MARTA, as how it would integrate with MARTA—what it could do for the city, and for the region—it is just tremendous! I mean, moving people—there's just so many things it accomplishes . . . the opportunity for development—housing, and office, and work development—around these stations—it's a tremendous opportunity for getting people out of their cars and into transit!

This in spite of the fact that, realistically, the Beltline has little hope, even in the best-case scenario, of effecting much in the way of changing patterns of car behavior, notwithstanding the fact that of all the transportation improvements under consideration, the Beltline projects the highest ridership. Speaking specifically to the Atlanta case, Bae (2004) compares Atlanta's transit system to that of Barcelona, Spain, to demonstrate what extent of simple rail addition would be necessary to have a significant impact on mode choice. To accomplish Barcelona's ridership (30 percent of trips made on public transit versus Atlanta's current 4.5 percent) before even touching attitude, major infrastructure changes would be necessary. Largely because of Barcelona's density as opposed to Atlanta's sprawl, MARTA's forty-six miles of rail and thirty-eight train stations, would have to grow to 2,125 miles and 2,800 stations respectively to begin to match Barcelona's ridership capacity (364–65). And speaking directly to the Beltline's transit potential, a September 30 AJC article (Donsky 2005) tells us:

> A panel of transportation experts issued a report Thursday that questions the need for Atlanta's proposed Beltline to have mass transit along its entire 22-mile loop.

As we shall see, this report had an impact on Beltline enthusiasm, but for now suffice it to say that the panel noted insufficient ridership potential on some segments of the loop. A MARTA executive must certainly be aware that a few more lines will not significantly impact ridership—yet this presentation of the Beltline potential is simpler and more readily appealing than more nuanced explanations of its capacity to allow Atlanta to "change the way it thinks about itself." Pucher (2004) reminds us that hopes for public transit are always about more than meets the eye, and most certainly about more than ridership. He cautions us that perception is as important as results when it comes to such matters. Inasmuch as subsidies for public transit in the United States come in at about twenty-three billion dollars per year and the system transports less than 2 percent of the population, the cost-benefit analysis cannot explain government and voter choices to continue this funding. Pucher explains that it is perceptions that keep us paying in: perceptions about "indirect social and environmental benefits far beyond the direct benefits of riders themselves" (209). We continue to hold on to and cherish the notion "that public transit helps to relieve congestion, save energy, reduce pollution, revitalize cities, provide mobility to the disadvantaged, and ensure basic mobility options for everyone" (209). Even persons who have enough knowledge about how cities and transportation systems work to logically know that notions of dramatically increased ridership are overblown nonetheless embrace that belief. Such is the power of persuasion, even working on the persuaders.

As to the second point regarding the demand for conformity of opinion once a decision has been reached, it remains to be seen whether this will be the case with the Beltline. Whispers of concern and dissension that are now being heard will be a testing ground on which to see if this censure arises. The public relations campaign up until quite recently has been so effective that it appeared as though no coercive demand for conformity would be necessary. One influential private sector actor remarked:

> I mean, there's something there—if you are ever going to write about how to create a public atmosphere to support public projects, that one's a great place to start—and Cathy Woolard gets a lot of credit for that, I think! The Beltline—the more you look into it, the more difficult it gets to be in terms of finding a solution.

Despite logistical and ideological stumbling blocks, to be discussed more fully below, the Beltline has been hailed, as one transit authority executive noted, as "a developer's dream." It has likewise been lauded as a "political dream" (Hairston 2005), and "an urban planner's dream" (Coppola 2005). One area developer called the Beltline "the most exciting redevelopment project since Sherman burned Atlanta" (Coppola 2005). However, as evidenced in the preceding chapters, sometimes people find that realizing their dreams can have the unanticipated side effect of simultaneously realizing their worst nightmares. When that begins to appear true for a large enough or powerful enough group, the brakes are applied—as has been the case with the Northern Arc, and various other proposed road projects in the Atlanta region, and to a certain extent with GRTA. While it may be true that grassroots efforts have advanced the project so far, other private and public sector actors have had an enormous influence and will have more and more power in determining where it goes from here. The Beltline's potential to transform Atlanta's image and mobility patterns is in large measure dependent on who claims ownership of its dream power.

The smart growth laissez-faire style promoters are certainly working to capture the Beltline precepts as an embodiment of their dream. As a Florida consultant told Atlanta developers in a 2003 meeting, "Context sells, and walkable context is what really sells now" (Sundquist 2003). In keeping with the commodification of space and the sexiness of New Urbanism as product, the content of a Beltline Web site reads in part as follows:

> Imagine walking a few steps from your Grant Park home, catching a European-style tram, and zipping off for lunch at the King Plow Center.[5] Imagine bicycle and pedestrian paths that engage diverse parts of the city. Imagine opening 4,000 acres for redevelopment that could accommodate 100,000 new residents—all of whom are a short walk from environmentally friendly transit. Imagine a smart growth idea that does not cut through historic neighborhoods, but instead brings them together. (www.cathyatlanta.com/work/issues/belt_line_transit.html)

The language and imagery in this passage target people with eco-friendly sensibilities, educated palates, and refined tastes. It might not appeal so readily to people whose major concerns are about social justice and connecting the poor and socially disadvantaged to the full benefits of the city. This latter group's dream for the Beltline would hinge more fundamentally on missing linkages and creation of opportunities for groups that do not currently have access to even the basic amenities of urban living. So for many Atlantans, catching a Euro-style tram and zipping off for lunch at pricey restaurants is about as far from their reality as that alternate mode of transportation, the SUV or Lexus, that many proponents of that dream have waiting in their driveway in case the Beltline does not work out for them.

The middle-class residents of some Beltline neighborhoods also have reservations, related to the pace and type of development that the Beltline will likely inspire. So green, growth, and equity goals once again find points of convergence and disjuncture around yet another major transportation-related Atlanta project. The Beltline is so expressly emblematic of efforts to address spatiality that it is inevitably beginning to elicit criticism from both ends of the ideological spectrum.

HONEYMOON OVER BEFORE IT BEGAN?

As previously mentioned, perhaps the Beltline's popularity could be in part attributed to its vagueness. Echoes of this sentiment are beginning to surface. An October 3, 2005, op-ed in the *Atlanta Journal-Constitution* noted:

> The plan to connect Atlanta's intown neighborhoods with a ring of parks, condos, shops and a brand new transit system called the Beltline always had a warm and fuzzy ring to it. What's not to love? But it seems the warm reception the Beltline had been getting was mostly because details about it were so fuzzy. That's changing. ("Beltline Buckles," A 12)

As Beltline plans are beginning to congeal and become more solid and more public, there are three major areas of concern that are drawing attention, some of which have already been touched upon but will be more clearly drawn in this section. These are: (1) how the Beltline is to be funded; (2) who is included and who is left out, looking at both inclusion in decision-making processes and inclusion in (or exclusion from) the benefits accrued upon completion; and (3) where transit will be installed and enhanced.

Funding

There was a push for the TAD to be approved very quickly (by December 31, 2005). Two items are relevant in regard to this push: one is upcoming local elections and the other is that in Georgia TADs must begin at the first of the year (January 1) or be postponed until the next year.[6] This rush, however, caused some concern from various quarters. Some interested parties, particularly the Neighborhood Planning Units (NPUs), requested that the process be slowed down a bit. The mayor was anxious for it to move forward quickly, and in a meeting with NPU leaders in late September she entreated, "My appeal to you is to take the same leap of faith Atlanta has taken on other issues" (Pendered, 10/1/05). Some of the local spokespersons strongly expressed the need to have more questions answered before a vote moved forward. Mayor Franklin stuck with her resolve, noting, "Here's our dilemma. Despite the sense of unreadiness, the opportunity to create the Beltline will slip away if we do not act now" (Pendered, 10/1/05). Central to the concerns was the desire for more neighborhood input in the planning process.

Cindy Dennis, NPU-D Chair, at an October 4 meeting of the City Council's Community Development/Human Relations and Zoning committees, voiced specific worries about the TAD:

> Dennis wanted to know if city taxpayers who live outside the TAD area will have their taxes increased in order for the city to provide the required services (police, fire, garbage, etc.) to thousands of new people forecast to be moving into the TAD area, since TAD monies cannot be used to pay for such services, only capital infrastructure needs . . . Dennis also cautioned that the city may lose a large amount of tax revenues—millions of dollars over the next 25 years—if the

> TAD is passed this year using real estate tax assessments within the TAD area "which we know are bogus,"[7] and which will be frozen at their present level, which is lower than they should be, for the 25-year duration of the TAD. (Schaffner 2005)

At an October 6 Public Hearing held by the Atlanta City Council, objections were also raised about possible legal deficiencies with the TAD. A woman identifying herself as an attorney noted that TAD monies can only be collected and used in economically and socially depressed areas. She pointed out that many sections of the Beltline do not meet these criteria. She further noted that in order to achieve TAD status, it must be proven that redevelopment would not be possible for the TAD without government involvement. Again, she noted that this was not the case for some sections of the Beltline. Several other Virginia Highland and Morningside residents echoed some of these concerns and voiced a desire for the process to slow down, expressing fears that the TAD might make the Beltline "development-driven rather than transportation-driven."

From an equity perspective, Vincent Fort (Senator) voiced concerns that the TAD would act as an "engine for gentrification," and do harm to his constituents. Residents of District 11 noted that theirs would be the only district left out of the Beltline, and there is now talk of a spur to tie it in. These concerns relate to issues of inclusion and exclusion.

Inclusion

Several aspects of inclusion need attention, including: involvement in the decision-making process; direct and indirect effects of development; and who picks up the tab for the project in the short and long runs. Each of these aspects is relevant to numerous actors: developers, the city's administrative body, the NPUs noted above, as well as those primarily concerned with social justice. Robert Bullard's important remarks bear reproducing at length and touch on all aspects of inclusion:

> I think there needs to be a lot of discussion about the implications of implementing a Beltline at the same time that MARTA is struggling. You understand? The major transit system in the region is struggling! And how do you strengthen the existing system at the same time—not carve off a piece and give it priority and let the other piece drown—and how do you create a system that is equitable so that you do not somehow shortchange those people who have to wait . . . So it's almost like a catch-22—you built in inequity and . . . money follows power, you know, and in order to get the acceptance of this whole idea, to get it to pass—to fly—the first line is going to be in the northern part of the piece. And so

> that is something that really has to be thought through in terms of resource allocation, particularly when resources are very, very scarce . . . So when you talk about making sure that your main service constituency is not impacted in a negative way . . . we're not talking about riders who have—choice riders or discretionary riders—we're talking about, you know, basically transit-dependent—those services are being cut and impacted even before this thing [the Beltline] is being talked about! So, I guess you're going to have to do some type of—not just cost-benefit analysis, but really a social equity analysis of implementation and what that means for, not just mobility, but also in terms of access to basic stuff . . . When you start raising those kinds of questions people think you are trying to stop it, or block it, or that you are opposed to trying to make it work . . . but even this area is changing as we speak—West End—this area over here—in terms of lofts and those old warehouses—and you know we didn't even have a grocery store in this area! And it is like, you know, you gotta eat! So when we talk about basic amenities, most people don't think of basic amenities as a grocery store—but you know, a lot of neighborhoods do!

Bullard gives voice to several important questions and concepts here: First, is it right that we as a city should give our limited resources to creating a major new transit loop when MARTA, the region's primary provider, can barely stay afloat? Secondly, he notes that the northern spur is likely to go in first as this is where the money is. Once again, this will benefit those with more and inconvenience those with less. Thirdly, Bullard points out that to raise these kinds of objections potentially brands one as a naysayer, when in fact he thinks the Beltline is a fine endeavor, but must be approached with caution and care so that equity may be achieved. Finally, he reminds us that some neighborhoods are still struggling to partake of basic amenities such as grocery stores, while others are flirting with notions of increased greenspace, convenient transit loops, and lovely restaurants.

The initiator of the Beltline concept also has serious concerns about the equity piece. He told me:

> I think it's important to make the project happen, just politically, there are also environmental justice issues, uh, I mean the whole project needs to move forward together. It would be a huge problem if pieces of it started to get broken off and seen as different from the rest of the project—you know, we can do this, but we can't do that. That's what makes me nervous about the MARTA study, because they're looking at the northeastern quadrant which has a lot of economic activity right now . . . already it's easy to see that growth continuing and there being a need for that . . . but it's not as

> easy to see for some people that the south and the west are equally suited to that kind of growth and that those communities need that kind of growth and that that growth is warranted . . . and that it gets designed and built in a way that is conducive to the bigger, longer-term picture of where the city is going to be.

Who is being centered and who is being left out of the fruits of this potentially wondrous Beltline depend on whom you ask. From one view, as expressed in the above passages, it appears as though the poor and black may once again reap most of the negatives of yet another major Atlanta project. Some middle to upper-class neighborhoods fear that their wants and needs will likewise be neglected and overridden.

Wayne Mason, the developer who bought up about four and one-half miles of the Beltline specifically in anticipation of the project, has begun to make plans for development on that strip that are stirring up some fears and concerns. In mid-June 2005, two op-ed pieces appeared in the *Atlanta Journal-Constitution* taking opposing sides, and addressing some of the concerns. The hot issues are parking spaces, densities, and neighborhood destruction. In regard to the former, the concern is that increased parking potential will deter the actual building of the Beltline both by encouraging cars and by detracting from funding for transit:

> One important bellwether will be the outcome of a request to build 1,800 parking spaces for a pair of high-rise condos with a total 750 units on the eastern edge of Piedmont Park. The towers—38 and 39 stories respectively—promise to be the first residential component of the 22-mile transit loop that would run along little-used rail tracks through 45 neighborhoods, spurring the creation of new shops, parks, and trails . . . but the parking plan for the towers, which breaks down to roughly 2.4 spaces per unit, is troubling . . . Atlanta planning and zoning officials must strike a reasonable balance between competing interests, but they'd do well to remember this maxim: More parking only begets more traffic, which begets more parking. ("Not auto immune" 2005)

The opposing view holds that the beauty of the Beltline is that it will spur growth and development, in addition to adding parks, trails, and transit. The author argues that the NorthEast Atlanta Beltline Group is donating land for these civic uses but must realistically also get a return on its generosity. The residential properties will indeed be near transit lines, but, the author asserts, "residents will need to park their cars" (Whiddon 2005).

While the number of parking spaces requested for this project only slightly exceeds the current levels of car ownership in the United States,[8] it definitely does not link with notions of transit, bicycle, and pedestrian-friendly transformation of urban space. To place this discussion in a broader context, it is important to note the centrality, pervasiveness, and invisibility of parking procedures in the shaping of mobility patterns. Pucher (2004) reveals that according to the 1990 Nationwide Personal Transportation Survey (NPTS), "over 95% of car trips made in U.S. cities benefit from free parking" (219). Even that parking that is paid for by consumers is most often subsidized by employers or businesses. This is further subsidized by the government in that when businesses allow free or low-cost parking to their employees and customers, the businesses can in turn deduct their costs from their taxes, while the users pay no taxes on the privilege. The free-parking perk is huge, "estimated by some studies to exceed $1,000 per year per urban vehicle," and "the country's leading parking expert provides convincing evidence that free parking entails more subsidy—and more inducement to drive—than would the provision of free gasoline" (219).

Thus, the provision of such generous parking allotments in association with the Beltline encourages growth as usual and detracts from its transformative potential. In short, it lends to the potential to keep Atlanta growing in its car-oriented way. In response to fears of Beltline Mason-style, a group has already formed—the Beltline Neighbors Coalition—specifically geared toward ensuring that the giant buildings sitting right on the Beltline, and possible similar construction to follow, is not what the Beltline becomes. The concerns go well beyond parking spaces. Density issues and neighborhood preservation are key to the coalition's agenda. For instance, most seemed to believe that the greenspace loop (parks encircling the area) would be the first piece with transit coming last because of expense and logistical problems such as acquiring rights-of-way. But in fact, it would now appear that at least some redevelopment might precede either transit or greenspace. While development, particularly aimed at greater densities, is a desired feature of the Beltline for most proponents, the way that this is starting to take shape is already causing some consternation. As noted in a September 27 *AJC* article, fears are mounting that, "No longer was the Beltline a 22-mile greenbelt for intown residents. It was starting to look like a welcome mat for Buckhead-style[9] developments in neighborhoods that have no high-rise buildings" (Pendered 2005).

The Beltline Neighbors Coalition posted their mission statement on a Web site (MidtownAtlanta.org) detailing their hopes and fears:

> There is a vision of the Beltline that has inspired us all—a vision of linear parks, trails, and greenways; an emerald necklace with new opportunities for transit and recreation, which will enhance and strengthen our intown communities. Yet even before this vision has had the chance to take hold, we see another, more disturbing, vision of the Beltline emerging, where our parks and greenways are crowded out by mega-development, where neighborhood streets are

> choked by thousands of new cars while transit is still decades away, and where high rises tower over single family homes.
>
> Why is the promise of the Beltline in danger of being transformed into this disappointing reality? Because in our zeal to make the promise of the Beltline happen, we have confused the means with the ends. Development has replaced both public infrastructure and transportation as the driver and organizer of the plan. One-size-fits-all mantras about density have replaced appropriate safeguards to protect existing neighborhoods. And common sense protection and extension of existing parks and green space have been usurped by a desire to appropriate every usable acre for development.
>
> In order to recapture the promise of the Beltline, we must commit to a process that is careful, disciplined and responsible, that recognizes both its potential and its pitfalls. We must prioritize the core values of the Beltline: a linear park; continuous trails; a reinvigoration of existing parks and the creation of new green space; a plan that strengthens, protects and preserves the neighborhoods which it passes through, and new development based on transit and sustainable principles.

They go on to detail specific precepts to keep in mind as guiding principles for the project, including such things as, "a clearly articulated 'step-down' guideline to limit the scale of development adjacent to residential neighborhoods," and "quality-of-life zoning principles for all Beltline development." An op-ed piece in the December 7 *AJC* further demonstrates this position. In explicit opposition to the Towers in particular, and Mason-style development in general, Markwell (2005) asserts, "If Mason has his way, Atlanta will become like New York City. If I wanted to move to a city like that, I'd move to New York . . . Atlanta doesn't need growth that is unrestricted and unguided, except by the greed of wealthy developers." He further notes:

> Atlanta needs to have planned, intelligent growth, and that plan should include money for a public transportation system that binds our spread-out communities without creating strip malls and towering condos that will ruin them. The Beltline is our opportunity to do that: add transportation options and modest growth that can enhance our communities, not drown them. (Markwell 2005)

The residents of these neighborhoods (Virginia Highland, Morningside, Midtown) have considerable clout and significant influence with policymakers. Consequently, developers, in their turn, are becoming concerned that they may be pushed out of the inner circle of planners of this project. In a September 27 *AJC* article, entitled "Land donor snubbed in Beltline plan," the author details the dissatisfactions of Wayne Mason and his NorthEast

Atlanta Beltline Group. Mason's intentions were to donate up to one-half of the nearly seventy acres he acquired for greenspace, transit, and so on to the city. This generosity is understandably contingent upon being able to realize a sizable profit from his investment. Mason's son, a key player in the company, expressed that they were "puzzled, disappointed, and bewildered" by the exclusion of the NorthEast Atlanta Beltline Group from the planning process (Pendered 2005). It seems as though the city has begun to distance itself from Mason and his plans since it has become evident that the proposed high-rises slated to be built by Trammell Crow Residential on land they intend to buy from Mason on 10th and Monroe is, as referenced above, an unpopular project. In addition to being excluded from the Beltline Partnership, Mason's people believe that the city is deliberately interfering in rezoning applications in response to this public hue and cry:

> [Mason's team] sent a letter August 26 to the city's zoning administrator demanding an end to what it called "official interference" in its rezoning application. "ADA's factual misstatements have confused the public and frustrated our efforts to educate the public about our applications and seek support in the same manner as other applicants for rezoning," the letter states. "At a minimum, ADA's actions are unique, extraordinary, and potentially irreparably harmful to the [rezoning] process and our proposal." (Pendered 2005)

According to an article in Georgia Trend, a local business and politics publication, Mason situates himself as central to the Beltline realization. He is quoted as saying, "Without me, everything else is a pipe dream . . . I put real dollars in there. I've gone through the process and through the hoops and taken the abuse" (Coppola 2005). This is not a white-gloves battle. Both sides are determinedly married to their positions and leave little room for compromise. The vice-chair of NPU-F (Virginia Highland/Morningside area), noted, "The neighborhood doesn't want towers in Piedmont Park . . . There is no deal. We're at zero stories and the neighborhood is not budging from zero stories." While Mason asserts, "I was raised on a farm . . . when you sell a man a mule, don't tell him how to work it." He also noted:

> I have a clear shot, but it comes down to the bottom line: Is the mayor and council going to have enough political will to work for the best interests of the population as a whole, or are they going to listen to a handful of people who bitch about everything that happens downtown? This handful in the Morningside area and the Midtown moaners terrorize everybody. They defeated I-475. They defeated the Stone Mountain Freeway. Anytime anything comes up they threaten everybody and try to intimidate everybody. (Coppola 2005)

Mason, avers, however, that he is not to be intimidated by these "intown moaners." He says, "I'm not Fortune 500. I'm not worried about my public image. Not worried about where I'm going to sell Coca-Cola or plywood. It's my money and I'll make the decisions" (Coppola 2005). Mason also argues that the type of development he proposes is necessary for the kind of transit the neighborhoods want and envision. "You can't have public transportation without density," he reasons (Coppola 2005). As noted, the transit piece of the Beltline is not without its own specific controversies.

Transit on the Beltline

Another development, which has inspired a more cautious approach to the heretofore headlong trajectory of the Beltline vision, relates to the findings of a panel of transportation experts convened to determine transit efficacy. The panel, headed by Catherine Ross (former GRTA executive director and now the director of Georgia Tech's Center for Quality Growth and Regional Development), issued their report in September 2005. While the report was far from negative regarding the Beltline plans in general, it "questions the need for Atlanta's proposed Beltline to have mass transit along its entire 22-mile loop" (Donsky 2005). The panel is in favor of the TAD and enthusiastic about the greenspace and other components of the Beltline, including transit. Nonetheless, the study found that significant sections of the Beltline will not fulfill the basic aims of public transportation, namely getting people where they need to go. The article points out that the routes do "connect trendy neighborhoods" but fail to hook into the "biggest job centers in Midtown, Buckhead and downtown." Donsky reports that since much of the Beltline is located in "low-density, low-income neighborhoods on Atlanta's southwest and northwest sides," there are grave doubts that it will sustain the kind of ridership needed to support transit. He quotes a transportation consultant, also a Georgia Institute of Technology professor, Mike Meyer, as among those who doubt its efficacy (Donsky 2005). This report, while far from startling or disapproving, seems to have had a significant impact on some proponents. In a story enumerating some of the criticisms the Beltline is currently receiving, the author posits:

> But the development that may have raised the most concern among Beltline backers in the past week was the transit panel's report, which found that portions of the loop—mainly the northwest and southwest sectors—would not have sufficient ridership to support trains, trolleys or other mass transit options. (Schaffner 2005)

This north/south split, so prevalent in Atlanta politics, and which so often serves as a proxy for racial divides, is highly salient in the Beltline discussion also. Southside politicians are particularly attuned to this potential for Beltline decisions to pick at old wounds. For instance, Atlanta City Council member Harris of southwest Atlanta said that "she doesn't understand all the fuss over the Beltline given that the city won't lift a finger in her neighborhood to buy a piece of land that's been vacant 30 years and build it into a park" (Pendered, 10/01/05). And speaking more directly to transit concerns, other council members, Fellers and Bryant, both voiced concerns that the Beltline would do little in the way of connecting their neighborhoods to the rest of the city (Pendered, 10/01/05). While concerns appear to be mounting, nevertheless, Beltline plans would seem to be proceeding relatively smoothly, as compared with other major area projects. For instance, despite all the cautions and wariness, the approval of all three entities needed to create a Beltline TAD was garnered prior to the December 31 deadline. The Atlanta City Council voted twelve to three to pass the Beltline TAD on November 7, the Board of Education approved it on December 12, and the Fulton County Commission signed off on it on December 21.

The Atlanta Public Schools' (APS) approval was contingent on four concessions, sought and gained: (1) $150 million for construction and maintenance of school facilities; (2) up to 840 low-cost housing units for teachers and other school staff; (3) a site (within two years) within the TAD for athletic fields and $10 million to build recreational facilities; and (4) all developers receiving money through the TAD will be required to pay $25,000 to the school system for enhancing educational programs (Pendered 2005). The Fulton County Commission asked for and received assurances that $27 million from the TAD will go toward the Atlanta-Fulton Public Library System. This demand is in part meant to assuage the concerns of those outside the city that the Beltline would do little for them. Karen Handel, Fulton County Commission Chair, noted, "We were looking for a service that would benefit all citizens of Fulton County—children, adults, and seniors . . . It's a huge win for the citizens of Fulton County, whether they live in Alpharetta, Atlanta or Palmetto or anywhere in between" (Pendered 2005). Notwithstanding these crucial authorizations, what the Beltline will become has by no means been ascertained and is dependent upon a number of factors, at the heart of which lie power and politics.

WHERE WILL THE BELTLINE LEAD?

In addition to ideological obstacles, the practicality, enormity, and logistics of the Beltline are posited as stumbling blocks that may in part determine its fate. Current estimates put the cost at about $2.5 billion and the time-frame at as much as twenty-five years or more (Donsky 2005). As a Georgia Regional Transportation Authority respondent noted, "It's a wonderful urban plan—extraordinarily expensive! Can they get the rail right-of-way? A portion of it, yes—a portion of it, no!" While access to that right-of-way is looking increasingly promising, there is many a slip twixt the cup and the lip. Because of cost and related problems, some believe it is imperative to create a supportive environment before trying to put the transit piece in place. That means land-use manipulation, and we have seen in the study of GRTA how much resistance that can foment. A long-time area transportation consultant informed me:

> What you will end up with is, you will have higher density buildings facing, you know, this amenity [the greenspace]. And they will push up to it like the apartment buildings do on Central Park, and that sort of thing. And you've got to do everything that you can to continue to stimulate that concentration of development along that line so that once you cross that threshold and you put the train in, it's an immediate success. Because it really ends up being the missing link! What we've always done, is put in the transportation resource and neglected the land use that would support it.

The mode of public transportation that will be used for the Beltline is also related to concerns about cost and balancing those concerns against ones related to effectiveness. A transportation executive board member told me:

> Yeah, even the mode is unclear. Uh, I think the four routes that they're looking at in the alternative analysis phase now, uh, the modes, I mean, theoretically at least—you know, it could be light rail, bus rapid transit—uh, I think—one of the things that—because it is so dependent on attracting private funding, it has this sort of ironical twist—because of that I think it's more likely to be rail than bus rapid transit. Bus rapid transit is what the federal government is pushing everywhere that they're funding—because it's, you know . . . forgive me for . . . for you know, stereotyping, but that's the Republican way . . . you know, anything that ordinary folks use—do it as cheap as you can! But the bus rapid transit does not attract development at stations—it's just not shown to do that in the places it's been used—light rail does. So developers that are interested in having this as a development tool—or as an aid in development, prefer light rail.

All of this once again emphasizes how astonishing the popularity of the Beltline notion is considering how uncertain its mode, costs, timetable, order of operations, and even its purposes are to the public and to those involved in its creation. Not to mention what entity will be in charge of planning and developing it, much less actually be in charge of operations. Some say GRTA, some say MARTA, some believe a new entity will be developed for its implementation. As a GRTA informant explained:

> I'm on the technical advisory committee for the Beltline. You know, there are so many people doing Beltline! MARTA is doing a Beltline evaluation of alternatives, Cathy Woolard (before she ran for office) has her own committee and it's doing a Beltline evaluation of services, ARC—yeah—everybody is looking at the Beltline! It is part of the ARC Mobility Twenty-Thirty plan—it is part of my RTAP [Regional Transit Action Plan] study . . . It's a great project, but an expensive project! Everybody doesn't mind owning the study, the interesting thing will be to see who owns the project!

And that ownership will in large part determine what the Beltline becomes—what issues it is framed to solve and what measures are put forward as answers. Even staunch proponents of the Beltline, when pressed, confide that there is widespread uncertainty as to the likelihood of it becoming much more than another "pretty face." An area transportation planner, after telling me at great length that the Beltline could transform both the image and the mobility patterns of Atlanta, finally noted toward the end of the interview:

> The Beltline has been described as a solution trying to find a problem! I mean, who's going to ride it? Lots of people will probably ride it to Piedmont Park every Sunday, but is that an important way to spend their money? I don't know!

Yet, the hopes for the Beltline, as with the hopes of most popular projects, are greater than the sum of its parts. Everyone agrees, for instance, that the transit piece in itself will do little to mitigate congestion, pollution, or to address other traffic woes, including issues of equity. Nevertheless, it is well-loved. While desperation, high hopes, perceptions, and hegemony all aid in the promulgation of particular projects, none of these, alone or in combination, is enough to make them effective.

Making the Beltline live up to even a modicum of its desired potential will be a daunting task. In How Cities Work, Marshall (2000) describes what would be necessary to transform Ghent (a suburb of Norfolk, Virginia) from what he describes as "urbanism as ornament" into a useful and lively community. The issue there is the lack of utilitarian items for sale on the trendy main boulevard. His point is that it is not as simple a matter as it might at first appear to merely add stores with useful items in them, it requires reassembling the entire fabric of the system as it now exists:

> To convert Colley Avenue back into an actual utilitarian shopping district, rather than the specialized mecca it has become, the transportation system and the growth policies of the entire metropolitan area would have to be reworked. Some of the big highways

> would be torn down; the development of new subdivisions further out would be restricted, money would be put into bus service and light rail. Then, as older neighborhoods revived under the pressure of a more limited housing market and the structure of commerce changed, you'd actually see more practical stores reappear in the center city. (Marshall:91)

I use this excellent example to illustrate that changes in isolation are neither practical nor practicable. Furthermore, even with a chain of changes, the desired result still may not be achieved. For instance, even if in the long term the Beltline manages to contribute to higher densities:

> There is as yet no convincing evidence that higher densities reduce automobile dependence or even (at least significantly) result in lower VMTs [vehicle miles traveled] . . . Greenwald (2003) found that higher densities resulted in more walking but had no influence on automobile use . . . In addition, the environmental gains are not substantial. (Bae 2004:366)

The likelihood of substantial gains in air quality, for instance, from increased transit alone is slim to none:

> In the United States, even if transit ridership could be doubled, the environmental impacts of automobile use would be little effected because the transit ridership share is so low and continues to decline (4.7% of work trips in 2000 compared with 5.3% in 1990 and 12.1% in 1960; for all trips, the 2001 transit share was only 1.6%). (Bae 2004:364)

To truly have a significant effect on how we "do" Atlanta, or on how "Atlanta thinks about itself," we will need to allow the Beltline to lead us in new directions. Some of those directions may appear at first to be counterintuitive. As noted in the discussion of GRTA, one planner told me that we needed to "get out of the market's way" in order for GRTA to do its job. Dialectically, what we may need to do for the Beltline to accomplish its tasks is to get the market out of the way, or more precisely to rein in that unruly hand.

CONCLUSION: TOUGH CHOICES—BUSINESS AS USUAL OR CONSTRAINING OURSELVES

I have made reference several times to what I call Smart Growth laissez-faire style. Smart Growth without corresponding limitations is Dumb Growth. Adding a Beltline in Atlanta for example, without simultaneously limiting the auto-centric trajectory of that city, may do little good, and could even conceivably worsen some conditions, especially for the already socially disadvantaged. As Marshall (2000) notes, "Cramped, awkward spaces are what New Urban developments create through their attempt to have the car and get rid of it, too" (28).

To meaningfully reconfigure space we must decide what it is we want it to accomplish. Mobility for its own sake is an empty asset. Whitelegg (1997) speaks of "the status of distant things," noting that it has contributed to our "obsession with speed and saving time, [which] has almost destroyed place" (75). Being able to traverse long distances quickly does not in and of itself make for a better life. Additionally, that time-space compression must be weighed against its side effects as well as its uneven distribution. Recognizing how we got here is the first step. The hard work of undoing—or redoing—space is the next. Historical patterns of transportation planning and its attendant infrastructure are part of the picture, explaining, for example, some of the differences between the Western European and the American models of transportation decisions. But most central are policies that can be implemented at any time if and when it becomes clear that how we currently enact mobility shortchanges ourselves, our neighbors, and future generations. It is choice, reflected in policy implementation, that determines mobility patterns. For instance, Pucher (2004) points out that Canadian and European suburbs have far greater densities than their United States counterparts. He notes that this is not a circumstantial accident but rather a result of "strict land use policies and the much higher price of land in Europe" (217). As a consequence of these very different policies, as of the mid-1990s, "suburban densities averaged 39 persons per hectare in Western Europe and 26 persons per hectare in Canada, but only 12 in the United States" (217).

In turning to the European model and its results, it becomes clear that incentives and "getting out of the market's way" are insufficient tools for meaningfully impacting transportation choices and patterns. A broad range of government actions is necessary, including but not limited to restrictions on automobile usage. Several examples of some European policies follow:

> higher prices for gasoline
> higher sales tax and import fees on automobiles (e.g., in Denmark there is a 180 percent sales tax on new cars)
> wider sidewalks; bus lanes; bike lanes; car-free zones
> traffic calming via lower speed limits and through physical barriers
> privileging buses, pedestrians, and bicyclists with right of way
> mandatory private (i.e., customer pays) lessons for aspiring drivers
> older age for licensing. (Pucher 2004:217–20)

Pucher also notes a number of strategies that Europeans employ for providing high quality public transportation services, such as simple fare structures; extensive bike parking offered; widespread publication and distribution of schedules; low, wide floors for easy loading, access, and comfort; and many more (221). The point is, though, that without the restrictions the amenities have little chance of changing the balance. The differences in transit use and in nonmotorized travel are dramatic:

> The lowest transit market share in Europe (7% in the Netherlands) is still more than three times higher than in the United States. Most other European countries have transit shares at least five times higher than the United States, with some over 10 times higher (e.g., Switzerland at over 20%). Similarly, walking and bicycling account for a very low percentage of urban trips in the United States (only 7%) compared to Canada (12%) and most Western European countries (30–40%). (Pucher 2004:215–16)

To achieve comparable levels of public transportation and nonmotorized modes of transport in the United States, with the attendant reductions in harms, would be no easy task even with the resoluteness to implement all the requisite policies. To add (and stir) more transit without them may be at best ineffectual and at worst counterproductive, as the MARTA case has proven. The political will to make the necessary changes seems to be an increasingly remote possibility. As noted in the GRTA chapter, to even suggest tying transportation dollars to land-use decisions that might privilege transit or nonmotorized modes of transportation is viewed in some quarters as un-American. Any of these more radical suggestions of imitating the European model in terms of asking automobile users to acknowledge how deeply they have been discounted and begin to pay the full cost of usage would undoubtedly be met with even stronger resistance.

Nevertheless, it is extremely likely that some version of the Beltline will take shape in the coming years in Atlanta. Its winning attributes are to some degree embedded in its vagueness. This imprecision allows for multiple versions of the vision and accounts in part for the wide appeal. Once realized, the Beltline will most probably have more difficulty pleasing all palates. Choices about its direction will have to be made before long. MARTA's Inner Core Alternative Analysis Study, which as discussed in the MARTA chapter has identified four possible transit routes—one of which is the Beltline—will likely to be decided upon in the near future. One alternative is what is called the C-Loop, which is a piece of the larger Beltline vision confined to the northeast quadrant. Many of the concerned parties (which, as noted, are multiple) are mindful of the danger and the politics of a northeast partiality. Some are working hard to ensure that this does not play out in the final analysis.

Despite this attentiveness, if my prediction is correct, the Smart Growth laissez-faire-style Beltline will be the one that emerges. Place entrepreneurs, eager to jump on ripe and juicy opportunities, recognize a gold mine when they see one and are lined up, mouths watering, all along the Beltline. Gentrification, already and always underway in the region, will undoubtedly increase, forcing many out of neighborhoods and farther and farther toward nowhere. The details of how this will play out precisely are beyond my premonitory powers, but will likely result in much automobile-oriented development, a northeast bias, and more focus on curb appeal than on utility. If this is the case, it will not be what the original envisioner intended, nor will it embody the transformative elements that many proponents have in mind. To dramatically alter the landscape will require revisioning our very notions of space and our movement within it. As Soja ([1989)] 2003) counsels:

> Given the effective empowerment of a neo-conservative opposition bent on burying again the exploitative instrumentality of spatial restructuring, it becomes even more urgent that all progressive social forces—feminism, the "Greens," the peace movement, organized and disorganized labour, movements for national liberation and for radical urban and regional change—become consciously and explicitly spatial movements as well. (173)

A basic aspect of rethinking space is reconsidering mobility; what it is for, who it benefits, and how it plays into the larger picture of production and consumption that shapes our daily journeys and destinations. To strike a sustainable balance between growth, green and equity goals—the fundamental components of urban equilibrium—will require a retreat from the commodification of mobility, manifested in part through overreliance on the automobile. Achieving such a balance will also entail a turning toward the reshaping of an urban landscape in the image of community, rather than commerce. The Beltline concept is in essence about such a revisioning. Whether Atlanta is ready remains to be seen.

SIX

CONCLUSION

The Cases in Relief—A Three-Tailed Tale

What is the story that an examination of MARTA, GRTA, and the Beltline can tell us? How do these cases add to our understanding of how mobility is produced and reproduced in the Atlanta region? I began this book by asking a set of related questions:

> What motivates groups of individuals to fight for or against a particular transportation policy?
> How does this motivation and the action(s) in response to it, vary temporally, geographically, by race, class, and so forth?
> How are transportation decisions arrived at?
> Who are the key players in setting the agendas and making the decisions?

I further noted that a trio of interests emerged as salient and deeply influential in understanding the urban power structure in the Atlanta region: Car-centered Growth advocates, Green (environmental) proponents, and Equity (social justice)[1] actors emerge as the triumvirate in the region determining transportation and land-use practices. This observation led to additional linked questions:

> Under what circumstances does each of these goals intersect with the others?
> When are they mutually exclusive?
> What makes them at times mutually supportive?
> When they are at odds, what forces result in the privileging of one over the others?

In the preceding chapters I have addressed these questions and the observations regarding growth, green, and equity actors have been well supported. In this final chapter I:

1. Summarize the answers to the research questions;
2. Identify and address two sets of actors who cannot always be fitted neatly into the Growth, Green, and Equity mold;
3. Expound on what is further revealed when we look at the cases in concert;
4. Venture to uncover where we may expect to go from here.

QUESTIONS ANSWERED IN BRIEF

The creation of MARTA was an effort by the business community to reinvigorate the downtown central city and simultaneously enhance Atlanta's image as a world-class city. Largely unanticipated resistance arose from two diametrically opposed camps. For the suburban contingent, MARTA appeared to threaten their sense of identity as independent, non-urban dwellers. Suburban communities had little interest in enhancing the urban core, especially through the provision of public transportation that might encourage "undesirables" to "leak" into their sacrosanct space. On the other hand, from the perspective of those so-called undesirables, MARTA appeared to be neglecting their needs and catering to big business. For the urban poor, and particularly people of color, MARTA's mission seemed a far cry from the mobility equalizer so desperately needed by this group. Thus, the African American community withheld its stamp of approval until MARTA made solid promises and concessions that would ensure black participation in the organization as well as in the distribution of its benefits.

The reality of what MARTA became mostly failed to meet the expectations of the downtown elite. In small measure, it did provide access to convention centers, downtown hotels, sports arenas, and other venues that the business community, tourists, and visitors could utilize. This modestly supported the impression of a cosmopolitan center. But because of Atlanta's layout, and the minimal routes that the trains navigated, Atlanta remained extremely difficult to negotiate without a private vehicle. The suburban refusal to jump on board via the one penny sales tax and the resistance to MARTA from counties outside the core ensured that MARTA would not serve to connect the metro region in a smooth and seamless fashion. Furthermore, MARTA's push-me pull-you practices with the transit-dependent (big promises, minimal delivery) managed to alienate both those who used it most and those who used it least. Because of MARTA's failure to revive downtown in the hoped-for fashion; its inability to properly serve the transit-dependent; its checkered history with accusations of corruption, and contract and union problems; and lack of support from and reach to the suburbs, MARTA has essentially created a trio of allied enemies who otherwise make strange bedfellows.

As for GRTA, its creation really grew out of a mandate. Threatened with loss of federal dollars for transportation projects unless or until air quality issues in the region were addressed, the Chamber of Commerce and the governor's office both had high stakes in ensuring that something was done—and quickly. Created by Democratic governor Roy Barnes, with input from the Chamber of Commerce's Metropolitan Atlanta Transportation Initiative (MATI), GRTA was granted unprecedented statutory powers to change land-use practices and coordinate regional transportation planning. Much of GRTA's potential was appealing to politicians, environmentalists, and businesspersons alike. Vehement opposition came from counties outside the city of Atlanta. Suburbanites perceived GRTA as MARTA all over again—only worse. This time, the entity would be endowed with the authority to insist on their participation and force the counties to modify their land-use patterns in ways that might de-center the automobile and increase housing densities. This kind of power was unacceptable. Conversely, social justice activists, particularly transit advocates, were hopeful that GRTA would work to enhance mobility for all from the city to the suburbs, from suburb to suburb, and from the suburbs to the city.

As with MARTA, what GRTA became was an entity that did not do enough for any of its promoters. It did, however, assuage the fears of its strongest detractors (the counties outside the city) by utilizing so little of its land-use powers as to make those powers nearly invisible. The services that GRTA provided, express bus routes from a few counties to downtown Atlanta, pleased suburban commuters. GRTA and its sister transit providers allowed for a clean, safe (read non-MARTA) commute from the suburbs to downtown without substantially altering the transportation landscape or the home-rule "rights" of the suburban communities. Thus, in GRTA's case its friends and foes have to some extent been reversed, with its initial enemies now being some of its few remaining supporters. The business and political leaders were initially pleased because GRTA's creation appeased the federal government and helped to reinstate federal monies for transportation projects. The Republican administration of Governor Sonny Perdue that replaced Roy Barnes saw to it that GRTA's role was one that did not intrude in suburban governance and did little to shift away from automobile dependence for the region. Environmentalists and equity actors have been disappointed in GRTA's actions, and most especially in its lack of initiative regarding land use and public transit policies.

Motivations for involvement in the Beltline project are also evolutionary. The concept started with a graduate student's master's thesis, was picked up by political and environmental actors and polished and honed, received support from the city with the approval of a tax allocation district (TAD) by the City Council, Atlanta Public Schools Board, and Fulton County Commissioners' Office. The Beltline concept has most recently been the recipient of criticism from social justice actors and neighborhood groups fearful of unwanted consequences. Reminiscent of MARTA, the Beltline has been framed as the centerpiece, crowning glory, and shining jewel of the city, with promises of greater mobility and image enhancement for the city and the region. It has been held up as a means for Atlanta to refashion an identity in keeping with other world-class urban centers. Atlanta's longstanding pursuit of a spectacular image on the world stage has been one of its noted features for some time. This image enhancement has long been chased by politicians and the economic sector, and is an important point of convergence of their interests. Keating (2001) speaks of this common goal, asserting that promoters have long tried to position Atlanta as a "progressive, enlightened city" despite the fact that it is located in the often presumed backward South. This strategy is not only aimed at attracting residents, he argues, but also an outgrowth of "the way in which business interests have dominated the city's politics." He asserts that selling image is as fundamental to private enterprise as is selling products, and because of the conflation of interests between the two, this focus on image has spilled over from the world of commerce into the governmental sphere (202).

Thus, the image-making aspect of the Beltline has enormous appeal, and politicians and the business community have been strong advocates of the Beltline for these reasons. Some environmentalists are likewise extremely enthusiastic because of the Beltline's promise to increase greenspace and provide bicycle, pedestrian, and transit alternatives for movement. Once again, however, as the reality of how this all might play out begins to jell, not everyone remains wholeheartedly committed. Fears of exclusion of the poor, drastic changes to neighborhood compositions and densities, and costs unequal to benefits, begin to erode the unmitigated support for the Beltline project.

Another possibility must also be considered concerning the Beltline. Perhaps, as with MARTA, the projections of its contribution might turn out to be quite overblown. The preeminent developer, Tom Cousins, put many of his eggs in the MARTA basket in the 1980s and was severely disappointed. The Omni International Complex was supposed to be invigorated by MARTA. "Cousins believed rapid transit would draw them [tenants and customers] in from the suburbs by the tens of thousands, filling the empty office space with workers and the boutiques with well-heeled shoppers" (Allen 1996:217). There was much hoopla around the opening of MARTA's West line in 1980 and "Cousins remained convinced that MARTA held the key to the future" (217). These high hopes failed to pan out. It seemed in this case that Cousins backed the wrong horse. The bulk of the passengers passing through the Omni MARTA station was from largely black and less-wealthy neighborhoods, "and they had little interest in shopping at Hermès or Givenchy or dining at the French Restaurant" (217). The North Line was not even open yet and so we cannot know whether it would have transported the requisite wealthy whites from the suburbs who would perhaps fill the pricey shops and restaurants. Allen also notes that those who did come for sports games and concerts mostly came by automobile and mostly departed without so much as a glance at the retail options (217–18). It is quite possible that a similar fate might await the Beltline. Its costs may well exceed its benefits, it may be underutilized, and its probable uneven development may result in equally uneven usage.

TWO WILD CARDS

What I have further discovered in the course of this investigation is that two interest groups who hold enormous sway in the region are not always an easy fit with the Growth, Green, and Equity model. First, suburban groups cannot always be fully subsumed under the interests of those three groups. Although suburban interests tend in many cases to be growth oriented, when it comes to transportation policies they sometimes are not. In the MARTA case, for instance, suburban actors were interested in stemming the tide of urban expansion and in maintaining autonomy at all costs. This meant that from a suburban perspective public transportation should be contained and not encroach on counties outside the city. In the GRTA example, fears of encroachment were even more pronounced. Suburban actors felt that GRTA threatened home-rule prerogatives and had the potential to impose unwanted changes on local communities. In regard to the Beltline, little resistance has been evidenced from the suburbs as their interests do not (as of yet) seem to be directly concerned. Suburban interests and influence have been extremely salient in determining the fates of both MARTA and GRTA, however.

The other set of actors who do not fit neatly into the Growth, Green, and Equity trio are politicians. Political economy scholarship and regime analysis have alerted us to the fact that most often politicians, not least in Atlanta, ultimately cater to business interests, albeit through circuitous routes. Keating (2001) points out that while Atlanta's political and economic climates have shifted dramatically over the last several decades, the relationship between the two spheres has remained fairly constant, "Despite the reduced range of their powers, business interests continue to dominate city politics" (197). Similarly, one of the private sector transportation planners that I spoke with averred:

> I contend we are the most privatized city in the country. We have the weakest government in the country . . . just look at this stuff [pointing out the window]—the government had virtually nothing

> to do with this! Just look at the Aquarium—virtually nothing to do with it—not even—not only did they have nothing to do with it, they didn't even take the time to do the planning around it. All the planning was done by Central Atlanta Progress. I've sat down with the ex-planning director for the City of Atlanta, and said you know, I'm doing fifteen projects around the Aquarium and we're trying to hold these things together and have some continuity—but I can't BE the city! You've got to be the city—and you need to direct some of these things.
>
> Question: So you're saying that the private sector runs Atlanta?
>
> Absolutely!! Has for years! Back to the Woodruffs—and it's harder now, because nobody—because there's not a Dan Sweat anymore—there's not a Woodruff sitting behind the scenes pulling the strings—it's—the influence is so diverse now, it's complicated and difficult . . . and I say sometimes, we're successful in spite of ourselves.

This dominance of the private sector is nevertheless modified by and implemented through politics. An examination of political actors as separate and distinct from—yet interacting with—the economic sector is therefore useful. One of the most important ways in which politics informs transportation policy is through decisions regarding public versus private expenditures on projects. Mobility is distinctive in that determining whether it is a private good or a public right is not a straightforward proposition. Taylor (2004) explains:

> So-called pure public goods share three characteristics: (1) no one can be excluded from consuming them, (2) consumption by one person does not affect consumption by others, and (3) they can only be provided through collective action. But transportation systems lie on a continuum between pure private goods and pure public goods (295).

Taylor points out that most public transit systems were initially private enterprises and have only since become, at least in part, public because of the vast areas, large numbers of people, and times of day that they must accommodate. They still have private features in that "[p]eople can be excluded from transit vehicles, and consumption of transit capacity does affect others" (295–96). He contends that sidewalks are "pure public goods" in that "it is very difficult to exclude people from sidewalks. Sidewalks are only rarely congested, so use of sidewalks does not significantly affect others. And without public regulation, interconnected networks of sidewalks would not exist" (296). This complexity in determining whether transportation options are private commodities or public provisions informs the debate around who should pay for what in regard to mobility. Automobile usage is perhaps most difficult to disentangle because cars are private conveyances that carry people over public space. That space is heavily subsidized by the collective body, yet neither the vehicles nor the space they share have any of the other features of a public good; that is, both cars and roads allow for exclusion from consumption, and consumption by one person does affect consumption by others.

Whose interests are served by which kinds of movement, to where, in what conveyance, and toward what end all inform the debate as to whether public or private sources are the most appropriate for financing mobility. Taylor (2004:295) provides an array of salient questions in regard to this debate. Looking at them in turn, we can determine what the Atlanta answers have been in each case:

> Should transportation revenues be collected from user fees (such as bridge tolls, transit fares, or fuel taxes) or with more general instruments of taxation (such as income, sales, or property taxes?

In MARTA's case, the answer has been to collect fares from riders (user fee) and to get the balance of operating expenses paid through the one penny sales tax levied in Fulton and DeKalb counties (public contribution). GRTA's bus operating funding comes mostly through Federal Congestion Mitigation and Air Quality (CMAQ) dollars, soon to expire. How these buses will then be funded is as yet undetermined. In the case of the Beltline, a tax allocation district (TAD) is the funding mechanism. The TAD is a kind of compromise between private and public dollars, in that private bonds are purchased and then repaid by public dollars. As property values increase in the TAD area, property taxes increase, the revenue generated by this increase is then used to pay back the bonds.

> Should people pay for transportation systems based on ability to pay? Benefits received? Costs imposed? Should, for example, income-regressive sales tax revenues be used to pay for commuter rail lines that primarily serve high-income suburban commuters?

For MARTA, ability to pay has certainly not been the criterion. It has also been argued that benefits received has not been the basis for MARTA funding either, in that suburban residents receive ample benefits from MARTA but do not contribute to its major funding mechanism. In terms of costs imposed, it has been suggested that in the construction of MARTA, areas were cleared of black low-income residents (those who ride MARTA most) in order to augment its appeal for white riders (Keating 2001:108).

Additionally, poor service to low-income areas, uneven distribution of clean fuel buses, and inadequate service for disabled patrons have all been cited as sources of disproportionate burdens on low-income riders (Bullard et al. 2000). Thus, MARTA cannot be said to be priced by costs imposed. As for GRTA, the issue of how expenses are distributed across populations is becoming more salient as CMAQ monies come due for expiration. In the case of the Beltline, the TAD is an attempt to have transportation options paid for according to benefits received. In other words, those who live along the Beltline corridor will presumably benefit most from its amenities and will be the primary supporters through the TAD.

> Should streets and highways receive funding priority because they are so heavily used, or should public transit and bicycling receive priority to create more environmentally friendly alternatives to private vehicle use?

The Atlanta Regional Commission's Mobility 2030 plan details the regional spending projections. To date, the Atlanta region has chosen streets and highways as the funding priority. Nineteen percent of the $53 billion allocated for transportation expenditures is projected for transit capital and a scant 3 percent for bike and pedestrian initiatives; clearly, the emphasis for the region is still on highway projects. The bulk of federal money is for highway maintenance and expansion and nearly half (46 percent) of all the monies are to maintain the current infrastructure for all modes (www.atlantaregional.com/transportationair/2004/factbook). Additionally, the aims of the Congestion Mitigation Task Force and the new highway projects planned along the I-75 corridor suggest that that priority is not likely to budge any time soon. Within the city limits, the Beltline endeavor is an attempt to shift those priorities, but funding (as the ARC plans illustrate) is unlikely to come from government sources.

> Should transportation taxes and fees collected in one jurisdiction be spent in other places? If so, on what basis should the funds be geographically redistributed? Should transportation projects be distributed equally among states and jurisdictions, or should the most needed projects be funded first, regardless of location?

These issues of geographic equity have been knotty ones for Metropolitan Atlanta as well. The controversy surrounding the Congressional Balancing Bill (detailed in chapter 4) exemplifies the region's concern with the issue. The regional battles over MARTA (who pays in and who does not) and GRTA's suburban reception (spare us your "sprawl martial law") also speak to matters of distribution of transportation dollars across jurisdictions. In addition to funding determinations, politics shapes transportation projects in various capacities. In the MARTA case, local politicians advocated for it, the political process decided its jurisdiction through referendums, and state laws determined its powers. From MARTA's inception and throughout its life thus far, political actors (including the polity) have influenced its direction and not always in the express interests of business. For instance, the political decisions of the suburban counties to decline participation in the system by not paying into the one penny sales tax determined where MARTA would go. On the other hand, Cobb's and Clayton's representation on the MARTA board has been influential in setting its level of service and fare determinations. Additionally, public participation has been steadfast and has perhaps stemmed the tide of fare increases and service cuts that MARTA regularly employs. Although the public participation has by no means stopped these cutbacks, it has brought attention from broader audiences to MARTA's wounds, and perhaps the public meetings and protests have been instrumental in garnering action from the state through the ARC, even if that action, likely the reduction of MARTA's autonomy, is not quite what some of the advocates had hoped for.

In GRTA's case, the change at the state level from a Democratic governor to a Republican one was highly determinative in its trajectory. GRTA was created in response to significant air quality concerns under Governor Barnes. It was granted the authority to transform the region in potentially dramatic ways through land-use regulation and regional transportation coordination. With the change of administration, GRTA's goals (or at least its actions) became far less "green," and far more suburban oriented, focusing largely on moving commuters along the highway. The business community's reception to GRTA has been mixed. GRTA's powers over Developments of Regional Impact (DRIs), though untapped, were somewhat intriguing for in-town developers—for whom increased densities equate with a potential goldmine—and quite threatening for suburban development, which continues to rely heavily on automobile-oriented, low-density use of space. Inasmuch as GRTA's actions promote growth opportunities it is welcomed; to the extent to which it restricts such opportunities, it is viewed as suspect by growth promoters.

Political ties with the Beltline are also complex. Initially promoted by Cathy Woolard (a local politician), with an intensive study performed by urban planner Alexander Garvin, it continues to be backed by political leaders, including the mayor. Of the three, the Beltline project seems to be most straightforward in its alignment with growth interests, yet even this is complicated by the fact that some neighborhood and environmental groups fear that the development emphasis may detract from its aesthetic and "green" goals. Its funding mechanism (the TAD and other state and federal monies allocated for its capital and operating expenses) are and will remain politically charged as well. Monies that go to the Beltline, for example, are monies not going to other transportation needs, such as MARTA, road and bridge infrastructure, and regional transportation solutions.[2] In the development of a project such as the Beltline, politicians have the added burden of at least appearing to attend to Growth, Green, and Equity goals all at once—even when those goals seem to suggest actions that operate at cross-purposes.

Yet the Metropolitan Planning Organization—the Atlanta Regional Commission—largely responsible for coordinating transportation planning decisions for the region is not an independent entity. It is compelled to privilege some of those goals over others. The ARC is hardly a disinterested party, free to judiciously and objectively dispense planning decisions for the region. As Rutheiser (1996) points out in Imagineering Atlanta, "The ARC ultimately reflects the interests of the suburban politicians and developers who dominate the board" (288). Nonetheless, they are not entirely free, either legally or from public pressure, to ignore Green and Equity goals. While the discovery that there are some groups that do not fit easily into the Growth, Green, and Equity camps complicates the investigation, these three nevertheless remain useful categories of analysis. For suburban and political actors, issues of development (Growth), environmental concerns (Green), and problems of social (in)justice (Equity) remain the core social problems. These actors simply need to juggle them in different ways than groups that clearly privilege one above the rest.

THE CASES IN CONVERSATION

Paying fuller attention to the ways in which the cases speak to each other further enhances our understanding of the processes involved in urban decision making. Apparent contradictions become reconciled when viewed through this broader lens. For instance, taken in isolation it might appear as though developers' enthusiasm for the Beltline concept could represent a sea change in attitude, contradicting the idea that the business community promotes growth at any cost. This zeal for higher densities and walkable communities might be interpreted as signaling a shift in emphasis from unfettered growth to smart growth precepts. However, if viewed in concert with the other cases, the consistency of the growth position becomes apparent.

Smart Growth—Shmart Growth—So Long as We Keep On Growing

The business community has had somewhat of a schizophrenic relationship with MARTA. Developers at the outset loved the MARTA potential for downtown revitalization and expansion opportunities. In its earliest incarnation, MARTA was imagined as a vehicle for changing land-use patterns. The idea was that high-density development near rail stations would generate enormous growth. Steps were taken in this direction. For instance, Keating (2001) speaks of the city's hiring of Fred Blair, a renowned planning consultant, to help rewrite city ordinances in ways that would promote development near rail stations. The plan was to create zoning regulations that would allow for lower densities farthest from MARTA lines and high-density developments closest to stations (129). However, when it came time in 1976 for the ordinance to be implemented, the business community capitulated. Keating posits, "Forsaking their commitment to nodal development around rail stations, coalition members [of the City Council] argued instead for a laissez-faire approach" (129). They succeeded in defeating the ordinance and substituted for it one implemented in 1980 that allowed for high-density development in any of the city's business districts. Because this high-density development did not take place, MARTA has been unable to generate either the kind of ridership or the kind of downtown revitalization that early proponents had hoped for. "A laissez-faire approach to development has left the city with a rail system that has not significantly changed commuting habits" (130).

Largely due to these choices by the business community, MARTA was doomed to failure. "Instead of billions of dollars of public investment leading the way to a more sensibly and healthily organized region, the region's growth has condemned heavy rail to chase new development" (141). MARTA was then perceived (since little else was left to it) as providing limited and insular job opportunities and contracts for minorities and mobility for the poor and carless, transforming its image for some from that of "town darling" to that of "town demon." It was not allowed, for the most part, to provide occasions for large-scale development. There are now some opportunities through the Transit Oriented Development (TOD) nodules, which have thus far had limited success. In keeping with the growth orientation, developers are proponents of the TODs (as long as they do not seem to limit other growth opportunities).

In the case of GRTA, the Chamber of Commerce was instrumental in its creation, and has stuck with it, even encouraging the current Republican administration to allow GRTA to exercise its powers over land use. When I asked John Sibley if GRTA's powers had been curtailed under Governor Perdue (R), Sibley explained:

> Well actually over that period of time [since the Republican administration has been in office] the mission statement of GRTA has been reclarified, and it's become clearer than it was when GRTA was organized, for the transportation mission of GRTA to be done well, there also has to be a lot of thinking about land use—that you have to tie land use together with the transportation thinking to get the job done. And that GRTA has to take a role on the land use side is clearer than ever, there's a better understanding of that than there was, so that—I'm saying that because it's sort of counterintuitive, the shift from a Democratic administration to a Republican administration—you'd think—might think that it would

> have gone in the other direction—it has not. There's just been a continuing momentum in this region, led largely by the business community through the Metro Atlanta Chamber of Commerce, in the direction of understanding that you can't get transportation right until you get land use right. And, GRTA has come more and more to understand that, sort of intellectually, although GRTA—is not, uh, does not want to get overeager in that role, and is sort of very cautiously working out its relationships with the other major transportation agencies.

While this emphasis on tying land use to transportation planning has not been evidenced under the Perdue administration, at least in the conversations of business leaders, it is considered to be a sound principle. This clearly New Urbanist leaning might appear to be in conflict with the business community's equally zealous support of the Congestion Mitigation Task Force, an entity intent on highway expansion and automobile-centered solutions to transportation problems. Yet by scrutinizing the responses and behaviors over time and across cases, we can see that the business community demonstrates consistency in all these cases. Taking free-market capitalism to its logical and extreme conclusion—growth is growth, be it "smart" or unfettered is of little consequence, so long as it provides opportunities for massive development.

I Don't Want Sprawl, But I Want My Mall

Looking at Green goals across cases also sheds light on urban decision-making processes. In this instance, a cross-case examination helps us to recognize the concealed contradictions rather than the hidden consistencies. MARTA, GRTA, and the Beltline all seem to address, in relatively straightforward ways, Green goals. MARTA speaks to air quality and traffic mitigation. GRTA addresses these also and has the potential to do so more profoundly by changing land-use patterns. The Beltline is a Green dream—combining greenspace, transit, and housing densities in ways that support sustainability and urban re-imagining. The Trust for Public Land, a venerable national conservation organization, is fully immersed in the Beltline project—ideologically and financially. Transit advocates, the Sierra Club, the Center for Quality Growth and Regional Development, Park Pride, the PATH Foundation, the Atlanta Bicycle Campaign, Pedestrians Educating Drivers on Safety (PEDS), and many other smart growth proponents are eager Beltline backers. These smart growth allies also for the most part support MARTA (advocating for the state to do so more explicitly), and wish for GRTA to exercise its "greening" authority. There are no apparent contradictions in this scenario.

Yet the zest for greening transportation practices is not as clear cut as it appears at first blush. There is ambiguity in the embrace. I have alluded within this work to "smart growth laissez-faire style." To some extent, this is an oxymoron. Marshall (2000) notes that one of the precepts of laissez-faire economics is that the market "operates efficiently and for the benefit of everyone" (142). Yet, he points out, "Not only do markets not always maximize public or individual good, they actually often degrade it through the same mechanisms meant to produce value" (142). Marshall uses environmental degradation and traffic issues as two illustrative examples of instances in which "people all pursuing their maximum self-interest, make things worse for everyone, themselves included" (142). In the case of treatment of the environment he posits that "left to themselves, people and companies will pollute the air, water, and land to the detriment of all without some larger system of control" (142). And regarding traffic, Marshall notes, "Everyone trying to get to work quickly and easily by car creates a traffic jam where no one gets to work quickly" (142–43).

Marshall sees New Urbanism as just the sort of laissez-faire smart growth that I speak of. He writes at length about this connection, positing that New Urbanism has unique appeal for American sensibilities because it is free of restrictions. "Under its rubric, Americans are told they can eat their cake and have it, too" (37). Through its precepts it is possible to grow ever outward and simultaneously enjoy the fruits of urbanism. Marshall claims that New Urbanism supports the illogical proposition that we can build our way out of sprawl. He implies that Americans breathe a sigh of relief when presented with solutions that suggest bigger and more rather than restrictions and less. But, he asserts, if we really want workable cities, the only way to get there is through "such things as growth control, a big gas tax, investment in mass transit, prohibitions on parking. None of which are sexy advertising slogans" (37).

Yet laissez-faire-style smart growth is finally the only type of "smart growth" that is tolerable—or even imaginable—in a capitalist context. In speaking of GRTA's most "radical" powers, Jeff Rader (who worked with Alex Garvin on the Beltline study as well as having been on the initial staff of GRTA) informed me:

> There is an authority in there [in the GRTA statute] and it's, you know, expressed in a very convoluted way—but basically GRTA can deny access between a piece of property and the state or local transportation system. Now, what exactly does that mean? Probably you'd have trouble denying, you know, existing access, but what you might be able to do is, for instance, if they were going to do a development and they wanted a series of traffic lights or new curb cuts or something like that, that you would need to serve the vehicle demand there—they could probably undercut their ability to do that. And they can do it in a fairly unilateral way . . . Theoretically, you could say, no more access. I mean, you know, it's sitting there in the legislation. I think that there's obviously concern about using

> it and how you would approach that, but it's one of those pieces of the kitchen sink that [was thrown] into the legislation.

He further pronounced GRTA's powers "breathtaking," chuckled at the mere idea of them actually being utilized, and declared that "of course no one ever suggested implementing them." The cases show us that so long as "smart growth" does not interfere with the market, it is a welcome addition to growth options in the region. This explains the wide and warm embrace the Beltline is receiving. However, when new urbanist precepts begin to intrude into the market arena, as was feared with GRTA, the brakes are applied. Another eminent transportation planner (so fearful that his opinions might sound too Left-leaning that he did not want to be identified) displayed his own ambiguity by simultaneously aligning himself with and distancing himself from the "radical" smart growth position in the following statement about his onetime advocacy for the Northern Arc (outer perimeter):

> I used to be—not so much a fan of the outer perimeter—but a believer that the outer perimeter was essential for this area to be a reasonable place to live. Have you ever been up to state route Twenty in Cherokee County where it goes across the top in the afternoons? I mean, it is just one of the most miserable places on the face of this earth, in my opinion. And I finally got the point that after the people started fighting it, I finally concluded that, if you don't want it, why should we spend any money on it? If you want to choke up there, have at it, I don't care anymore! And maybe we shouldn't spend money up there in places like that. I'm not so far—I don't go so far as to believe with the Georgia Conservancy and the Sierra Club that you should choke people off in order to change the way they live, but . . . and I heard [it said once] at a speech . . . I thought it was kind of interesting—[the speaker] says, you can control land use through congestion, but when you get done you're not going to like what you have. So, I think you have to be careful sometimes.

What exactly is he saying? On the one hand, he is advocating for allowing—or even abetting—the situation (traffic congestion) to get so bad that people will be forced to make some other choices. On the other hand, he cautions that such actions might have consequences that are too extreme and undesirable, and further, he implies that such encouragement is coercive in an unacceptable way. What these and other respondents ultimately advise is to allow market forces to dictate land use and transportation planning.

In a similar vein, Jay Bookman, deputy editorial page editor for the *Atlanta Journal-Constitution*, wraps smart growth precepts in a cloak of free market language:

> The free market, left to its own devices, would produce growth patterns more like "smart growth" policies . . . since developers want to put as many units as possible on their property, because that's how they make the most profit. [Smart growth advocates] ask only that zoning laws be relaxed enough to allow smart growth developments to compete for customers, so that people can be given a real choice. Given the success of smart growth projects around metro Atlanta, when people are given that choice, they jump at it. (*AJC* 12/5/05)

Attempts to retrofit smart growth precepts into a free-market frame is one of the techniques employed to give smart growth a broader appeal. Another stumbling block for smart growth proponents is that even for environmentally conscious actors, there is the question of "walking the walk," demonstrating the courage of their convictions. As a planner from GDOT told me, "Everybody wants transit, but for somebody else!" In my own neighborhood, goodhearted, green-loving neighbors spoke out at a public meeting held by MARTA in favor of discontinuing the Number 3 bus run to the far end of our residential street, arguing that the noise of the bus frightened their children. Losing that battle to the louder voice of transit advocates, including a block of riders for a church that houses homeless men located on the same street, they later won the war by having a turnabout installed that prevents the passage of a bus. The Number 3 no longer services that stretch of road. Many of the same neighbors are strong proponents of the Beltline, the Peachtree Streetcar, and similar transit-oriented initiatives.

Similarly, "every" green-minded urbanite wants density—but not too much, too fast, or in the "wrong" places, as the current controversies around the Beltline development are teaching us. Change is good, but not too close to home and not with too much government interference, as GRTA illustrates. Sustainability is paramount, so long as it does not require too much sacrifice—lessons learned from MARTA, GRTA, and the Beltline. The cases help us to recognize the tension between what we want and what we can stand.

The Distance between Fair Play and a Fair Playing Field

Even more than questions of environmental sustainability, issues of social justice are a constant nag on a capitalist society's collective conscience. Even for those who espouse the free-market rhetoric most vociferously, equity discourses problematize and confound notions of market-driven decision making. Despite the pronounced tendency to sweep race and class under the rug, these issues stubbornly refuse to be silenced. They insinuate themselves into every transportation planning conversation. Most blatantly present in discussions of MARTA, which is almost code for minority and poor in the minds of many, race and class are "handled" through various techniques.

One technique is to never mention them directly—whichever side of the social justice divide you stand on. I have been to many transportation meetings in which the words race and class were never uttered, despite the fact that the issues being discussed often revolved around them. "transit-dependent" is a term often heard in such venues and geographic designations ("southside," "west-end") are often substituted for race and class. In addition to studiously avoiding using the words race and class, another technique is to adopt a fatalistic, resigned stance to the negative consequences of being black, or Latino, and poor. An area planner remarked:

> Where my wife taught school in the Decatur system—in the Oakhurst District, I mean, the gentrification is just rampant. I don't know how bad that is, how good that is—but it sure is something that's happened! It certainly—it might be unfair to some folks who could rent houses very cheaply when it was undesirable—but I want to think that it's better for all of us in general that it's happening! I guess! I don't know! I mean, I don't know where those folks go!

These statements imply that there really is nothing that can be done about it so we might as well hope that it is better for everyone in the long run. They also demonstrate a bit of shame and regret. For many, race is a dirty word and equity is impossible in the context of "freedom" or "progress." The most utilized technique for managing issues of social equity (other than pathologizing the poor) by planners and politicians is to assert that a rising tide lifts all boats. In regard to his emphasis on congestion mitigation, I asked Mike Kenn, "How does making congestion the main focus address the concerns of the least among us?"

> Well, that's what I'm saying is that—they go hand in hand—you know, one doesn't do well without the other. You know, I mean, transit—you have to develop a well-connected transit system that fulfills the need, not only for the transit-dependent population but for the business community. And you know what a consequence is for increasing the quality of life for the people who are transit-dependent? They get to be able to afford to buy a car!

Kenn was assuming that my reference to "the least among us" was speaking to the need for public transportation and responded by suggesting that congestion mitigation increases the quality of life, which is good for everyone concerned. A Chamber of Commerce representative also indicated that what's good for the area as a whole incidentally pulls up those on the bottom. In a similar discourse, Jeff Rader discounted poverty and venerated transit use out of desire (versus need) in the same breath—thus implying that those "few" who still need it will benefit from those who choose it:

> JR: We do have to recognize that personal mobility is now ubiquitous. Everybody's got a car. That's one of MARTA's big problems is they can't rely upon a captive market anymore because even, you know, people of very limited means end up having cars and if they're not treated well by the system and if it doesn't serve their needs, well, they just get behind the wheel of a car. But . . .
>
> M: There still are some transit-dependent.
>
> JR: Oh, yeah, there are absolutely, but they're a smaller and smaller as a proportion of the total population.
>
> M: Mmmhmm . . .
>
> JR: But there a lot of other cities where you are transit-reliant, not because you are unable to afford other means of transportation but because it's the best way to get around.

This trickle-down perspective on social justice issues was echoed in many of the conversations I had with planners and transportation authority representatives. Environmental justice advocates obviously hold a different view, asserting that it takes both a deliberate effort and a race and class-conscious lens to alter existing inequalities.

While no one wants to talk about race and class, they persist in remaining on everyone's mind (recall the words of an area planner who asserted, "Our racial problem is our biggest transportation problem in Atlanta! And we don't talk about it!"). Partly through the efforts of social justice actors such as Robert Bullard, we are constantly reminded that we really cannot delink race, class, and transportation. Additionally, a profound sense of fairness is as fundamental a part of the American ethos as a belief in hands-off government. Therein lies one of capitalism's deepest contradictions. Freedom and equity are like oil and vinegar; an appealing combination but resistant to smooth blending. Thus, fair play is held up as essential, but the creation of a fair playing field is viewed as coercive and counterproductive.

MARTA reeks of unfulfilled promises to the poor on one side of the tracks, and of too much service to that constituency on the other. GRTA's potential to level the playing field is unrealized (and perhaps unrealizable). The Beltline, unborn, is already plagued by equity issues in terms of the distribution of its benefits and burdens. Yet despite a larger conversation bent on marginalizing issues of equity, a quiet whisper endlessly echoes the word "justice"—a persistent reminder that triumph for some at the expense of others is ultimately no victory for anyone. The enduring ravages of transportation inequity, manifested by impediments to social mobility through physical mobility constraints, serve as capitalism's conscience and will not succumb to complacency. Fortunately, we need not depend entirely on abstract notions of conscience for these issues to receive attention. Laws and mandates also require that environmental justice be taken into consideration. As Chick Krautler, executive director of ARC, stated:

> Equity is a significant issue for us, it always has been, but it became more important when President Clinton signed an executive order [Executive Order 12898 in 1994] directing that transportation decisions take into account what's called environmental justice—making sure that one segment of the population, one area of the region, doesn't suffer or benefit more than others. And the Atlanta area has actually been a leader in that whole issue. We spent probably three years working with DOT out of Washington, to do an analysis of transportation benefits and burdens, that provided us with the guidance that we need to look at those issues as we develop transportation plans [here he is referring to the Environmental Justice Report, a subsection of the Mobility 2030 Report—discussed more fully earlier in this chapter].

While the executive director of the ARC explains that equity issues are of central concern in their planning process, it is also true that Metropolitan Planning Organizations such as the ARC have a specific set of federal mandates they must address when performing cost-benefit analyses for transportation planning. In his "Reflections on the Planning Process," Wachs (2004) cautions that traditional planning cost-benefit analyses make less tangible but equally pressing concerns quite difficult to address. Quality of life issues that do not lend themselves to easy measurement—such as freedom from noise pollution in our yards and knowing that children can go out and play without being run over—are not generally included in such analyses. Additionally, Wachs reminds us that the benefits of most planning analyses are aggregated, so that it may appear that an area as a whole is benefiting from a project or projects, but the analysis does not look at the sometimes significant minority that is suffering because of those same projects (143). Despite the fact that of the triad—Growth, Green, and Equity—Equity has the least economic clout and weakest political voice, through the diligent efforts of equity activists; a collective inner voice that reminds us of fairness; and laws of the land that dictate a modicum of environmental justice, Equity remains a force to be reckoned with and affects long-range transportation planning alongside Green and Growth goals, albeit in a second fiddle position.

When Clarence Stone did his reexamination of regime dominance in Atlanta in 2001, he concluded that the shift to regional concerns coupled with interest-group splintering had left little room for a coalition powerful enough to dominate local plans of action. In his analysis, he noted that the business community had transferred its gaze to the larger area, no longer primarily concerned with in-town projects and events. African Americans with influence were still interested in garnering benefits for their constituents, but found in the current climate that this was best achieved piecemeal, through "informal understandings." As for the residents of the upwardly mobile in-town gentrified neighborhoods, Stone implies that their erstwhile enthusiasm for progressive change for the most part had settled into complacency and NIMBYism. Thus, he asserts, with all the fragmentation and inertia, things are no longer accomplished through firm and longstanding alliances but rather through "cronyism and patronage" (27).

This study of MARTA, GRTA, and the Beltline lends support to some features of Stone's assertions, while problematizing some aspects of them as well. It seems evident that the regional concerns of the business community had a guiding hand in GRTA's trajectory, reining in its land-use powers in the same way that they had earlier restrained MARTA's prospects as a land-use tool. This only seems counterintuitive if we neglect the eminence of free-market ideology; while GRTA regulations could have provided wonderful development opportunities, they would have also constrained unfettered growth. Consequently, GRTA's course seems to have thus far been in keeping with the greater goals of laissez-faire capitalism, if not entirely, or obviously, in line with the short-range plans of area growth and development.

The ever-increasing awareness that MARTA must be drastically reconfigured is also, finally, a business-led realization. This too is influenced by the push toward regional concerns, because it is increasingly evident that the area needs transit beyond the city limits and MARTA is not the entity for the job. As a Chamber of Commerce respondent put it, the MARTA image is just too badly tainted. While GRTA could be perceived as failing to live up to its potential, MARTA could be framed as falling apart. Yet in both cases, the directions they have gone were neither haphazard nor inevitable; they were shaped predominantly by the business sector.

The Beltline is a local project, perhaps drawing developer interest back into the city in a way that nothing else has for a long time. This denotes a shift from Stone's observation that "the city has simply become less critical to the business sector than it was in the mid-twentieth century" (27). A strong coalition seems to have developed around the Beltline, simultaneously testing and reinforcing the alliance between city government and the business community, as was fully drawn out in chapter 5 on the Beltline. Altogether, the examination of these cases suggests that while fragmentation and regionalism inform the details of project development and implementation, the business-dominated urban regime is alive and well in Atlanta.

Having demonstrated how MARTA, GRTA, and the Beltline have provided a glimpse into Atlanta's profoundly mired mobility patterns, in the concluding pages of this volume I will return to my early assertion that, with a Marxian twist on a Marxist concept, "It is the consciousness of men [humans] that determines their being, and their social being that determines their consciousness." The validity of this contention has been well supported by what we have learned from the three cases examined. It can also be used as a guide in imagining transportation's possible futures.

DEUS EX MACHINA

As promised at the outset, I investigated the interplay between discourse (the consciousness of humans) and the built environment (the "social being"), keeping in mind the recursiveness of the relationship between the two, and demonstrating that transportation policies and practices both create and reflect the mode of mobility. Somewhere along the way, this Marxian journey took a Weberian turn, depicting a landscape so hopelessly bogged down in its own mobility quagmire that escape seems scarcely possible. Environmental degradation, danger, excessive auto-reliance, traffic congestion, and perhaps most especially unequal distribution of mobility's benefits and burdens portray a virtual "iron cage" of gridlock. Perhaps a return to Marx, extending especially on his sometimes quixotic optimism, will point to possible means of egress.

A number of innovative and creative thinkers have for some time been putting their minds to the task of rethinking how we traverse space. While none of these suggested, and in some cases implemented, alternatives have exactly captured the American imagination in an overwhelming way to date (due largely to the conflicted nature of that collective body as has been described in the preceding chapters), some are catching on in pockets, and even those that have not are worth considering. Some shifts are ideologically driven, and some are forced upon us by changed circumstances (again, reflecting the Marxian notion that we are both products and agents in and of our environment). The effect of rising gas prices on transit use is emblematic of accommodation to circumstances. Clifford Krauss (*New York Times*, May 10, 2008) notes that transit ridership has been slowly but steadily increasing in various U.S. cities over the last several years:

> Americans took 10.3 billion trips on public transportation last year, up 2.1 percent from 2006. Transit managers are predicting growth of 5 percent or more this year, the largest increase in at least a decade. "If we are in a recession or economic downturn, we should be seeing a stagnation or decrease in ridership, but we are not," said Daniel Grabauskas, general manager of the Massachusetts Bay Transportation Authority, which serves the Boston area. "Fuel prices are without question the single most important factor that is driving people to public transportation." (nytimes.com)

Yet we know we cannot rely entirely on gas prices to dictate our modal choices, hence the need for new visions. At one extreme of urban transportation planning are spaces configured almost exclusively for the automobile. Many American cities are prime examples of that variety of urban layout. For instance, "In Houston, Texas and in Detroit, over 70 percent of the urban space is made up of streets, parking lots, and garages . . . The architecture and urban design is relegated to an insignificant sideshow" (Hamilton-Baillie 2004:45).

At the other end of the spectrum are auto-free zones. Globally, there has been much experimentation with this notion. The term pedestrianization has been employed to describe converting a street or an area from one that accommodates automobiles into one that does not. Early examples of such efforts in the United States were pedestrian malls. There were a few cities that tried out this option in the late 1960s through the early 1970s. These included Ann Arbor, Michigan; Boulder, Colorado; Fresno, California; and St. Charles, Missouri, among several others. In these cities, certain malls were restricted to street traffic for several surrounding blocks and beautified with attractive amenities (fountains, playgrounds, public transit access, and so forth). The majority of these experiments failed to draw in the requisite customers and reverted back to their former configurations within twenty years (Auto-free zone 2005:2). One of the exceptions to this general rule of failure is the San Antonio Riverwalk, which continues to provide aesthetic and practical pleasure to shoppers and visitors. Such areas are far more prevalent (and successful) in other parts of the world. For instance, "A large number, perhaps the majority, of European towns and cities have made part of their historic centers carfree since the early 1960s" (2). Moving gradationally from both extremes—auto-dominated versus carless spaces—there are a wide variety of compromises, concessions, and experiments underway in many places aimed at de-centering the automobile, or at least ameliorating its ill effects.

The financial costs of automobility are remarkable. Even in the United States where both auto purchasing and fuel costs are lower than in many other (notably European) countries (even with the daily price hikes on gas in the United States in the late 2000s, the price of gas in Europe is still much higher), ever-greater percentages of the average household's income go to covering the costs of personal vehicles and their maintenance. This can be "as much as 22 percent of an average family's income yearly in such sprawling, auto-oriented regions as Houston, Atlanta, Dallas, Miami, Detroit, Minneapolis-St. Paul, and Phoenix" (Peirce 2001:2). And of course this hits some citizens harder than others; the lowest quintile of earners spends an average of 36 percent of their income on vehicles. This is money not being saved or spent on investments such as a home. Historically (though perhaps not so much in the current crashing economy), homes increase wealth whereas cars decrease it (2).

That speaks to the most direct effects of automotive costs. Indirectly, as has been explicated throughout this book, poorer citizens, who are also disproportionally people of color, are often further disadvantaged by transportation policies and procedures. Sanchez, Stolz, and Ma (2003) describe some of these indirect costs. They note that the privileging of highways over transit has historically meant development far from central business districts increasing both income disparities and residential segregation. Additionally, housing development in poor neighborhoods has lost out to highway development in those same areas. Monies allocated to transportation projects in poor neighborhoods have also increased property values in some communities, making the cost of living prohibitive for some residents. And finally, this highway-heavy allocation of transportation dollars has increased spatial mismatch—"the disconnect that occurs when new entry-level and low-skills jobs are located on the fringes of urban areas that are inaccessible to central-city residents who need those jobs" (viii).

Beyond these issues of spatial mismatch, gentrification, and economic isolation, the poor and people of color are underrepresented in transportation decision-making processes and in the transportation construction industry (Sanchez et al. 2003). The study conducted by Sanchez et al. in 2003 at Harvard University, "Moving to Equity: Addressing Inequitable Effects of Transportation Policies on Minorities," makes several recommendations. Among them are: increasing funding for public transportation; more emphasis on researching equity impacts of transportation planning; focus on the ties between land use, transportation, and social equity; attending to local needs and actors for local transportation projects; encouraging low-income and minority participation in planning processes; and fostering job opportunities for low-income minorities in the transportation industry (38–40).

Other (more car-centered) approaches to fiscal constraints on mobility include car sharing and programs to help low-income individuals purchase vehicles. In regard to car-sharing programs, variously referred to as Zipcars, common cars, flex cars, shared cars, or community cars, the CarSharing Network (www.carsharing.net) asserts that car sharing offers an easy, convenient, and inexpensive way to have access to a car without the burdens of ownership. They advise that "[i]f you drive less that 12,000 km (7,500 miles) a year . . . car sharing will likely save you thousands of dollars . . . give you greater mobility—and actually reduce pollution." This same source notes that as of December 2004 there were fifteen car-sharing programs in the United States with about 61,650 members and about 940 vehicles. Many of these programs seem to be geared toward middle-class and environmentally conscious consumers. More directly targeting low-income and minority individuals and families are the programs aimed at helping people purchase cars. It is often argued that, particularly for rural residents who have little or no access to public transportation, car ownership is a necessity. One such program is the "Wheels to Work" endeavor established in 1999 in New Hampshire. Here, the state offers tax credits to companies that get on board with the "Wheels to Work" program.

This latter approach (low-income auto programs) clearly favors resource distributions that privilege the existing arrangements. Programs such as this not only pose no threat to the current mode of mobility, but also reinforce both its precepts and its ability to continue unabated. Conversely, the recommendations laid out in the Harvard study challenge the underlying assumptions of automobile dominance as well as the taken-for-granted tenets favoring environments configured with built-in racial and class privilege.

The links between traffic and air pollution have become an enormous problem globally, and policymakers have been grappling with this issue for many years now. As evidenced in chapter 4, this air degradation also has implications for transportation funding for various locations and broadly impacts growth and development issues. Thus, many localities search for measures that will reduce vehicular impacts on air quality, including road pricing, no-driving days, and pushes for public transit use, some of which include land-use decisions. Much of the discussion on land use and regional ties to environmental issues has been well explicated in the preceding chapters. Here, I merely wish to emphasize some points relating specifically to environmental justice concerns. As Sanchez et al. (2003) note:

> While many lament the trend toward "suburban sprawl" as unaesthetic or damaging to the environment, those who support social equity should also be concerned about this trend. Substantial investment in highway development and other transportation programs that encourage private automobile use has encouraged and supported low-density developments that extend increasingly farther and farther from the central city and to residential and commercial areas that are increasingly spread out—edgeless cities. (1–2)

They assert that beyond the high cost of such development for local and regional authorities, this also impacts low-income residents socially and economically in terms of increasing residential segregation and spatial mismatch (2). Their report specifically addresses the need for land-use regulation and regional decision-making processes as essential in rectifying social inequities. They cite the emphasis on increased mobility via automobile use as culpable in maintaining inequalities. Also, in terms of regional issues, this report notes that the national suburban bias in transportation spending ignores the fact that "most of the nation's population is located in metropolitan areas" (16), thus deepening disadvantages. As noted throughout this book, the distribution of decision-making power profoundly informs emphasis and direction of decisions. As has been demonstrated in the Atlanta case, many MPOs have disproportionate suburban representation because of notions of "geographic equity." This arrangement impacts both levels of participation (with poor minority areas participating less) and decisions about where funding goes (less to transit in many cases) (Sanchez et al. 2003:33). These inequities in the distribution of burdens and benefits often affect life chances in personal as well as broadly social ways. One consequence of transportation inequities is a disparity in health outcomes. Many scholars place at least some of the blame for differences in asthma rates among racial and income groups at the feet of transportation decisions.

While some measures aimed at addressing these problems are relatively simple to undertake, such as converting bus fleets to clean fuel, others, like changing, strengthening, and/or enforcing rules and regulations, are more complex and long-range. These harder challenges must be faced and met however, if spatial equity issues are to be seriously addressed. Some other ideas about changing mobility patterns focus on the oft-neglected world of nonmotorized transport. In the Atlanta context, Sally Flocks of PEDs (Pedestrians Educating Drivers on Safety) told me some of the foci of her organization are: sidewalk maintenance; speed camera installation; working to get the GA driver's manual updated to include a more comprehensive section on pedestrian safety issues; deceleration lanes; and better enforcement of and changes to local speed limits, among others.

Such invitations to think about creating space for nonmotorized movement, implicitly (if not explicitly) speak to issues of density and a preference for turning our gaze away from the city as "carchitecture" (Holtz Kay 1997) and toward one reconfigured via rebuilding the environment for multimodal mobility. The perspective of the nonmotorized vehicle advocates departs dramatically from that of congestion mitigators. The former seek to de-center the automobile while the latter accept its centrality as a fact of life and merely ask what we can do to make it more bearable. This leads to drastically different interpretations and treatments of the landscape. Germane to this divide, Sally Flocks told me that "from a pedestrian perspective, traffic congestion is not a bad thing," because it slows drivers down and makes them more aware of their surroundings. For traffic reduction actors, this could not be farther from their desired results.

Many policymakers concern themselves first and foremost with congestion mitigation. This has certainly been the case in the Atlanta region, much to the chagrin of many social and political actors because the focus on congestion mitigation in no way challenges the automobile as the centerpiece of mobility. At the request of Governor Perdue, the Congestion Mitigation Task Force was formed in May 2005. This Task Force consists of two board members each from GDOT, ARC, and GRTA and two appointees from SRTA. Their mission was to reduce congestion by: emphasizing congestion relief and safety; utilizing quick-fix operational initiatives; identifying and prioritizing major capital initiatives to expedite; and adopting a congestion target against which progress will be measured (www.grta.org/news_section/2005_Articles/CMTF_Announcement.pdf).

Their goal was to come up with recommendations by December 31, 2005, and they had a public hearing on October 31, 2005, to get public input. I attended this meeting at which about forty people spoke (and more gave written comment). Without exception, all speakers spoke strongly in favor of the provision of more transportation alternatives. None spoke out for more roads, though many expressed fears that that would be the direction and focus of the Task Force. Several people spoke to the glaring omission of MARTA from the Task Force and remarked on how detrimental such an omission might be in light of the fact that MARTA is the backbone of the public transportation system in the region. On December 15, 2005, I received a communication in the mail from the ARC outlining the recommendations that the Task Force determined that it will send to the governor. The gist of the recommendations is very much in keeping with the road-centered approach to congestion management. There were three recommendations proposed. The first of these is that the Task Force recommends refining the current project selection process for the financially constrained Atlanta Regional Transportation Plan to increase the weighting of the congestion factor to 70 percent. This is up from its current weight of 11 percent, equal with other factors such as safety and air quality. Secondly, "The Task Force recommends that all four agencies [GDOT, ARC, SRTA, and GRTA] develop and implement a technically consistent and transparent methodology for cost/benefit analysis." The third recommendation states, "The Task Force recommends a Travel Time Index be used to measure improvement in congestion. The Task Force recommends a regional Travel Time Index goal of 1.35 by 2030 for the Atlanta nonattainment area." They go on to explain:

> The Travel Time Index is the ratio of travel time in the peak period to travel time in free flow conditions (speed limit). For example, a Travel Time Index of 1.35 indicates a trip that takes 20 minutes in free flow conditions would take 27 minutes in the peak (35% longer) . . . The Task Force proposes that a Travel Time Index goal of 1.35 be adopted or the Atlanta region. Movement towards this goal recognizes that some level of congestion is to be expected in a vibrant, growing urban area but that improvement can be made over current congestion levels and certainly over future expected congestion levels region-wide.

The communiqué also lists some of the ways in which they anticipate producing this Index level; "increased highway and transit capacity, improved incident management, operational efficiency improvements, flexible work hours, telecommuting and prompting land development initiatives that reduce vehicular travel."

The technical, efficient, goal-oriented, impersonal, and businesslike tone of this report, coupled with its content, made it perfectly clear that the focus of the Task Force will be on improvements of detail and that the automobile and its driver will be the recipients of any benefits accrued. Clearly, many of the fears expressed by respondents at the public hearing were realized. As seems to be the case with the Congestion Mitigation Task Force, typically, congestion mitigation efforts have to do with road treatments: expansions, additions, and modifications. The phrase itself transmits the paradigmatic perspective; relief for cars and their users. The total appropriation of the public realm for automobiles sometimes reaches the level of absurdity. A private sector planner told me:

> DOT says, "But our goal is to move cars and not people," and . . . and then you have some idiot from DOT who says, you know, "Yeah, we like to have our sidewalks as recovery zones for automobiles"! Or you know . . . things that just make you want to cringe!

The organization that lobbied heavily for the Congestion Mitigation Task Force in Atlanta, Georgians for Better Transportation, is a group that favors highway projects and believes strongly in roadway solutions to transportation impasses. For instance, when discussing transportation solutions with Mike Kenn, the head of this organization, he spoke of truck-only lanes as very important:

> Truck-only tollways . . . not only does it allow in freedom of movement, it would eliminate the safety issues relating to trucks interacting with cars, and the beneficiary of it would be the motor vehicles from a congestion relief standpoint. Because if you look at I-Two-Eighty-Five, and these are GDOT's numbers, if you took every tractor-trailer off of I-Two-Eighty-Five, you would reduce congestion by forty-two percent. Now there's not a traffic—a traditional traffic improvement, or transportation improvement out there that has that type of impact.

Notice the language employed regarding beneficiaries—"the beneficiary of it would be the motor vehicles." He had also talked about designated lanes for BRT. When I voiced concern about all of these restricted lanes resulting in sixteen-lane highways, he responded:

> No, because you don't have to build them out, you can build them up! You actually can . . . because of the advancement in construction technology, you don't have to build them on the ground, you can build them up in the air—and they can even hang over the existing general-purpose lanes.

Double-decking highways and designating lanes for trucks and commuter buses (not with the emphasis on relief for truckers and bus riders but rather to get them out of the way of automobile traffic) are his principal recommendations for relief from highway horrors. Another increasingly popular notion in efforts to reduce congestion is telecommuting. Mike Kenn also praised this option:

> Employers are asking a lot more from their employees now [in terms of] time commitment than they have in the past. I believe that business could have a tremendous impact on reducing congestion if they would change their antiquated mindset and allow eligible employees to telecommute. There's an unbelievable amount of people, because technology now . . . sole job responsibility now revolves around a PC, that they shouldn't be measured on what time they punched the clock, but [rather by] their productivity in relationship to doing their tasks on that PC—and you can telecommute from home. But there's an antiquated mindset of business that's fearful, very fearful to a certain degree, but they just haven't developed a way that they're comfortable yet to make sure that those employees are accountable for their production without making sure that they're sitting at their desk when they walk by to see if they're there. I think that that's got more potential than anything—anything we could do, to allow people to telecommute.

This respondent and many other transportation scholars posit that telecommuting and flexible work schedule options are forward-thinking and more likely to grant significant gains than either carpooling or public transit. There is much debate over the efficacy of these measures. Many assert that telecommuting is as yet too young for us to be able to adequately judge its potential. One relevant piece of information is that "work trips account for less than one-fifth of total trips" (Bae 2004:372). Additionally, whereas telecommuting does cut down on work trips, some studies have indicated that this reduction may be offset by an increase in nonwork trips (Giuliano and Hanson 2004:396). Social issues of isolation and inequity also must be taken into consideration in regard to telecommuting. The suitability of telecommuting varies by type of job, access to equipment, and importance (both personally and for the job) of face-to-face communication. There is also for some the fear of becoming "invisible" to their employers if they are physically absent too much of the time (396). Class and gender issues regarding telecommuting are also worthy of attention:

> [Holcomb] notes that for women with career aspirations, working from home might deny one the same opportunities enjoyed by those who are in closer personal contact with the job environment. More importantly, she observes that most of the women who work at home are involved in low-pay activities, such as data entry, catalog sales, ticket sales, processing insurance claims, and

> other routine tasks. Concerns over low job security, few worker benefits, and poor prospects for job advancement are at the root of labor union opposition to widespread adoption of telecommuting. (Janelle 2004:104)

On the other hand, this same author notes that despite the fact that "fears persist that the telecommuting option may exacerbate urban sprawl and related transport-generated pollution," this may be an unwarranted concern, because "findings show that telecommuting has had very little impact on choice of residential location; indeed, the telecommuters were more heavily concentrated in the larger metropolitan centers than the workforce as a whole" (Janelle:107). As noted, it remains to be seen whether virtual travel will have a significant impact on traffic patterns. What we can already determine is that the benefits and burdens of such "travel" so far follow the same patterns as physical travel—that is, the already disadvantaged seem to be further disadvantaged through its distribution. This alerts us to the fact that if we are to turn to information technology as a partial solution to mobility problems, we need to be attuned to the same social issues in this arena as in the ones we currently inhabit.

Another measure gaining currency, which has the double benefit of reducing congestion and generating revenues, is tolling. There are a number of appellations for and ways in which tolling options can take shape. Road pricing, congestion pricing, value pricing, cordon tolls, HOT lanes, and FAST lanes are among them. Freeing Alternatives for Speedy Transportation (FAST) lanes are a variety of HOT lane owned and operated by private companies who partner with the state. When I spoke with the then director of programming and policy at SRTA, Daniel Drake, he indicated that from his perspective tolling is the best possible way to ensure that drivers pay the true costs of driving. He also acknowledged that it is hardly the most popular way.

There are many other proposals and practices emerging around the country and the world that principally focus on congestion mitigation. Many of these creative ideas hold out real possibilities for changing the way we move about. A possible future would include numerous options employing feet, wheels, motors, and various sizes of conveyances, allowing for a mobility mosaic in urban, suburban, and rural settings quite different from that which we have come to think of as the only way. Such a re-visioning and reemployment of space brings us to the final set of solutions to mode of mobility problems.

Cityscape Renaissance

A quiet revolution is underway at the intersection of architecture and city planning. This fresh look at how to configure and utilize the spaces of mobility is essentially a psychological model based on the precept that "behavior follows design" and that traffic may be calmed and environments enhanced through the manipulation of space (Lyall 2005). This in itself is not a radical notion, as all planning is to some extent based on this idea. What distinguishes this new view from the traditional one is the deconstructive emphasis—aiming toward removing impediments to shared space. This vision of space uses the notion of the *woonerf* (sometimes just *erf*) as a jumping off place. This is a Dutch word which I have seen variously translated as residential yard; street for living; home zone; living street; legible street; environmental area; urban room; and self-reading street. The definition is best understood through example. The Dutch designer Hans Monderman has designed several such areas in parts of Holland that have been (counterintuitively) successful in reducing accidents and raising comfort levels. In a 2005 *New York Times* article, Lyall explains:

> He [Monderman] led the way to a busy intersection in the center of town, where several odd things immediately became clear. Not only was it virtually naked, stripped of all lights, signs, and road markings, but there was no division between road and sidewalk. It was, basically, a bare brick square . . . To make communities safer and more appealing, Mr. Monderman argues, you should first remove the traditional paraphernalia of their roads—the traffic lights and speed signs; the signs exhorting drivers to stop, slow down and merge; the center lines separating lanes from one another; even the speed bumps, speed-limit signs, bicycle lanes and pedestrian crossings. In his view, it is only when the road is made more dangerous, when drivers stop looking at signs and start looking at other people, that driving becomes safer. (4)

Monderman is by no stretch of the imagination a car hater: "[A]s a car enthusiast and owner of a driving school, he dislikes anything that smacks of a 'war against drivers'" (van den Boomen 2001:31). Monderman also eschews the term woonerf, which he associates with streets configured for pedestrians but relying on "traditional" traffic engineering techniques such as speed humps and speed limits. He distinguishes his vision from that of the woonerf, in that the latter relies on signs and standards to affect behaviors whereas his model depends on the removal of them (31).

Traffic engineers, for at least the last half-century, have been the dominant controllers of the majority of city-space. From the new design perspective, this makes no sense. "Traffic engineers [are] alone responsible for more than half the space between buildings in European cities, and often 70% of urban land in the United States. If anywhere should reflect our urban values and priorities, it should be our streets" (van den Boomen 2001:31). The British urban designer Ben Hamilton-Baillie is one of the leaders in this urban design revolution, and he emphasizes that it is this disconnect between traffic engineers and urban designers that has resulted in auto-centric and uncomfortable spaces for people. Hamilton-Baillie (2004), in keeping with the work of Hans Monderman, draws a distinction between "the traffic zone and the public realm." He asserts that traffic zones, like highways, are regulated, unsurprising, standardized, and relatively unvarying. On the other hand, what he refers to as the public realm inhabits the other end of the spectrum. Such spaces are "highly diverse, personal, and are governed by a complex web of ever-evolving social and cultural conventions. Cities are unpredictable, and rich urban environments offer surprise, serendipity, and ambiguity" (51).

The fundamental idea of the new urban design is to turn our notions of middle and edge on their heads by showing a third road, that is, neither a car-less nor a pedestrian-less environment, but rather one that is centered around sharing space. "Central to the approach . . . is the understanding that environmental context can strongly determine behavior, more powerfully than legislation and formal rules" (Hamilton-Baillie 2004:52). Thus, an environment that dictates for example, slow speeds, rather than a sign demanding one, is more likely in this view to meaningfully change behavior, for a number of reasons. Hamilton-Baillie notes that signs such as "'Caution: Beware of Pedestrians' are not only redundant but are demeaning to the intelligence. Monderman's work suggests they also result in accidents by absolving the driver from having to use intelligence and engage with his surroundings" (53). The importance of eye contact, which is impossible at high speeds, is emphasized as an essential component of urban legibility also. Hamilton-Baillie believes that "social rules and subtle messages" communicated through eye contact dictate use of space (54).

Many elements, both subtle and glaring, go into the creation of these kinds of spaces: physical markers (often in the form of art) that one is about to enter a "different" kind of place; subtle rises and falls in the pavement to draw attention to shared space; absence of a clear demarcation between walking and driving space (i.e., no sidewalks or streets in the traditional sense); and the omission of signs and symbols privileging the automobile. I offer one further example to help bring the concepts to life. In Christianfeld, Denmark, there was a high casualty rate at the town's central intersection with an average of three fatal or serious injuries per year. Rather than go the traditional route and put in more signs, warnings, and bumps:

> The notion of a "place" at the intersection has been emphasized through the surface treatment, the lighting columns, and the squared-up corners of the crossroads. It feels like the center of the town again. No special priority is afforded to direction of travel, and pedestrians, cars, buses, bikes, and trucks are thrown back on negotiating movement through eye contact. Many were surprised

> when records collected by the Danish Traffic Directorate . . . showed that not only had the KSI [serious injury] rate fallen to zero for three years, but the number of traffic backups during peak periods had also decreased. (Hamilton-Baillie 2004:56)

Hamilton-Baillie concedes that "[s]elf-explanatory streets of this kind are a distant dream for the USA or for the United Kingdom" (in van den Boomen 2001:31). Yet the notion that context and design ultimately guide and inform movement and behavior is a lesson worth learning. As Hamilton-Baille points out, "After all, nobody needs a sign in the living room saying 'Do not spit on the floor!' The architecture of your house and the values it reflects are enough to explain appropriate behavior" (in van den Boomen 2001:31). Streets, of course, are already quite "legible," most of them just tell a very different story. They inform us of a "pedestrian-beware" world, and, in concert with the discourse of the greater society, reinforce messages that speed and power win the day. They are also replete with signposts reminding us to consume goods, services, time, and space. To rewrite that story will take Herculean efforts and a will from the polity that is perhaps just beginning to emerge.

Returning to Atlanta, such dramatic twists in the road are nowhere in sight, yet the cases under examination in this volume certainly hint at recognition that some changes must occur due to changing demographics and priorities. What direction meaningful change will come from is still to be determined. MARTA certainly was not the unlikely savior, nor has GRTA proven to be that hero to date. The latest prospect is the Beltline. While the responsibility of pulling Atlanta out of its transportation-related quandary is far too large a burden to place on any one project, the successful accomplishment of such an enterprise might signal a shift in direction and commitment. It could serve as a catalyst for wider change in the region.

One might well ask, of course, what does the Atlanta Beltline project do, for instance, for a Cobb, Gwinnett, or Clayton County resident? The answer could be that it enhances the region as a whole by reinvigorating the core and attracting interesting and life-sustaining development to the area. The need for regional solutions to transportation problems is increasingly recognized by all actors. Toward what ends, varies with the holder of the lens. For "carchitecture" promoters (car-growth), regional solutions mean fewer restrictions, greater automobile mobility, congestion mitigation, and the capacity to attract businesses to the region. Representing this perspective, Mike Kenn notes:

> They [the business community] definitely need to be partners and stakeholders, because they are the ultimate beneficiaries of the improvements. When you've got a major investment in metropolitan Atlanta or in the state of Georgia, you want to make sure that

> you are operating in an environment that is least intrusive, least cumbersome, compared to competitors in other states. So from a business attraction and a business retention standpoint, the best investment and cheapest investment they can make is to support, you know, group or entities like us [Georgians for Better Transportation] that are focusing and addressing and proposing solutions to solve that problem . . . [I]f things improve their businesses grow and if things don't their businesses decline. Jobs go away, services go up, and the burden of underwriting the services now falls on the homeowner by property tax.

In that passage, he is referring to transportation improvements in general. As for transit, from this perspective the purpose of transit is to advance economic opportunities for those who are transit-dependent, and ultimately to allow them the prized social privilege of no longer needing to use it:

> You know, I mean, transit, you have to develop a well-connected transit system that fulfills the need, not only for the transit-dependent population but for the business community. And you know what a consequence is for increasing the quality of life for the people who are transit-dependent? They get to be able to afford to buy a car!

The focus of transportation dollars and initiatives, the thinking goes, ought to be on relief for the predominant mode of mobility: the automobile. As a Chamber of Commerce respondent expressed it:

> Our road infrastructure is at the point of breakdown now—with another two-point-three million residents coming by Twenty-Thirty . . . we'll see traffic up twenty-three percent by Twenty-Twenty, up somewhere around forty-six percent by Twenty-Thirty . . . Instead of spending about one and a half work weeks stuck in traffic if you're a commuter, you'll be looking at eighty to one hundred hours stuck in traffic a year. That's a long time to be away from your family, or your friends, or your hobbies, or whatever. Um, so we know that roads will be very important and they probably should predominate the spending . . . our transit patronage from a commuter standpoint, is some of the lowest in the country . . . um, but even if you look at the limited MARTA service area, we really can't expect to do better than a fifteen percent mode share . . . so eighty-five percent of the population is still going to drive . . . we need to recognize that.

From this business-as-usual lens, then, regional solutions need to center around measures that privilege and entice economic enterprise and infrastructure improvements that increase and enhance automobility for the greatest number. For the smart growth minded (Green), land use is the primary focus of regional solutions to transportation problems. Here, business interests are also centered, insofar as they correspond to shifting demographic patterns, and emphasis on issues of density. Jeff Rader, reflecting this perspective, says, "There's just been a continuing momentum in this region, led largely by the business community through the Metro Atlanta Chamber of Commerce, in the direction of understanding that you can't get transportation right until you get land use right."

Yet some environmentalists see a conflict in this arena between what the business community wants and what is ultimately the best way to grow the region. Brian Hager of the Sierra Club opines, "The Atlanta region does not have a mobility problem, it does not have a traffic problem, it has a land-use problem." He asserts that the problems plaguing the region—congestion, air quality, water pollution—will never be fully addressed because of conflicts of interest, with efforts that continue "taking more money from the pockets of Jane Q. citizen to put into the hands of road builders, engineers, or even transit providers that don't actually improve Jane Q. citizen's quality of life." In his view, area transportation projects, largely,

> [a]re not about improving transportation. What they're about is funding more construction—that's their number one goal. If you were trying to come up with a good user pay system, you'd use the existing highways, you'd put some toll lanes on those highways, you'd use the money from those toll lanes to pay for transit service in that corridor. That'd give people true choice and do more to deal with congestion than this expansion stuff that they're talking about. But the engineers and the road construction companies don't make money from that and they're the ones who are driving all of these projects—and driving so much of the regional decision making on this.

From this view, it will be difficult to align economic interests with land-use priorities, and yet there is widespread acknowledgment that land use must come first. Regional solutions must include transit, but transit follows land use, not the other way around. So in response to a question regarding a regional transit authority, the business-minded Jeff Rader noted:

> The real question is how do we get land use right that will support transit being a useful mode of transportation to people. And you know, from that perspective, we probably need a regional land use agency before we need a regional transit agency.

From the smart growth standpoint land use comes first, the business community must be brought into the fold, and regional solutions mean growing the region in a way that focuses not so much on congestion mitigation but rather on reconfiguring the landscape for mobility choices and for reducing harms to the environment. Finally, the social justice (Equity) lens sees regional solutions as paramount in order to address issues of spatial mismatch, reduce automobile dependence, and ensure greater parity of opportunity across social classes. As Robert Bullard expressed it:

> Regions are so important! We're not just individual little places, you know, we're not just Cobb County, or Gwinnett County, or Clayton, or city of Atlanta. We're so integrated and tied together that I think if we could create a regional system that would . . . work throughout, and work in a way that would tie our different places together—I'm talking place-space integration right now. In terms of making sure that, for example, our downtown somehow could be tied to these economic activity centers that are emerging and that have already emerged . . . the way the population has grown . . . to anticipate in 2030, for example, we're going to add a couple more million more people, if we somehow could shape that development in a way that could . . . channel people to the places that we were talking about trying to grow, as opposed to just saying that, well, you know—they're going to be growing anyway . . . you know what I'm saying? . . . So that we could support a way that would not just make everybody automobile dependent. That's doable, and it's doable right now—but I think it means sitting down and getting people together to say, okay, we're gonna make sure that the dollars that we spend on transportation, that a substantial portion goes into real transit—not just HOV lanes, and calling it transit. That to me is a big one.

So public transportation that actually benefits the public is a crucial aim from this perspective; a regional system that links people and places in a meaningful and just way. Another precept of this view is that the burdens of mobility's distribution should not fall disproportionally on the shoulders of the least advantaged. In this regard, Robert Bullard and the Environmental Justice Resource Center were parties to the air quality lawsuits against the ARC and the Environmental Protection Division (EPD). Bullard explained their involvement to me in this way:

> Yeah, we were involved in terms of the environmental justice piece and the equity piece. We worked with a lot of the civil rights groups and the environmental justice groups . . . because a lot of this stuff slipped off the civil rights agenda. You know, transportation has always been a civil rights issue, going back to Eighteen Ninety-Six with Plessey, and the Freedom Riders, and Rosa Parks and the bus

> boycott and all that stuff—so we got them to thinking, that the money that's being spent on roads—and very little on transit—you know, you're basically subsidizing roads [to take people] way out—and you can't even get to the jobs cause the jobs have left so we say, okay, we need to put this back on the agenda and three or four of our groups joined in with Sierra Club and the other groups on the air quality thing, and we also made sure that the equity piece was in there, in terms of making sure that—who benefits, and who is paying the cost, and how the benefits are distributed, and what we were able to do is . . . very innovative and creative, in terms of getting transportation planners and decision makers thinking about benefits, since [the thinking was] most everybody benefits—well everybody is NOT benefiting—there are some people who are paying the cost and paying . . . the price in terms of externalities, but in terms of benefits, they're not getting any benefits, and so we got them to start thinking about this.

Seen through this lens, a substantial component of the lawsuits, and of the transportation equity movement in general, is about consciousness raising. It is about bringing these issues to the table, allowing silenced voices to be heard, and drawing attention to taken-for-granted assumptions about beneficiaries and benefactors.

For the Atlanta region, it is clear that Growth, Green, and Equity goals are the competing strands of the mobility braid. Interestingly, the term three-legged-stool is often employed in discussions of transportation planning. This shared metaphor does not always share the same legs. The different appendages on the stools described reveal both the confluence among and distance between the driving aims of growth, green, and equity actors.

For car-centered growth advocates, I draw on the words of a Federal Transit Administrator, Jennifer Dorn, spoken at an annual American Association of State Highway and Transportation Officials (ASSHTO) meeting in 2001. Dorn's three-legged stool consists of: "safety and security; economic vitality; and personal mobility" (www.fta.dot.gov/2639_5720_ENG_printable.htm). This seems a neat summation of the perspective demonstrated by highway lobbyists, GDOT, some Chamber of Commerce members, and other area car-growth actors. Ryan Gravel's three-legged stool, emblematic of the smart growth view, includes "greenspace, redevelopment, and transit." For Robert Bullard, embodying the transportation justice perspective, the stool's legs are: "environment, economics, and equity."

While they all share an economic component, the word choices are telling. For the car-centered it is "economic vitality," invoking notions of growth and development. For the green-minded, it is "redevelopment," the emphasis being on reconfiguring the built environment in a more sustainable fashion. For transportation equity actors, it is "economics," drawing our attention to the political economy and mindfulness regarding who benefits. It is also noteworthy that for all three, by coincidence or by design, this component falls in the middle of their list—the pivotal position.

The first component for the "carchitects" is "safety and security," for the sustainability camp, it is "greenspace," and for those forefronting transportation justice, it is "environment." Again, we can read different messages in these expressions. The concept of "safety and security" reflects an emphasis on protection of persons and places—of maintaining the status quo. The "greenspace" appellation tells us that these actors want attention to environmental and aesthetic concerns to be paramount. The choice of the word environment from the equity promoters is intended to invoke notions of both sustainability and environmental justice.

The third leg also goes by three names, each remarkably emblematic of the positions of those who utter them. For the car-growth minded, even when talking about transit, the accent is on "personal mobility." As we have seen throughout this book, this "right" is almost sacred—profoundly embedded in the American ethos. For the green growth group, "transit" is representative of moving away from obscene fossil fuel consumption and toward, as is the fashionable phrase these days, "live, work, and play" communities. Lastly, for those who believe issues of social justice must be at the heart of transportation planning, "equity" is the operative word.

The blending of these three positions seems rather unlikely, as they are, in some aspects of their ideological stances, mutually exclusive. The economic leg of the stool has been the point at which there have been the most attempts at convergence—the notion of "allowing the market" to dictate an environment that accommodates growth, green, and equity goals. The problem is that unfettered growth supersedes and excludes other aims and has so far won the day in the Atlanta region's transportation landscape. For the Beltline to become anything other than a "gentrified doughnut," or for any other project with profound mobility implications to be more than a Band-Aid, will require a paradigm shift that has not yet arrived. In this vein, the executive director of the Atlanta Regional Commission, Chick Krautler, expressed his frustration with regional politics and priorities in speaking of the Georgia Department of Transportation:

> Well, you know this is a Department of Transportation—but it's never built a transit system! It's trying to build a commuter rail system and while I think long-range commuter rail may wind up being a valuable piece of the puzzle, it's not what we need short-term. We need better connectivity within the region and, you know, I don't think—if we had all the money in the world, commuter rail to Athens or commuter rail to Bremen, would be a great thing to have—to me it's not the high priority, but that's where there's

> certain elements of the Department of Transportation—that's the only kind of transit that they're dealing with! And that leaves the issue of, well, then who is going to do everything else?!

The emphasis on distance consumption at the expense of reasonable access within and around the city is only a piece of the frustrating agenda. In his view, worthy projects are at best underfunded, and at worst thwarted by inattention and lack of cooperation from authorities:

> I mean, we're doing the engineering and environmental work on the transit system on Two-Eighty-Five North, GRTA is doing the engineering and design work on the transit system on Seventy-Five—and Cathy Woolard and a little band of—of—committed people, passionate people, are really doing the planning work on the Beltline right now—and Michael Robinson and a group of passionate people are doing the work on a proposed streetcar line for Peachtree Street! Well, it's great that we've got—if we didn't have passionate people moving these things forward they wouldn't be moving forward at all!!!

In Krautler's estimation transit is crucial to moving the region forward, and support from the government is the only way to achieve it. He expresses the need to propose plans, despite the better judgment of the agency, that do not really achieve the goals they see as most significant, for fear of making promises they simply cannot keep:

> So, that I think is the key, I think that is just SO important—is to figure out how we're going to institutionalize the development and operation of transit. You know, four years ago when we adopted the last long-range transportation plan, we got sued by the environmentalists, because they said we fudged that air quality stuff, and we didn't do this and we didn't do that, and we won the suit. But one of their allegations was, that you were planning for transit that you could not build. And to some extent they were right! Now, we won the case, we won the case, we moved forward and while we've got a long range transit plan built into Mobility Twenty-Thirty, if you look at the funding there's very little transit with any funding allocated to it because we don't want to make the same mistake—we don't want to promise transit we can't build . . . we're trying through our study to at least get some proposals to lay on the governor's desk and say, you know, what are you in the legislature going to do about this because they're not issues that we can deal with at the local level!

If the MPO is unable to leverage the clout to push through policies that even modestly shift the mobility patterns in the region, what hope is there for more marginal actors?

The politics of race and regionalism are so firmly entrenched in the fabric of the Atlanta decision-making bodies that escape from "carchitecture" seems distant and improbable. The commodification of movement appears alive and well. The "status of distant things," coupled with the fear of democratization, keeps palms greased and wheels rolling. Despite vocal, compelling, and reasoned opposition (and despite my attempt at Utopian propositions to the contrary), mobility fetishism—with its attendant car-centered panorama and its uneven distribution of impediments and advantages—is likely to reign in the Atlanta region for quite some time to come.

APPENDIX A: METHODS

My sampling choices for interviews were based on the decision to speak with civic, political, and economic actors in the transportation arena. The literature on transportation decision making suggests that these three sectors are crucial to the process (Stone 1989; Marshall 2000; Giuliano and Hanson 2004). My sample was purposive (that is, I selected respondents on the basis of their expertise and/or interest in the projects under study) and in some cases snowballed (meaning some respondents referred me to others who they believed might add valuable information to the study). I spoke with people who were in positions of authority and/or influence in the agencies (MARTA, GRTA) and project (The Beltline) I was studying. I also spoke with representatives of other area transportation organizations (SRTA, GDOT, ARC), as well as grassroots and/or lobbyist organizations whose aims were primarily or prominently engaged with transportation issues (Georgians for Better Transportation, Sierra Club, The Environmental Justice Resource Center, Center for Progressive Transit, Pedestrians Educating Drivers on Safety, conservationists, homeless advocates) and also Chamber of Commerce Transportation Division members. I then spoke with other area actors as suggested to me by those respondents who were believed to have an intimate knowledge of, or influence over area transportation decision making. For instance, one private sector planner was recommended to me by three different respondents as someone with voluminous knowledge on area transportation matters.

I continued interviewing until I believed that my investigation had reached the point of saturation (twenty interviews). That is to say, I stopped when I was no longer learning anything new from respondents. The respondents were all between the ages of twenty-five and sixty. All were educated beyond high school and professionals (thus middle-class). Thirteen of the respondents were white males, three white females, one Latina and one African American female, and two African American males. This overrepresentation of white males and exclusion of poor people is in keeping with the area transportation decision-making body. As my focus is on the decision-making process, and only implicitly on the experiences of recipients of those decisions, for the purposes of this work I chose not to interview the transit-dependent, or nonprofessionals in general, but rather focused on the elite who constitute the planning regime (see Appendix B for a fuller description of the respondents).

I conducted open-ended interviews, allowing the respondents to lead me in new directions when appropriate, but guided by my primary concerns regarding power negotiations within transportation decision-making processes. Appendix C is a sample interview guide. The interviews ran between forty-five and ninety minutes. Some respondents and I continued to communicate by e-mail, and I spoke with one respondent in person one additional time for another hour (the initiator of the Beltline project). Several respondents also had me on their mailing lists, so that I received general communications about transportation work that they and/or their groups were conducting. Several of these communiqués led to further meeting attendance (for example 9/29/05 Inner Core Transit Feasibility Study meeting).

In addition to area meetings and symposia, newspaper articles and communiqués from a wide variety of transportation-related agencies—these interviews were further supplemented by my involvement in a transportation-centered fellowship (GSU Urban Fellowship) running Spring 2005-Spring 2006. This fellowship brought speakers to a small group of scholars in an intimate setting, allowing for intensive question and answer sessions, as well as the opportunity to hear speakers such as Governor Roy Barnes, GDOT Commissioner Harold Linnenkohl, and Tom Weyandt of the Atlanta Regional Commission expound on current transportation issues.

APPENDIX B: THE RESPONDENTS

Anita Beaty—Executive Director, Metro Atlanta Task Force for the Homeless

Bill Bolling—Executive Director, Atlanta Community Food Bank

Robert Bullard—Ware Professor of Sociology and Director of the Environmental Justice Resource Center, Clark Atlanta University; author and expert on environmental justice issues

Daniel Drake—Director of Policy and Programs, State Road and Tollways Authority (SRTA)

Sally Flocks—President, Pedestrians Educating Drivers on Safety (PEDS)

Nathaniel Ford—Chief Operating Officer, MARTA (resigned 11/05)

Ryan Gravel—Belt Line Partnership; originator of the Beltline concept

Brian Hager—Director, Georgia Chapter of the Sierra Club

Matthew Hicks—Associate Legislative Director, Economic Development and Transportation, Association County Commissioners of Georgia (ACCG)

Mike Kenn—President, Georgians for Better Transportation

Chick Krautler—Executive Director, Atlanta Regional Commission

Joseph Palladi—State Planning and Program Administrator, Georgia Department of Transportation

Jeff Rader—Currently with Quality Growth Associates; former Executive Director, Regional Business Coalition; former Transportation Manager, GRTA

Rebecca Serna—President, Citizens for Progressive Transit

John Sibley—President, Georgia Conservancy

Four respondents chose to remain anonymous: a Chamber of Commerce representative; a transportation expert with involvement in various of the projects I interrogated; an influential private sector transportation planner; and a GRTA representative.

One respondent, though granting me permission to use his name, made statements during the course of the interview that I believe he would prefer not be linked with his name; therefore, I have chosen not to use it. This was someone with MARTA connections.

Additionally, I had the opportunity to hear speeches from and ask questions of several area transportation actors in a semi-private forum, through involvement in the Georgia State Law School Urban Fellows Program, a component of the Center on the Comparative Study of Metropolitan Growth, as follows:

1/20/05—Governor Roy Barnes

2/21/05—GDOT Commissioner Harold Linnenkohl and State Senator Mitch

Seabaugh

3/21/05—Greg Dunn, Georgia Commission Chair, Fayette County

4/18/05—Tom Weyandt, Director of Comprehensive Planning, Atlanta

Regional Commission

9/12/05—Luz Borerro, city transportation planner

10/17/05—Cathy Woolard, BeltLine Partnership, and Jim Langford, Executive Director, Trust for Public Land

11/14/05—Dr. Catherine Ross, former Executive Director of GRTA, current Director and Harry West Chair, Center for Quality Growth & Regional Development

8. 11/28/05—Dr. Truman Hartshorn, Atlanta transportation scholar/expert

APPENDIX C: SAMPLE INTERVIEW GUIDE

Tell me a little bit about this organization.

How long has [this organization] been in existence?

What is your role here?

How is [this organization] funded?

What is the primary goal of this organization?

What is the relationship of [this organization] to others [GRTA, MARTA, GDOT, etc.]?

Is there conflict between this and other organizations? How do you work to resolve it [when it arises]?

What is the role of public involvement in your planning process?

What about issues of equity?

What role do land-use considerations play in transportation planning?

In your opinion, what is the role of GRTA?

Can you tell me a bit about GRTA's history?

Talk to me about MARTA.

What about MARTA's struggles?

What is your impression of the Beltline Project?

In your opinion, what is the biggest transportation challenge in the Atlanta area?

What is your dream transportation scenario over the next five or ten years?

What is the biggest obstacle to realizing that dream?

NOTES

CHAPTER 2. THE TRANSPORTATION TRIO

1. This city ordinance banned the use of small dwellings in alleyways, which effectively eliminated much affordable housing for African Americans that had once been used as servants' quarters in many instances.

2. This administrative body (USHA) existed for only a three-year period from 1937–1940. It was a "New Deal" agency whose focus was public housing for poor inner-city United States residents.

3. This role of the state may be even more central in places outside of the United States, as, for example, Jonathan Davies (2003) points out in his article, "Partnerships versus regimes: Why regime theory cannot explain urban coalitions in the UK."

4. In 2005, Joel Rast published findings from a study of the Local Industrial Retention Initiative (LIRI) in Chicago. This was a case study performed in part to determine if "Imbroscio's optimism about the regime altering capabilities of alternative economic development" (54) was supported. Rast also wanted to find out whether Stone's cautions about overreliance on the economic side, to the neglect of a focus on coalition building, would be borne out in this study. Rast found that they were both right, noting, "In the case of the LIRI program, alternative economic development ideas had an impact, but only because they were advanced by a group of actors that held resources useful for governing" (66–67). Thus, Rast contends that there are valuable lessons to be learned from both Imbroscio's and Stone's positions. Looking at actual cases such as the one he studied, Rast asserts, will further the usefulness of regime theory. He notes:

> We should learn from such experiences. Programs such as LIRI may appear to be relatively modest innovations. Over time, however, they may point to new possibilities for more democratic urban governing arrangements of the sort that both Stone and Imbroscio seek. (67)

5. Mobility fetishism here refers to the global intensification of increased speeds and hasty departures from one place to another for no compelling purpose–movement for movement's sake.

CHAPTER 3. MARTA

1. According to the MARTA Web site: "Metropolitan Atlanta Rapid Transit Authority Act (S.E. 102) became a law having passed the Georgia General Assembly

205 to 12. It set up the agency to bring rapid transit to reality but required local referendum in the five counties and the city of Atlanta before the agency could begin operation. [In June 1965] the local referendum ratifying participation in the Transit Authority failed in one metropolitan county [Cobb] getting 43% of the vote and succeeded in the other four counties and the City of Atlanta getting 70% of the vote" (www.itsmarta.com/about/history01.htm).

2. From Bayor (1996) notes, p. 294: "Maynard Jackson and Leroy Johnson, representatives of the Atlanta Coalition on Current Community Affairs, to members, board of directors, Metropolitan Atlanta Rapid Transit Authority, 1 July 1971, Box 68, Mule to Marta Papers, AHS."

3. Metropolitan Atlanta Rapid Transit Oversight Committee (MARTOC) was created in 1973 by the Georgia General Assembly to oversee MARTA's fiscal operations—its further role is as ombudsman for the public (http://www.legis.state.ga.us/legis/2001_02/fulltext/hr395.htm).

4. Cobb Community Transit (CCT) had an average weekday ridership of 11,951 as of 2004, with Clayton County Transit (C-TRAN) averaging 1,171, Gwinnett County Transit (GCT) at 5,290, and the GRTA express (Xpress) carrying about 1,087 persons per weekday (www.atlantaregional.com/transportationair/2004factbook).

5. A major bargaining chip used to garner African American support for MARTA in the early days (starting in the 1960s) was the promise of a rail spur to a public housing development called Perry Homes that was located on the far west side of Atlanta and housed about three thousand low-income African Americans. In classic "white man speak with forked tongue" fashion, this vow was broken again and again, always with solemn oaths that it would one day become a reality. A spur reaching part way to this area was finally built in the 1980s. The full extension has yet to arrive (Keating 2001:131–41).

6. The four meetings were held: 12/13/01, City of Roswell Council Chambers; 12/18/01, DeKalb County Maloof Auditorium; 12/19/01, MARTA Headquarters Building in Atlanta; and 12/20/01, Atlanta City Council Chambers. These meetings were attended by concerned citizens including representatives of community action groups, concerned clergy, politicians, and a multitude of riders—elderly, disabled, homeless, and their advocates.

7. Between 1988 and 1993 about 17.3 percent of MARTA contracts were awarded to minority business enterprises. In 1993, nearly 70 percent of MARTA's full-time workers (n = 3,710) were black, mostly male, with good representation of black males at all levels—e.g., 50 percent of officials and/or administrators being black males (Davis 1997: 93–94).

8. "The C-Loop Concept, derived from the efforts of U.S. Representatives Cynthia McKinney and John Lewis (1998), focused on the development of transit access and connectivity to major activity centers, employment centers and points of interests. These points of access include the Clifton Corridor (Emory Complex), Atlantic Station, the Northside Drive corridor, Georgia Institute of Technology, the Atlanta University Center complex, Turner Field, Zoo Atlanta/Grant Park and South DeKalb Mall" (from www.itsmarta.com).

9. By "perception of a special right-of-way," this respondent meant that when there is a designated lane for public transit (either because it runs on rail or because a traffic lane is set aside for it, or at most shared restrictedly, as in an HOV lane)

the public is more likely to ride than when public transit shares space with general traffic.

10. The one penny sales tax is due to expire in 2030, increasing the pressure for area transit authorities to arrive at funding solutions as rapidly as possible.

11. The split from the one penny sales tax between capital and operating expenses for MARTA is frequently renegotiated in the state senate. For instance, in 2002, House Bill 1245 allowed for 55 percent of the revenues from the sales tax to be spent on operating expenses and 45 percent on capital expenses, changed from the previous fifty-fifty split. Currently (February 2006) two bills (SB 114 and SB 115) have just passed the Senate and are now awaiting the House approval that would again allow for the fifty-five–forty-five split, and even to go beyond and recapture some capital income as operating revenue when needed. If the bills do not pass, the sales tax distribution will revert to the fifty-fifty split (www.itsmarta.com/newsroom/press_releases; AJC January 9, 2006:4C).

12. In January 2006 a Transit Planning Board (TPB) was created to perform a two-year study addressing regional transit problems and solutions for metropolitan Atlanta. At the conclusion of the study, the board will provide recommendations for how to proceed, which may include the creation of a "superagency" to manage regional transit. See postscript to chapter 4 on GRTA for further detail regarding this planning board.

13. In College Park, a community near Hartsfield-Jackson Atlanta International Airport, MARTA is working with Enterprise Construction Co. Inc. to build a three-hundred-room hotel and an office park on MARTA property adjacent to the College Park MARTA station. TOD-like development is planned for many other places as well. For instance, Carter & Associates is planning an office building at the Medical Center Station; Harold A. Dawson Inc. has plans for 132 townhouses across from the Hightower MARTA station; the Integral group plans offices, lofts, and condos near the Ashby Station; and there are plans for mixed-use development at the North Springs Station (www.allbusiness.com/periodicals).

CHAPTER 4. GRTA

1. The thirteen counties were: Cherokee, Clayton, Cobb, Coweta, DeKalb, Douglas, Fayette, Forsyth, Fulton, Gwinnett, Henry, Paulding, and Rockdale.

CHAPTER 5. THE BELTLINE

1. Mason's mindset regarding suburban development is well illustrated in his remarks about Gwinnett County, his home and long-time area of development focus: "They ran the environmental people out of here a long time ago. You've got no trees. You've got no streams. You've got no mountains. It's a developer's paradise" (Kunstler 2001:41).

2. "Workforce housing" seems to be the latest appellation for low to moderate income housing. This is very telling in that it situates housing affordability squarely in the arena of production and consumption and who does which for whom. Having workers close to consumers once again becomes more compelling when the

current trend for many middle-class people is to live in-town with more close-by amenities.

3. The Northern Arc was a proposed highway project under Governor Roy Barnes's administration. It was to be a $2.4 billion addition of fifty miles of highway advocated by some as a means of traffic reduction in anticipation of the predicted massive new growth coming to the region. The Arc would have cut through four northern metro-Atlanta counties. It was soundly defeated through the efforts of an unlikely coalition of conservationists, smart growth advocates, suburban lifestyle proponents, and environmental justice activists—each with their own reasons for opposing it.

4. The Omni International complex never really got off the ground in the way in which developers (especially Tom Cousins) had hoped. As Allen (1996) reports, the hopes for the complex were very high; coupled with the MARTA station put in to deliver people to this site, it was expected to attract producers and consumers alike in vast numbers. The shops, skating rink, video arcade, and so forth did not draw the white, middle-class clientele anticipated: "As the weeks and months passed in 1980, the expected surge of white patrons at the Omni International failed to materialize. Cousins held out as long as he could, clinging to his fantasy, until at last the harsh realities of life in the heart of downtown Atlanta overtook him. Lenders disappeared. Federal grants withered with the advent of the Reagan era. Omnisouth languished on the drawing board. The block of land Cousins had assembled next to the Five Points station fell into foreclosure" (218). As for Underground Atlanta, its fate, also MARTA-related, has been similar. In the 1970s Underground went out of business for lack of interest, and although it reopened in the 1980s, it has always struggled, never reached the levels of attendance hoped for, and tenants have fought hard to keep their doors open" (Allen 1996:243). For a discussion of MARTA, see chapter 2 in this book.

5. "King Plow has been transformed from an antiquated plow factory into an arts community and center for commercial, performing and visual arts. In 1990, the owners designed a plan to build affordable Live/work studios, commercial artist spaces, art galleries, areas designed for the performing arts, and a restaurant within the buildings while preserving their historic and architectural significance. The project started with eleven different buildings. Several of the buildings were built at different periods of time throughout the Plow Company's existence. The oldest, as well as the only two-story building, was built circa 1890. Most of other buildings were built between 1936—38. Because of the different types of architecture involved the renovation of the building created spaces that are truly unique" (www.artery.org/KingPlow.htm).

6. As discussed later in this chapter, the TAD was approved prior to January 31, 2005.

7. This notion that real estate tax assessments are bogus in the region is predicated upon ongoing scandals in the Fulton County tax assessors' office regarding properties being appraised well under market values.

8. In 2001 the number of motor vehicles per household was 1.9, and of course considerably higher as income rises. Overall, 37 percent of households own two vehicles, and 21 percent own three or more (Pucher 2003).

9. Buckhead is a highly developed area of town with high rises, mixed-use sites, and an upscale and diverse nightlife.

CHAPTER 6. CONCLUSION

1. Throughout this document I have been using the word *equity* as synonymous with social justice. In the world of transportation planners, this is not always, or even most commonly, the understanding of the term. At least three types of equity are frequently referenced: geographic, individual, and group. Geographic equity refers to how transportation spending is distributed across jurisdictions (states, counties, legislative districts, and so on). Individual equity relates to how residents, voters, travelers, and so forth are priced or taxed in relation to the costs of travel on society. Group equity is the kind I refer to simply as equity in this context—having to do with how benefits and burdens of transportation policies and practices are distributed across races, ethnicities, and classes of people (Taylor 2004:300).

2. While this scarcity argument has been put forth by environmental justice actors, TAD supporters suggest that without the Beltline, these additional monies would not even exist. Therefore, the distribution of these TAD dollars is not taking anything away from anyone. The counterargument would be that while TAD dollars may be "newly generated" they are nevertheless dependent on local resources (e.g., tax dollars of local residents) that might otherwise go to different projects.

REFERENCES

Allen, Frederick. 1996. *Atlanta Rising: The Invention of an International City 1946–1996.* Atlanta: Longstreet Press.

AtlantaJokes. 2004. Glowport: AHAJokes.com.

"Auto-free zone." 2005. *Wikipedia* (en.wikipedia.org/wiki/Auto-free_zone).

Bae, Chang-Hee Christine. 2004. Chapter 13 in *The Geography of Urban Transportation*, ed. Susan Hanson and Genevieve Giuliano. New York: The Guilford Press.

Baxandall, Rosalyn, and Elizabeth Ewen. 2000. *Picture Windows: How the Suburbs Happened.* New York: Basic Books.

Bayer, Christine. 1999. "Crossing Cyber Cities: Urban Regions and the Cyberspace Matrix." Chapter 3 in *The Urban Moment: Cosmopolitan Essays on the Late Twentieth-Century City*, ed. Robert A. Beauregard and Sophie Body-Gendrot. Thousand Oaks, CA: Sage.

Bayer, Paul. 1978. *Urban Masses and the Moral Order in America 1820–1920.* Cambridge: Harvard University Press.

Bayor, Ronald H. 1988. "Roads to Racial Segregation: Atlanta in the Twentieth Century." *Journal of Urban History* 15: 3–21.

Bayor, Ronald H. 1996. *Race and the Shaping of Twentieth-Century Atlanta.* Chapel Hill: The University of North Carolina Press.

Bayor, Ronald H. 2000. "Atlanta: The Historical Paradox." Pp. 42–58 in *The Atlanta Paradox*, ed. David L. Sjoquist. New York: Russell Sage Foundation.

"Beltline buckles under pressure." 2005. *Atlanta Journal-Constitution*, October 3, p. A12.

Bollinger, Christopher, and Keith Ihlandfeldt. 1997. "The Impact of Rapid Rail Transit on Economic Development: The Case of Atlanta's MARTA." *Journal of Urban Economics* 42:179–204.

Bookman, Jay. 2005. "The free market would never pick sprawl." *Atlanta Journal-Constitution.* December 5, p. A15.

Bourdieu, Pierre. [1984] 2001. "Distinction: A Social Critique of the Judgment of Taste." Pp. 499–525 in *Social Stratification: Class, Race, and Gender in Sociological Perspective*, ed. David B. Grusky. Boulder: Westview.

Brottman, Mikita (Ed.). 2001. From "Introduction." Pp. xi–xliii in *Car Crash Culture.* New York: Palgrave.

Brown, Natalie. 1998. "Atlanta's Sprawl." *Southface Journal of Sustainable Building* 3 (Fall 1998).

Bullard, Robert D., and Glenn S. Johnson (Eds.). 1997. *Just Transportation.* Gabriola Island, BC: New Society Publishers.

Bullard, Robert D., Glenn S. Johnson, and Angel O. Torres. 1999. "Atlanta Megasprawl." *Forum for Applied Research & Public Policy* 14: 17–23.

Bullard, Robert D., Glenn S. Johnson, and Angel O. Torres. 2000. "The Routes of American Apartheid." *Forum for Applied Research and Public Policy* (Fall 2000).

Bullard, Robert D., Glenn S. Johnson, and Angel O. Torres. 2000b. "Race, Equity, and Smart Growth: Why People of Color Must Speak for Themselves." A discussion paper. Atlanta: Environmental Justice Resource Center.

Bullard, Robert D., Glenn S. Johnson, and Angel O. Torres. 2000c. "Dismantling Transportation Apartheid: The Quest for Equity." Chapter 2 in *Sprawl City: Race, Politics, and Planning in Atlanta*, ed. R. Bullard, G. Johnson, and A. Torres. Washington, DC: Island Press.

Bullard, Robert D., Glenn S. Johnson, and Angel O. Torres. 2004. "Dismantling Transit Racism in Metro Atlanta." Chapter 3 in *Highway Robbery: Transportation Racism and New Routes to Equity*, ed. R. Bullard, G. Johnson, and A. Torres. Cambridge, MA: South End Press.

Bullard, Robert D., Glenn S. Johnson, and Angel O. Torres (Eds.). 2004 (b). *Highway Robbery: Transportation Racism and New Routes to Equity*. Cambridge, MA: South End Press.

Burns, Peter. 2003. "Regime Theory, State Government, and a Takeover of Urban Education." *Journal of Urban Affairs* 25: 285–303.

Caesar, Terry. 2000. "In and Out of Elevators in Japan." *Online Journal of Mundane Behavior* 1: 1–7.

"Call to Action." 2005. Atlanta Jobs with Justice communiqué. September 19.

Calthorpe, Peter. 1994. "The Region." "Foreword" in *The New Urbanism: Toward an Architecture of Community*, by Peter Katz. New York: McGraw-Hill.

Cervero, Robert. 2003. "Coping with Complexity in America's Urban Transport Sector." Paper prepared for the 2nd International Conference on the Future of Urban Transport.

Chinoy, Ely. 1955. *Automobile Workers and the American Dream*. Garden City, NY: Doubleday.

"City-wide transit forum." 2005. "City-wide transit forum on service cuts, contract negotiations, and the Atlanta Regional Commission's transit proposal." E-mail communiqué sent September 19.

"Coalition dedicated to cleaner air." 1993. *Atlanta Journal-Constitution*, May 17, p. F14.

"Commutants come home." 2005. *Atlanta Journal-Constitution*, November 13, pp. C2–3.

"Congestion Mitigation Task Force Announcement." 2005. (www.grta.org/news_section/2005_Articles/CMTF_Announcement.pdf.)

"Congestion Mitigation Task Force Recommendations." 2005. Atlanta Regional Commission—Comprehensive Planning Department Community Outreach.

Coppola, Vincent. 2005. "In the Driver's Seat." *Georgia Trend* (on-line), October.

Cottrell, W. F. 1951. "Death by Dieselization: A Case Study in the Reaction to Technological Change." *American Sociological Review* 16: 358–65.

Cox, Wendell. 2001. "Demographia." (www.demographia.com.)

Cox, Wendell. 2004. "Why Not Just Buy Them Cars?" From the Heartland Institute On-line publication. (www.heartland.org.)

Davies, Jonathan S. 2002. "Urban Regime Theory: A Normative-Empirical Critique." *Journal of Urban Affairs* 24: 1–17.

Davies, Jonathan S. 2003. "Partnerships Versus Regimes: Why Regime Theory Cannot Explain Urban Coalitions in the UK." *Journal of Urban Affairs* 25: 253–69.

Davis, Sidney. 1997. "Race and the Politics of Transportation in Atlanta." Chapter 7 in *Just Transportation*, ed. R. Bullard, G. Johnson, and A. Torres. Gabriola Island, BC: New Society Publishers.

Deka, Devajyoti. 2004. "Social and Environmental Justice Issues in Urban Transportation." Chapter 12 in *The Geography of Urban Transportation*, ed. Susan Hanson and Genevieve Giuliano. New York: The Guilford Press.

"Dial-a-Llama." 1998. *Alaska* 64: 13.

Donsky, Paul. 2005. "Panel doubts Beltline transit goals." *Atlanta Journal-Constitution*, September 30, pp. E1, E8.

Donsky, Paul. 2005a. "Officials endorse new transit planning board." *Atlanta Journal-Constitution*, December 15 (from www.cobbrides.com).

Dorn, Jennifer L. 2001. Remarks at ASSHTO Annual Meeting Intermodal Luncheon. (www.fta.dot.gov/2639_5720_ENG_Printable.htm.)

Dowding, Keith. 2001. "Explaining Urban Regimes." *International Journal of Urban and Regional Research* 25: 7–19.

Duany, Andres, and Elizabeth Plater-Zybeck. 1994. "The Neighborhood, the District, and the Corridor." Pp. xvii–xx in *The New Urbanism: Toward an Architecture of Community*, ed. Peter Katz. New York: McGraw-Hill.

Duany, Andres, Elizabeth Plater-Zybeck, and Jeff Speck. 2000. *Suburban Nation: The Rise of Sprawl and the Decline of the American Dream*. New York: North Point Press.

Elkin, Stephen L. 1987. *City and Regime in the American Republic*. Chicago: University of Chicago Press.

Environmental Justice Resource Center—Transportation Equity Newsletter. Fall/Winter 2003. Vol. 6.

Feagin, Joe. 1998. *The New Urban Paradigm: Critical Perspectives on the City*. New York: Rowan and Littlefield.

Feaster, Felicia. 2003. "Color of Transit: Eyedrum Show Examines Race and Public Transportation." *Creative Loafing*, September 4: Arts Feature.

Ford, Nathaniel. 2002. "Approval of MARTA Cost Containment Measures." From Metropolitan Atlanta Rapid Transit Authority communiqué to community leaders, February 12.

Foucault, Michel. [1984] 1998. "Different Spaces." In *Michel Foucault: Aesthetics, Method, and Epistemology*, ed. James D. Faubion, trans. Robert Hurley (et al.). New York: The New Press.

Franklin, Shirley. 2003. Speech delivered at Georgia State University, March 25.

Frankston, Janet. 2005. "The Lord giveth and the Lord taketh away, Part II—The Other Georgia gave to the metro. Will the metro now take it away?" *Cracker Squire*. (www.crackersquire.blog.com/2005/02/lord-giveth-lord-taketh-away-part-ii.html).

Garvin, Alexander. 2004. *The Beltline Emerald Necklace: Atlanta's New Public Realm*. The Trust for Public Land.

Georgia Regional Transportation Authority Act. In *West's Code of Georgia Annotated Currentness*, Title 50, Chapter 32, 1–60.

Georgia Regional Transportation Authority website. (www.grta.org.)

Georgia Injury Mortality Statistics. 1997. (http://www.cdc.gov/ncipc/osp/states/1307.htm.)

Georgia Smart Growth News Articles. 1996–2004. Smartgrowth.org/news, a subset of www.sustainable.org: Sustainable Communities Network (SCN).

"Georgians Fear Traffic Crashes." 1999. *Traffic Safety Digest—National Highway Traffic Safety Administration* (nhtsa.dot.gov/people/outreach/safedige/Spring99/sp9924.htm).

Ger, Guliz, Hal Wilhite, Bente Halkier, Jeppe Laessoe, Mirjam Godskensen, and Inge Ropke. 1999. "Symbolic Meanings of High and Low Impact Daily Consumption Practices in Different Cultures." *Consumption, Everyday Life, and Sustainability: The Reader for the Summer School of 1999*. European Science Foundations' Term Programme.

Giuliano, Genevieve. 2004. "Land Use Impacts of Transportation Investments." Chapter 9 in *The Geography of Urban Transportation*, ed.Susan Hanson and Genevieve Giuliano. New York: The Guilford Press.

Giuliano, Genevieve, and Susan Hanson. 2004. "Managing the Auto." Chapter 14 in *The Geography of Urban Transportation*, ed. Susan Hanson and Genevieve Giuliano. New York: The Guilford Press.

Greenwald, Michael J. 2003. "The Road Less Traveled." *Journal of Planning Education and Research* 23(1): 39–57.

Greif, Gary, and Marcelo Cruz. 1999. "Reconstructing Urban Boundaries: The Dialectics Of Self and Place." *Cybergeo* 103: 1–10.

Hairston, Julie B. 2003. "Connecting the dots—potential of proposed 22-mile belt line transit loop excites proponents." *Atlanta Journal-Constitution*, July 14, p. E1.

Hairston, Julie B. 2005. "Bullish on the Beltline." *Atlanta Journal-Constitution*, January 19, p. B1.

Hamilton-Baillie, Ben. 2004. "Urban Design: Why Don't We Do It in the Road? Modifying Traffic Behavior through Legible Urban Design." *Journal of Urban Technology* 11(1): 43–62.

Hamrick, Dave. 2000. "GRTA gets a grilling at commission meeting." *The Citizen*. (www.citizennews.com/main/archive-000913/news/in-01.html).

Harvey, David. 1989. "From Managerialism to Entrepreneurism: The Transformation in Urban Governance in Late Capitalism." *Geografiska Annale* 71(B): 3–17.

Henderson, Jason. 1999. "The Crisis of Automobile Hegemony in Atlanta." Paper presented at the Conference on Social Change and Sustainable Transportation. March 10–13.

Hinkelman, Michael. 1997. "Pedestrians Overrun by Bad Urban Planning." American City Business Journals Inc. (http://www.bizjournals.com/atlanta/stories/1997/06/06/editorials.html.)

Hirsch, Jennifer S. 2000. "En el norte la mujer manda: Gender, Generation, and Geography in a Mexican Transnational Community." Chapter 15 in *Immigration Research for a New Century*, ed. Nancy Foner, Ruben G. Rumbaut, and Steven J. Gold. New York: Russell Sage Foundation.

Holcomb, Briavel. 1991. "Socio-spatial implications of electronic cottages." Pp. 342–53 in *Collapsing Space and Time: Geographic Aspects of Communications and Information*, ed.Stanley D. Brunn and Thomas R. Leinbach. London: HarperCollins Academic.

Holtzclaw, John. 2000. "Is Smart Growth Social Engineering? Or is Sprawl?" From On-line Sierra Club publication. (www.sierraclub.org/sprawl/articles/social_engineering.asp.)

Holtz Kay, Jane. 1997. Asphalt Nation: How the Automobile Took Over America and *How We Can Take It Back*. Berkeley: University of California Press.

Hunter, Floyd. 1953. *Community Power Structure: A Study of Decision Makers*. Chapel Hill: University of North Carolina Press.

Hunter, Tera. 1997. *To 'Joy My Freedom*. Cambridge: Harvard University Press.

Hutchinson, Sikivu. 2003. Imagining Transit: Race, Gender, and Transportation Politics in Los Angeles. New York: Peter Lang.

Imbroscio, David L. 2003 "Overcoming the Neglect of Economics in Urban Regime Theory." *Journal of Urban Affairs* 25: 271–84.

Imbroscio, David L. 2004. "The Imperative of Economics in Urban Political Analysis: A Reply to Clarence N. Stone." *Journal of Urban Affairs* 26: 21–26.

Irrante, Joseph. 1980. "The Road to Autopia: The Automobile and Spatial Transformation of American Culture." *Michigan Quarterly Review* 19: 502–17.

Jackson, Kenneth. 1985. *Crabgrass Frontier: The Suburbanization of the United States*. Oxford: Oxford University Press.

Jacobs, Jane. [1961] 1992. *The Death and Life of Great American Cities*. New York: Random House.

Jain, Juliet, and Jo Guiver. 2001. "Turning the Car Inside-Out: Transport, Equity, and Environment." *Social Policy and Administration* 35: 569–86.

Janelle, Donald G. 2004. "Impact of Information Technologies." Chapter 4 in *The Geography of Urban Transportation*, ed. Susan Hanson and Genevieve Giuliano. New York: The Guilford Press.

Jaret, Charles. 2002. "Suburban Expansion in Atlanta: 'The City without Limits' Faces Some." Pp. 165–205 in *Urban Sprawl*, ed. Gregory Squires. Washington, DC: Urban Institute Press.

Jargowsky, Paul. 1997. Poverty and Place: Ghettos, Barrios, and the American City. New York: Russell Sage Publications.

Jones, Mack H. 1978. "Black Political Empowerment in Atlanta: Myth and Reality." *Annals*, AAPSS 439: 90–117.

Katz, Peter. 1994. The New Urbanism: Toward an Architecture of Community. New York: McGraw-Hill.

Keating, Larry. 2001. Atlanta: Race, Class, and Urban Expansion. Philadelphia: Temple University Press.

Kostof, Spiro. 1991. *The City Shaped: Urban Patterns and Meanings through History*. Boston: Bulfinch Press; Little, Brown.

Kraus, Clifford. 2008. "Gas prices send surge of riders to mass transit." *New York Times*, May 10, p. A1.

Kunstler, James Howard. 2001. *The City in Mind: Notes on the Urban Condition*. New York: Free Press.

Lefebvre, Henri. [1974] 1991. *The Production of Space*, trans. Donald Nicholson-Smith. Oxford: Blackwell.

"Lindbergh Center TOD Hits Atlanta's Latinos the Hardest." 2001. *Transportation Equity Newsletter* 5. (www.ejrc.cau.edu.)

Logan, John R., and Harvey L. Molotch. 1988. *Urban Fortunes: The Political Economy Of Place*. Berkeley: University of California Press.

Lyall, Sarah. 2005. "A path to road safety with no signposts." *New York Times* (The Saturday Profile), January 22, p. 4.

Mann, Eric, Kikanza Ramsey, Barbara Lott-Holland, and Geoff Ray. 2001. "An Environmental Justice Strategy for Urban Transportation in Atlanta: Lessons and Observations from Los Angeles." Los Angeles: *Labor/Community Strategy Center Report*: March 2001.

Marcuse, Herbert. [1941] 1982. "Some Social Implications of Modern Technology." Pp. 138–63 in *The Essential Frankfurt School Reader*, ed. Andrew Arato and Eike Gebhardt. New York: Continuum.

Marcuse, Herbert. 1964. *One Dimensional Man*. Boston: Beacon Press.

Marcuse, Peter, and Ronald van Kempen (eds.). 2000. "Introduction." Pp. 1–21 in *Globalizing Cities: A New Spatial Order?* Oxford: Blackwell Publishers Ltd.

Markwell, Joel. 2005. "Towers endanger neighborhood feel." *Atlanta Journal-Constitution*, December 7, p. A15.

Marshall, Alex. 2000. How Cities Work: Suburbs, Sprawl and the Roads Not Taken. Austin: University of Texas Press.

Marx, Karl. [1846] 1978. "The German Ideology—Part I" in *The Marx-Engels Reader*, ed. Robert C. Tucker. New York/London: W. W. Norton.

Marx, Karl. [1859] 1978. From the preface to "A Contribution to the Critique of Political Economy" in *The Marx-Engels Reader*, ed. Robert C. Tucker. New York/London: W. W. Norton.

Massey, Douglas S., and Nancy A. Denton. 1993. *American Apartheid: Segregation and the Making of the Underclass*. Cambridge: Harvard University Press.

Mollenkopf, John. 1989. "Who (or What) Runs Cities, and How?" *Sociological Forum* 4: 119–37.

Molotch, Harvey. 1993. "The Political Economy of Growth Machines." *Journal of Urban Affairs* 15: 29–53.

Morcol, Goktug, Ulf Zimmermann, and Bethany Stich. 2003. "The Georgia Regional Transportation Authority: A Smart Growth Machine?" *Politics & Policy* 31(3): 488–511.

"Moving Beyond Sprawl: The Challenge for Metropolitan Atlanta." 2000. The Brookings Institution Center on Urban and Metropolitan Policy.

Mumford, Lewis. 1938. *The Culture of Cities*. New York: Harcourt Brace.

Mumford, Lewis. "The Highway and the City," originally published in *Architectural Record*, April 1958, pp. 179–86, later in *The Highway and the City*. New York: Harcourt, Brace and World, 1963.

National Highway Traffic Safety Administration. 1999. *Traffic Safety Digest*.

"Not auto immune." 2005. *Atlanta Journal-Constitution*, June 16, p. A18.

O'Toole, Randall. 1997. "ISTEA: A Poisonous Brew for American Cities." Cato Institute on-line publication. (www.cato.org/pubs/pas/pa-287.html.)

Peirce, Neal. 2001. "Imagine a Future with Car-Free Cities." Seattle *Times*, March 1, editorials and opinions.

Pendered, David. 2004. "Transit loop on fast track—Atlanta makes Belt Line project 'huge priority.' " *Atlanta Journal-Constitution*, June 28, p. E1.

Pendered, David. 2005. "Land donor snubbed in Beltline plan." *Atlanta Journal-Constitution*, September 27, pp. B1, B5.

Pendered, David. 2005. "Mayor pitches Beltline 'courage.' " *Atlanta Journal-Constitution*, October 1, p. E3.

Pendered, David. 2005. "Schools sign off on Beltline." *Atlanta Journal-Constitution*, December 13, pp. B4, B6.

Pendered, David. 2005. "Beltline to aid Fulton Libraries." *Atlanta Journal-Constitution*, December 23, p. D1.

"Personal Mobility." 1997. *Transportation Statistic Annual Report 1997*.

Pomerantz, Gary M. 1996. *Where Peachtree Meets Sweet Auburn: A Saga of Race and Family*. New York: Penguin Books.

"The Principles of New Urbanism." 2004. Newurbanism.org.

Pucher, John. 2003. "Increasing Reliance on the Automobile Documented in the Latest Survey." *Innovation Briefs* 14:3.

Pucher, John. 2004. Chapter 8 in *The Geography of Urban Transportation*, ed. Susan Hanson and Genevieve Giuliano. New York: The Guilford Press.

Putnam, Robert. 2000. *Bowling Alone*. New York: Simon and Schuster.

Raphael, Steven, and Michael A. Stoll. 2000. "Can Boosting Minority Car-Ownership Rates Narrow Inter-Racial Employment Gaps?" *Joint Center for Poverty Research—Working Paper Series*.

Rast, Joel. 2005. "The Politics of Alternative Economic Development: Revisiting the Stone-Imbroscio Debate." *Journal of Urban Affairs* 27: 53–69.

Reed, John S. 1991. "New South or No South? Regional Culture in 2036." Pp. 225–35 in *The South Moves Into the Future*, ed. by Joseph S. Himes. Little Rock: University of Arkansas Press.

Reid, Lesley Williams, and Robert M. Adelman. 2003. "The Double-edged Sword of Gentrification in Atlanta." *Footnotes*: 31.

Reiman, Jeffrey. 2001. *The Rich Get Richer and the Poor Get Prison: Ideology, Class, and Criminal Justice*. Boston: Allyn and Bacon.

Ritzer, George. 1996. *The McDonaldization of Society*. Thousand Oaks, CA: Pine Forge Press.

Roth, Darlene K., and Andy Ambrose. 1996. *Metropolitan Frontiers: A Short History of Atlanta*. Atlanta: Longstreet Press.

Rutheiser, Charles. 1996. *Imagineering Atlanta: The Politics of Place in the City of Dreams*. London/New York: Verso.

Sachs, Wolfgang. 1992. *For Love of the Automobile: Looking Back into the History of Our Desires*, trans. Don Reneau. Berkeley: University of California Press.

Samuel, Peter. 1999. "Traffic Congestion: A Solvable Problem." *Issues in Science and Technology* 15: 49–56.

Sanchez, Thomas W., Rich Stolz, and Jacinta S. Ma. 2003. "Moving to Equity: Addressing Inequitable Effects of Transportation Policies on Minorities." Center for Community Change: The Civil Rights Project. Harvard University.

Sawers, Larry. [1978] 1984. "The Political Economy of Urban Transportation: An Interpretive Essay." Pp. 223–54 in *Marxism and the Metropolis: New Perspectives in Urban Political Economy*, ed.William Tabb and Larry Sawers. New York: Oxford University Press.

Schaffner, John. 2005. "Beltline TAD backers lobby for Council vote." TheStoryGroup.com, 10/6.

"Smart Growth Retarding the Quality of Life." 2001. (www.demographia.com/dib_smg.htm.)

Snell, Bradford. 1974. "American Ground Transport: A Proposal for Restructuring the Automobile, Truck, Bus, and Rail Industries" (from an online reproduction of the original 1974 United States Government Report).

Soja, Edward. [1989] 2003. *Postmodern Geographies: The Reassertion of Space in Critical Social Theory*. London/New York: Verso.

Southern California Association of Governments. 2001. "Growth Visioning for Sustaining A Livable Region" (Summary Report).

Southern Party of Georgia. 2005. "Legislative Alert—SB4—why are they changing highway fund allocations?" (Southern Party of Georgia Alert, March). Morganton, GA: Southern Part of Georgia. Retrieved May 21, 2005. (www.spofga.org).

Staley, Samuel R. 2003. "Libertarians at the Gates of New Urbanism" (Reason Public Policy Institute blog, May 30). Los Angeles: Reason Public Policy Institute. Retrieved May 16, 2005. (www.rppi.org/libertariansathtegates.html).

Stone, Clarence N. 1989. Regime Politics: Governing Atlanta 1946–1988. Lawrence: University Press of Kansas.

Stone, Clarence N. 1991. "The hedgehog, the fox, and the new urban politics: Rejoinder to Kevin R. Cox." *Journal of Urban Affairs* 13: 289–97.

Stone, Clarence N. 1993. "Urban Regimes and the Capacity to Govern: A Political Economy Approach." *Journal of Urban Affairs* 15:1–28.

Stone, Clarence N. 2001. "The Atlanta Experience Re-examined: The Link Between Agenda and Regime Change." *International Journal of Urban and Regional Research* 25: 20–34.

Stone, Clarence, and Carol Pierannunzi. 2000. "Atlanta's Biracial Coalition in Transition." Presented at the American Political Science Association annual Meeting, Washington, DC. August 31-September 4.

"Stuck in traffic—Roads and transit need commitment." 2000. Editorial from Startribune.com. April 1.

Stein, Rob. 2004. "Study links sprawling suburbs, sprawling waistlines." *Seattletimes.com* (syndicated from the Washington *Post*) May 31.

Sundquist, Eric. 2003. "Experts share ideas to make area walkable." *Atlanta Journal-Constitution*, June 16, p. E2.

Surman, Mark. 1994. "From VTR to Cyberspace: Jefferson, Gramsci, and the Electronic Commons." (From appendix, "What is a hegemony anyways?") Paper presented at the 1994 Canadian Community Networks Conference.

Swanstrom, Todd. 1993. "Beyond Economism: Urban Political Economy and the Postmodern Challenge." *Journal of Urban Affairs* 15: 55–78.

Swint, Mary. 2006. "MARTOC reports transit authority concerns to General Assembly." *The Story*. (http://www.thestorygroup.com.) January 5.

Taylor, Brian D. 2004. "The Geography of Urban Transportation Finance." Chapter 11 in *The Geography of Urban Transportation*, ed. Susan Hanson and Genevieve Giuliano. New York: The Guilford Press.

Towson University Center for Geographic Information Sciences (CGIS). 2004. (http://Chesapeake.towson.edu/about.asp.)

"Traffic Congestion." 2003. Federation of American Immigration Reform (on-line newsletter).

van den Boomen, Tijs. 2001. "Beyond the Home Zone—Toward the Legible Street." *NCR Handelsblad*, June 2, p. 31.

Vasconcellos, Eduardo. 1997. "The Demand for Cars in Developing Countries." *Transportation Research Part A—Policy and Practice* 31: 245–58.

Veblen, Thorstein. [1973] 2001. "The Theory of the Leisure Class." Pp. 491–98 in *Social Stratification: Class, Race, and Gender in Sociological Perspective*, ed. David B. Grusky. Boulder: Westview.

Wachs, Martin. 1989. "U.S. Transit Subsidy Policy: In Need of Reform." *Science* 244: 1545–49.

Wachs, Martin. 2004. "Reflections on the Planning Process." Chapter 6 in *The Geography of Urban Transportation*, ed. Susan Hanson and Genevieve Giuliano. New York: The Guilford Press.

Wall, Michael. 2004. "The Beltline is Dead." *Atlanta Creative Loafing (on-line)*, May 13. Retrieved 9/27/04 (atlantacreativeloafing.com).

"Wheels to Work." 2005. National Service Resource Center. (www.epicenter.national servicesources.org).

Whiddon, Alycen. 2005. "Beltline plan incorporates trees, transit . . . and cars." *Atlanta Journal-Constitution*, June 16, p. A19.

Whitelegg, John. 1997. Critical Mass: Transport, Environment, and Society in the *Twenty-first Century*. London: Pluto Press.

"Who Shudda Shot the Author of 'American Ground Transport.'" 1998. *Sci.econ.* (http://www.geocities.com/Capitol Hill/4834/gas6.txt.)

Whyte, William H. 1980. *The Social Life of Small Urban Spaces*. Washington, DC: The Conservation Foundation.

Wilson, James Q. 1997. "Cars and Their Enemies." *Commentary* 104: 17–23.

Wolf, Winfried. 1996. *Car Mania: A Critical History of Transport*. London: Pluto Press.

Woods, Walter. 2004. "A developer bets big on city's Belt Line." *Atlanta Journal-Constitution*, October 13, p. A13.

Wooten, Jim. 2005. "Makeover, not takeover, for MARTA." *Atlanta Journal-Constitution*, June 14, p. A11.

www.allbusiness.com/periodicals

www.atlantaregional.com/transportationair/2004/factbook

www.artery.org/KingPlow.htm

www.beltline.org

www.beltlinepartnership.org

www.bizjournals.com/atlanta/stories/2006/01/23.html

www.carsharing.net

www.cathyatlanta.com/work/issues/belt_line_transit.html.

www.demographia.com

www.grta.org/news_section/2005_Articles/CMTF_Announcement.pdf

www.halfass.com/blah/2002/03/13/atlanta-beltline

www.itsmarta.com

www.itsmarta.com/about/history01.htm

www.itsmarta.com/newroom/press_releases AJC 1/9/06

www.MidtownAtlanta.org

www.NewUrbanism.org

Xpress Homepage: Commuter Service for Metropolitan Atlanta. www.xpressga.com.

Yago, Glenn. 1978. "Current Issues in U.S. Transportation Politics." *International Journal of Urban and Regional Research* 2: 351–59.

INDEX